Econometric Sourcebook

Betty J. Blecha

San Francisco State University

Wadsworth Publishing Company
Belmont, California
A Division of Wadsworth, Inc.

Economics Editor: Kristine M. Clerkin
Production Editor: Leland Moss
Designer: MaryEllen Podgorksi
Editorial Assistant: Melissa Harris
Print Buyer: Barbara Britton
Copy Editor: Betty Duncan-Todd
Technical Illustrator: Joan Carol
Signing Representative: Stephanie Surfus

Printed in the United States of America   49

1 2 3 4 5 6 7 8 9 10—93 92 91 90 89

Library of Congress Cataloging-in-Publication Data

Blecha, Betty J.
    Econometric sourcebook / Betty J. Blecha. — 1st ed.
      p.   cm.
    Bibliography: p.
    ISBN 0-534-09882-7
    1. Econometrics.   I. Title.
HB139.B57   1989
330'.028—dc19   88-19126
                                                  CIP

Contents

Instructor's Preface   vii

Lesson 1
Estimators and the Random Error Term   1

Consumption Function Model   1
Estimating a Consumption Function   2
    Lesson Note 1.1   Did Monetary Forces or Spending Forces Cause the Great Depression?   6
Estimators and Estimates   7
    Lesson Note 1.2   Evaluating the Econometric Evaluations of Training Programs with
                Experimental Data   8
Justification for the Random Error Term   15

Lesson 2
Expected Values   18

Rules of Summation   18
    Sigma Notation   18
    Three Rules of Summation   20
Means, Variances, and Covariances   22
    Double Sigmas   28
Algebra of Expectations   30
    Expected-Value Rules   30
    Variances and Covariances   33

Lesson 3
Specifying a Model   36

Specifying a Model   36
Keynes and the Consumption Function   39
Problems with the Simple Consumption Function   42
    Lesson Note 3.1   Using the *Survey of Current Business*   45

Lesson 4
Single-Equation Models   51

Transforming Variables   51
Inflation and Money Supply Growth   52
    Lesson Note 4.1   A Comment on Statistical Significance   55
Productivity and GNP   56
    Lesson Note 4.2   Using the *Business Conditions Digest*   60
Suggested Reading   65

Lesson 5
More Single-Equation Models 66

Okun's Law 66
Fixed Business Investment 70
The Demand for New Autos 71
    Lesson Note 5.1   Some Issues in Measuring Inflation 73
    Lesson Note 5.2   Different Base Periods for Price Indices 76
Suggested Reading 77

Lesson 6
Making Nonlinear Functions Linear 78

Logarithms 78
    Three Rules of Logarithms 79
Exponential Function 80
Double-Logarithmic Function 83
Reciprocal Function 86
Polynomial Function 87
Logistic Function 89
    Lesson Note 6.1   Hybrid Corn and the Economics of Innovation 91
Suggested Reading 95

Lesson 7
Parameter Constraints 96

A Simple Constraint 97
Testing Hypotheses About Constraints 98
Conceptual Difficulties in Estimating Production Functions 103
Specification Search 105
    Lesson Note 7.1   The Six Varieties of Specification Searches 106
Suggested Reading 108

Lesson 8
Dummy Variables 109

Seasonal Adjustment with Dummy Variables 110
Decomposition Method 114
    Lesson Note 8.1   Seasonal Variations Seen Causing Big Swings in Economic Statistics 117
Suggested Reading 119

Lesson 9
Heteroscedasticity 120

Residuals as an Information Source 121
Causes and Problems 123
    What Causes Heteroscedasticity? 123
    Why Is Heteroscedasticity a Problem? 123
Treatment 126

Lesson 10
Autocorrelation 132

Interest-Rate Model 132
    Lesson Note 10.1   Measuring the Money Supply 134

Causes and Problems   140
Treatment   143

Lesson 11
Geometric Lags I   147

General Distributed Lag Model   147
Geometric Function   150
Partial Adjustment Behavior   152
Adaptive Expectations Behavior   155
    Lesson Note 11.1   Price Expectations and Core Inflation   158

Lesson 12
Geometric Lags II   161

Consumption Function   161
Permanent Income and Consumer Durables   167

Lesson 13
Polynomial Lags   170

    Lesson Note 13.1   The J-Curve   171
Estimating a Polynomial Lag Structure   173
    How Lag Parameters Are Generated   173
    Estimation Procedure   174
    Restrictions   175
Investment Functions in Differenced Form   177
Suggested Reading   179

Lesson 14
Simultaneous Equations   180

Solving a Simultaneous Model   181
    Graphical Analysis   181
    Algebraic Solution   185
New Estimator Criterion   190
Suggested Reading   202

Lesson 15
Econometric Case Study: The Phillips Curve   203

Natural-Rate Hypothesis   204
    The Beginnings   204
    Testing the Natural-Rate Hypothesis   208
    Lesson Note 15.1   Using the *Journal of Economic Literature*   210
The Rational Expectations Challenge   214

Data Bank   216

Notes   223

Instructor's Preface

The *Sourcebook* is addressed to the needs of undergraduate students taking a beginning course in applied econometrics at a state university or similar institution. It is aimed specifically at courses that use computer support to teach the principles of econometric application. The *Sourcebook* is a supplement and should be used along with a beginning econometric text. It is not a replacement for a text. With a few exceptions, students using the *Sourcebook* are assumed to have had two economic principles courses and a beginning statistics course.

Purpose

Most undergraduate students take beginning econometrics hoping that they will learn to use econometric methods. It is usually the only econometric course they take, and they are usually disappointed. They quickly come to think of econometrics as a course in statistics, rather than a course in the science and art of building and estimating models. By the end of the semester, they can estimate models and interpret regression results, but they cannot formulate problems on their own.

We often try to bridge this application gap by asking students to write an econometric research paper. They typically fumble for a topic, are overwhelmed by journal articles, have difficulty collecting data, and puzzle over interpreting their results. We end the course grading a stack of extremely uneven papers. Some are not satisfactory because the topic is too advanced for the beginning course. Others are well done but leave major, unanswered questions in econometric applications. Most importantly, we have a sense that students could learn much more if both their time and manner of posing questions were more structured.

The *Sourcebook* develops curricular structure for bridging the application gap by presenting a series of lessons that build in modeling complexity. The lessons are structured around the basic pedagogical premise that students best learn to use econometrics when they are constantly forced to structure problems in model form and to address the issues posed in estimating these models. Because the use of econometric software is a critical element in developing application skills, each lesson is linked to specific software procedures. There are, of course, distinct limits to what we can expect of students in the beginning course. I have tried to recognize these limits in the development of the modeling problems.

Application Features

Because the *Sourcebook* is designed to teach application skills, it includes a number of special features to facilitate the learning of such skills.

Use of Economic Data Sources

Throughout the *Sourcebook*, students are asked to go to published data sources to answer questions. By the end of the course, they know where to go for data on basic economic activity. They also develop an understanding of the difficulties inherent in collecting and interpreting actual data.

Lesson Notes

A series of Lesson Notes are included in the *Sourcebook*. Lesson Notes give descriptions of data sources, examples of econometric applications, and discussions of research methodology. These brief readings are addressed specifically to undergraduate students. One of the major frustrations in teaching the beginning course is the lack of supplemental material for beginning students, with most published material being addressed to more advanced students. I have tried to keep this frustration in mind in selecting the readings.

Nontrivial Problems

Although students can structure the models required by the lessons with little background in economics, most lessons nevertheless deal with actual issues discussed in empirical research. I have tried to select topics that students can relate to their economic principles courses. My choice of topics may appear a bit dated in the earlier lessons. But the basic questions involved in explaining topics like consumption and investment spending have developed over the years, along with increasing econometric sophistication. The topic selection thus allows students to see by example that empirical investigation is not separate from theoretical investigation. It also allows students to examine some of the most significant parameters used by economists to explain real-world economic activity.

Emphasis on Modeling

The standard econometric text gives students data and an equation and asks them to estimate the equation's parameters. The *Sourcebook* changes this procedure. Students are first given a problem and asked to address the problem by constructing a model. Only after they have constructed a model do they turn to the extensive Data Base that supports the *Sourcebook*. The order of addressing questions is thus much more consistent with the way economists actually conduct empirical investigation. More generally, students construct their own models. They are not given models to estimate.

Easy Course Integration

The *Sourcebook* is obviously a very different kind of course supplement. Allowing students to construct their own models yields diverse answers on lesson questions, which must be evaluated by the instructor. I have tried to structure the lessons such that this evaluation takes no more time than grading the homework normally associated with the beginning course. I have also done a number of things to make the lessons easy to integrate into existing courses.

Lessons Follow Course Outline

The lessons are titled to fit comfortably into the chapter headings used in a standard econometric text. The lessons can thus be easily integrated into an existing course outline. The quality of modern software occasionally changes the emphasis of the lessons from the emphasis of the standard text. For example, modern software makes it very easy to examine lagging assumptions in models, a topic previously considered too esoteric or time-consuming for the beginning course.

Use of Existing Software

The software currently used in a course will support the lessons. Although there would be some gain in clarity in linking the *Sourcebook* to a software-specific product, I have chosen not to do so. The general usage of the lessons would be restricted if they included specific software instructions. More importantly, I believe that the choice of software should be left to individual instructors. This choice is guided by available computer support and curricular judgments, both of which are more significant than the small gain in clarity that would result from a software-specific supplement. I teach at an undergraduate institution and have access to a microcomputer laboratory. I use MicroTSP, which is consistent with both student needs and the available computer support. An instructor at an institution with a strong graduate program teaching undergraduates motivated toward more advanced work might well select a more integrative statistical package such as SAS. This selection is also consistent with student needs and available computer support. Thus, the choice of software is a significant curricular question and hence is not limited by the *Sourcebook.*

Software Instructions Linked to Lessons

To make the integration of software with the lessons as easy as possible, I have included the instructions for my own course on the data disk in a separate file (TSP). These instructions link specific software features with each lesson. The file, written in WordStar, can be easily modified with any standard word processor. You need only edit the file to be consistent with your own choice of software.

Format

The *Sourcebook* has been printed on perforated paper so that students can clip the lessons, along with software instructions, into a loose-leaf binder. When students are asked to modify models developed in earlier lesson, they simply go back to the earlier lesson and pull out the relevant pages for inclusion in the current assignment. This makes it easy for students to hand in lesson assignments and for you to grade the assignments. The format also makes it easy to extend the material normally taught in the beginning course. For example, I have not included a lesson on pooling of cross-sectional and time-series data, because most beginning courses do not cover this material. But the Data Base contains a data set (STATES) that is suitable for a pooling problem. And the beef-demand model assignments can be extended to discuss how econometricians test for and deal with problems of changing structural parameters.

Clearly Defined Exercises

It is unlikely that you will assign all the exercises in a *Sourcebook* lesson. Time constraints and different learning priorities make some selection desirable. All exercises are clearly marked, making it exceptionally easy to isolate and assign them.

Extensive Data Bank

A glance through the Data Bank shows that many variables are included on the data disk. The extensiveness of the Data Bank allows you to create laboratory exams or generate additional problems. A copy of the Data Bank is available on microcomputer disk to adopting instructors. The disk is supplied in one of three formats: DIF, Lotus 1-2-3 (.PRN), or MicroTSP.

Theory and Research Style Left to Rigorous Text and Instructor

Explanations of econometric theory and research style are left to the text and the instructor. For example, while multicollinearity is likely to be an issue in several lessons, it is not discussed explicitly in the *Sourcebook*. This minimizes the notation used in the *Sourcebook*, making it much easier to integrate with the text. Although general issues of research methodology are discussed, explanation of specific research style in approaching the lesson questions is left to instructors.

Text Link to Lessons

Despite the lack of rigorous theory development in the lessons, I have found that some explanation of econometric structure is needed to link the lessons to the course text. I have tried to supply this structure by giving clear explanations of basic concepts. In this sense, the material emphasizes the obvious and leaves the full development of concepts to the rigor of the assigned text. If you feel that this material is too basic, it can easily be skipped. But it has been my experience that the obvious cannot be stated too often in the beginning course.

A Note on Microcomputers

Although the *Sourcebook* can be used with any mainframe batch-processing or time-sharing system, its fullest curricular potential is realized in a laboratory setting using microcomputers. In this way, the estimation portion of the lessons can be discussed with students in a step-by-step fashion, going over questions that occur as the process of estimating a model develops. Students can be given immediate feedback to their questions. In turn, you can raise new issues to challenge or expand their current level of understanding. This kind of classroom interaction was not possible prior to the development of microcomputer technology. For large classes where a laboratory setting is not possible, a microcomputer with a projection device can be used to go over the modeling issues for the entire class. I also suggest that you combine the Sourcebook lessons with one of the very inexpensive data bases now available for microcomputers (BCD Data Base or Citibase, for example). Learning to use a department data base encourages students to use the skills they learn in their econometric course in other economic courses.

Concluding Comments

Since the *Sourcebook*'s purpose is to help students learn to apply econometric methods, I would very much like to receive comments on the extent to which the material succeeds or does not succeed in meeting this purpose. Suggestions for revisions, new problems, or information on errors will be most welcome.

I must thank a great many people for their assistance in helping me complete the *Sourcebook*. Special thanks go to my students at San Francisco State University. In many ways, the *Sourcebook* is as much theirs as mine. They remain the *Sourcebook*'s most critical readers. Mark Green and Dag Syrrist compiled sections of the data base and improved the content of the lesson material. Michele Torrey, Barbara Castleberry, and Yoshimasa Terada helped correct the manuscript for errors and identified unclear language. I owe a special debt to my first Wadsworth editor, Stephanie Surfus, who gave me the necessary time to develop the initial concept into a mature product, at some expense to publishing deadlines. Her support is reflected in the quality of the pages. I must also thank my second editor, Kristine Clerkin, for her care in the production of the manuscript. Kris entered the process at a late date and refused to be daunted by the likes of heteroscedasticity. I am indebted to the anonymous Wadsworth referees, whose suggestions substantially improved the content of the lessons. One referee did not remain anonymous over the drafts. Carter Hill critiqued the manuscript with a professionalism that is often alleged but rarely achieved. His comments greatly strengthened the manuscript. Any remaining errors or deficiencies are my responsibility alone. Finally, I must thank the special people in my life who saw less of me than they felt reasonable over the last two years but nevertheless supported me in finishing this project.

Estimators and the Random Error Term

1. To understand the random error term and how it affects observed data generated by a simple linear model and influences the distributions of ordinary least-squares estimators

2. To learn how to estimate an ordinary least-squares regression using econometric software

3. To review the derivation of selected properties of ordinary least-squares estimators

Consumption Function Model

Aggregate consumption spending (C) in an economy often is explained as a **linear function** of aggregate disposable income (Q):

$$C = \beta_0 + \beta_1 Q \qquad (1.1)$$

The function's **parameters** are β_0 and β_1. Parameter β_1 is the marginal propensity to consume and shows the change in consumption spending associated with a one-unit change in disposable income. Product $\beta_1 Q$ indicates the amount of induced consumption, the amount of consumption spending that is dependent on income. Parameter β_0 is referred to as autonomous consumption and shows the amount of consumption spending that is independent of income.

Economic theory examines relationships between variables like consumption spending and income. When studying economics, you learn how one variable is related to other variables. These relationships can be stated in qualitative terms or, like the consumption function shown above, specified in mathematic form. Although specified in mathematic form, it is the *economic meaning* of variables and parameters that is of interest to economists. Economists are concerned about specifying a consumption function because they want to know the marginal propensity to consume and autonomous consumption.

Relationships among variables are usually presented in the form of a **model**, which is nothing more than a grouping of relationships. For example, the consumption function can be presented as part of a simple model of income determination:

$$C = \beta_0 + \beta_1 Q \qquad (1.2)$$

$$I = \bar{I} \qquad (1.3)$$

$$Q = C + I \qquad (1.4)$$

Variable I indicates planned investment spending. You may have used this model to solve for equilibrium values of income and consumption spending in the macroeconomic principles course.

Mathematical economists classify the equations that constitute a model into three types: **behavioral equations, equilibrium conditions,** and **definitional equations,** which are sometimes called **identities.** Equations 1.2 and 1.3 in the simple income-determination model are behavioral equations. A behavioral equation shows how a variable responds to other variables. Planned consumption spending responds to income in Equation 1.2; planned investment spending is equal to be some fixed amount $\bar{I}$ in Equation 1.3. The first two equations thus explain the behavior of planned consumption spending and planned investment spending. To the econometrician, Equation 1.3 also indicates that investment spending is not determined by variables within the model. It is determined outside the model. Variables determined outside a model are **exogenous;** variables determined within a model are **endogenous.** Consumption spending and income are the endogenous variables in the income-determination model.

Equation 1.4 is an equilibrium condition and indicates that the model is in equilibrium when the sum of planned consumption spending and planned investment spending equals the level of output. The three equations taken together model the structure of the economy. For this reason, they are referred to as the **structural form** of the model. We will see in coming lessons that it is sometimes useful to express the model in other forms.

Notice that the model does not include an example of the third type of equation, an identity. To estimate the model, however, an econometrician would very likely redefine the equilibrium condition as an identity. This has the effect of treating all *observed values* of consumption spending and income as *equilibrium values,* greatly reducing the complexity of the econometrician's problem.

The econometrician's problem is to estimate the parameters associated with models. Given the income-determination model shown above, the econometrician uses actual data to arrive at numeric values or estimates for β_0 and β_1, the parameters of the model. The first part of the econometrics course deals with single-equation, linear models estimated by the **method of ordinary least-squares.** The complications that arise when dealing with models comprising more than one equation or with nonlinear relationships are discussed later in the course. For this lesson, follow your text and assume that consumption spending is explained by a single-equation model. That is, assume the consumption function is *not* part of a larger model like that shown in Equations 1.2–1.4. The complications of estimating a more realistic consumption function are discussed in later lessons.

Estimating a Consumption Function

In this section the parameters of the single-equation consumption function will be estimated by using the following **regression model:**

$$C_i = \beta_0 + \beta_1 Q_i + u_i, \quad \text{for } i = 1, \dots, n \tag{1.5}$$

Subscript i shows that the model is now related to a data set with n cases. This data set can consist of values for consumption spending and income for the same economy observed at different times (**time-series data**) or for a representative sample of different economies observed at the same time (**cross-sectional data**). Consumption values are assumed to be generated by Equation 1.5 for given values of income in either type of data set.

Notice that a **random error term** is now included in the model. This is an exceptionally important addition to the model. Let's examine how the random error term affects consumption spending. We will discuss the justification for including this term later in the lesson.

Begin by assuming that we know what an econometrician never knows, the *true model* generating observed consumption spending for a representative cross-sectional sample of countries. The model is

$$C_i = 1000 + .8Q_i + u_i \qquad (1.6)$$

where u is a **random variable**, uniformly distributed between –$2000 and +$2000. The distribution of u has a **mean** of 0 and a **standard deviation** of $1155. All figures are in millions of dollars. *Circle the values for the mean and standard deviation of the random error term. This information will be used to answer some of the questions later in the lesson.* Notice that the random error term is *not* normally distributed.

EXERCISE 1.1

Table 1.1 shows a series of values for u, which were generated randomly by a computer program. Select ten values at random from the table and record them in Column u_i below. Using Equation 1.6, solve for consumption spending for the representative sample of economies whose disposable incomes are shown in Column Q_i. Record the consumption values in Column C_i.

Q_i	u_i	C_i	$\hat{C}_i$	$\hat{u}_i$
4,000	_____	_____	_____	_____
5,000	_____	_____	_____	_____
5,000	_____	_____	_____	_____
5,000	_____	_____	_____	_____
6,000	_____	_____	_____	_____
7,000	_____	_____	_____	_____
12,000	_____	_____	_____	_____
20,000	_____	_____	_____	_____
25,000	_____	_____	_____	_____
30,000	_____	_____	_____	_____

This is where an econometrician begins his or her work. The econometrician sees a sample of economies with varying levels of consumption spending and disposable income, the values shown in Columns Q_i and C_i. The econometrician does not know the values in Column u_i. The econometrician *assumes* that consumption is linearly related to disposable income and a random error term. You know that this assumption is correct because you know the true model. The econometrician, however, would have to accept the linear model as an assumption, which could be incorrect. Using your econometric software, estimate the consumption function and write it in the space below. Use the form $\hat{C}_i = \hat{\beta}_0 + \hat{\beta}_1 Q_i$ to record your estimated function. An example is $\hat{C}_i = 961 + .81 Q_i$.

Use your estimated function to find the predicted values of consumption spending for each country. Record these values in Column $\hat{C}_i$. Next, find the difference between each country's observed level and its predicted level of consumption spending. Record these values in Column $\hat{u}_i$. Your software should do the calculations for you. Notice that an estimate is indicated by the symbol ^.

Table 1.1
Random Values for u

-602	-541	973	-805	282	1765	-927
1453	-738	-393	1218	110	206	1791
1580	850	832	-395	-958	1430	18
1796	-1779	-1377	251	-953	-519	-182
0024	1459	-1052	1248	-1950	395	-793
-1623	514	-175	542	-1838	-1923	110
-1270	1332	-682	174	1353	-1434	638
-805	-1998	-649	-1908	1548	-98	-1330
1696	468	1941	335	859	33	314
297	-1224	1061	852	1209	955	-503
923	-1130	916	-623	-299	-476	1716
1031	490	-70	308	-1101	-148	-1226
-1464	1949	1500	1566	1212	-1024	-602
140	-799	-353	1097	565	-1065	1558
-231	-1667	386	944	-1025	1678	-677
-560	1245	1642	-854	-1542	1246	-1388
1215	1932	1480	1603	985	-365	1490
-977	-1516	1870	-1595	575	-1212	1930
-1076	843	829	-456	-754	795	1901
-1156	-1038	376	-1031	-1034	-395	-530
893	-1028	-1519	-1327	1801	1255	603
-1050	-1272	1113	743	1629	-303	-724
-923	316	-1659	-917	560	920	1501
-707	1733	83	-223	518	-983	1348
1520	972	454	773	-431	-114	690
-127	-19	1331	67	-319	1566	1640
225	845	824	-347	-1174	-1945	-1877
690	1514	811	1569	-932	-608	200
-808	-17	-597	-186	-1621	-476	1798
1793	-1757	-1430	376	-1271	445	980
-1581	-1664	1629	1144	-1557	-702	-1512
-214	229	665	-1946	1664	-397	-478
1312	1711	-1740	-712	-45	-1250	121
-1152	-1013	429	-1157	-716	-1314	-1693
1500	-1951	1145	-1287	1716	1405	46
-1807	984	-1621	890	1175	997	-641
-53	1695	-1760	-628	-273	-638	-1738
1776	-1777	-1347	149	-659	-1461	-1321
1654	559	1588	1265	1987	569	-1326
1597	-1252	1112	713	1731	-645	217
-376	-1312	-806	440	543	982	1327
1702	-1533	1849	-1511	394	-553	23
1853	79	-900	850	-697	694	-1726
-1954	1472	866	1521	-716	-1232	-1904
297	734	1214	-1505	-1689	-387	1461
-1373	-233	-1885	1812	-1601	1317	-1611
-997	607	1537	1420	1567	1829	-1106
-555	1253	1594	-638	1833	-857	948

Everyone in your class generates values for consumption spending using the same values for income, the independent variable. This is in accord with the specification of the general regression model, which assumes that the values of the independent variable are fixed values that do not vary from sample to sample. This assumption is questionable in the empirical world, where it is usually more realistic to assume that the independent variable is itself a random variable. The **fixed value assumption** causes few difficulties, however, because the properties of **ordinary least-squares estimators** can be shown to hold when the independent variable is a random variable. Beginning econometric texts assume that the independent variable is a set of fixed values because the properties of the ordinary least-squares estimators are easier to prove in the fixed value case than in the random variable case.

More significantly, assuming that the independent variable is either a set of fixed values or a set of random values follows from the consideration of the regression model as an experiment. In a true experiment, the values of the independent variable must be completely under the control of the experimenter. The experimenter must be able to change the value of the independent variable, in either a patterned or random manner, and observe the resulting change in the dependent variable. Econometricians usually observe different values of the dependent variable associated with different values of the independent variable *after* these values have been generated in the empirical world. In this sense, the typical estimated regression model does not represent a true experiment. Econometricians assume that the values of the dependent variable are what would be observed *if* they could experimentally manipulate the independent variable. It is important to realize that this assumption could be incorrect. When observing data "after the fact," we must be very cautious about inference. Correlations among variables can reflect chance occurrence or the influence of unknown variables.

The possibility that regression results can be significantly at odds with experimental results is seldom discussed. Economists recognize that they cannot do controlled experiments to address most empirical issues. The "all-other-things-being-equal" assumption used so often in economic theory allows for the analytical analysis of how two variables are related when all other variables are fixed. This assumption, however, is not helpful in resolving empirical issues when several variables change together.

Two lesson notes included in this section show the problems raised by the lack of true experimental data. Lesson Note 1.1 is a brief reading on the two major conflicting causes of the Great Depression: Was it a decrease in the real money supply or a decrease in real autonomous spending?[1] As the reading indicates, the analytical dispute over the cause of the depression is easily resolved by the *IS–LM* model. If you are not familiar with the *IS–LM* model, Figure 1.1 shows that the real interest rate does not move in the same direction for a reduction in the money supply (Figure 1.1a) as for a reduction in autonomous spending (Figure 1.1b). We should be able to decide which panel tells the true story by checking to see if real interest rates increased or decreased. But, as the reading reveals, the concurrent movement of the price level and the existence of disequilibrium observations make the apparently clear-cut analytical result difficult to assess.

Lesson Note 1.2 summarizes a recent study contrasting experimental results with econometric results for a set of job-training programs.[2] The reading includes an introduction to the study and the study's conclusions. While the conclusions may not be typical, they nevertheless indicate the importance of caution in evaluating regression results. The assumption that regressions can be considered as true experiments should never be blindly accepted.

Did Monetary Forces or Spending Forces Cause the Great Depression?

It turns out that explanations of the Depression can be classified into two groups, one group offered generally by those who believe that monetary policy would have been the best tool to alleviate the Depression and the other by adherents of fiscal policy. While this correspondence of views is apparent, there is no logical need for it. One can believe that the Depression was caused by events having nothing to do with the financial markets and yet that monetary policy would have been effective in offsetting the deflationary shocks. Or one can equally well believe that the economy declined due to financial developments, but that fiscal policy is the most effective expansionary tool. The question of what happened in the early 1930s is distinct from the question of what policy an omniscient economic dictator should have pursued.

The two classes of explanations for the Depression have different events at their cores. What I have called "the money hypothesis" asserts that the collapse of the banking system was the primary cause of the Depression, while "the spending hypothesis" asserts that a fall in autonomous aggregate spending lay at the root of the decline. The following chapters represent an attempt to discriminate between these two hypotheses.

The difference between them can be suggested by reference to the familiar IS–LM diagram of macroeconomic textbooks. These two curves jointly determine the equilibrium level of operation of the economy. For this equilibrium level to shift, one or the other of the curves has to shift. The money hypothesis asserts it was the LM curve; the spending hypothesis, the IS curve.

But although the two hypotheses may be distinguished by this stark statement, a simple test of their empirical merits does not emerge from it. There are several reasons for this unhappy fact. First, the simple model of IS and LM curves assumes that the economy is continuously in equilibrium. But adjustment to changes in the economic environment is never instantaneous. At any moment of time, the economy is in transition from one equilibrium to another, and it may never reach an equilibrium if the external influences change sufficiently rapidly. In any empirical test, therefore, the mechanism by which the economy adjusts to changes needs to be given as much prominence as the location of equilibrium points.

Second, the conventional IS–LM model is static. It assumes, for example, that income would stay constant in a stable equilibrium. But if investment is positive at this equilibrium—as it is in most actual economies—income must be growing. And if one important variable like income is changing, then others must be changing too, and the way they change will have important repercussions.

One possibility is that prices will change in response to the interaction of changes in income and movements of other variables. The IS and LM curves typically are drawn under the assumption of constant prices, and the tendency of prices to change is another reason why the simple IS–LM model does not lead directly to a test of the two hypotheses.*

Source: Temin, P. *Did Monetary Forces Cause the Great Depression?* (New York: Norton, 1976), 7–8.
*The nominal stock of money fell in the early 1930s, but the real stock did not. It makes a big difference whether the curves are defined in real or nominal terms.

Figure 1.1
Causes of the Great Depression

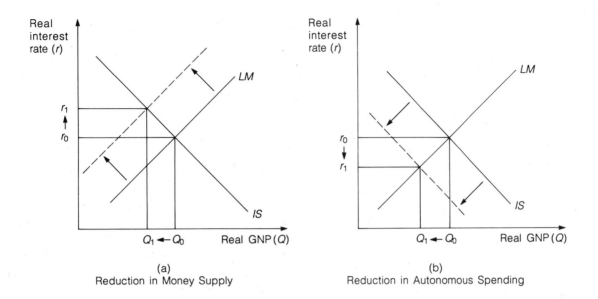

(a)
Reduction in Money Supply

(b)
Reduction in Autonomous Spending

Estimators and Estimates

How close are your estimates to the true values of β_0 and β_1? This is an easy question to answer because you know β_0 and β_1. But how do you evaluate the "goodness" of your estimates if all you know are the data shown in Columns Q_i and C_i in Exercise 1.1? Notice that this is really a question about evaluating the formulas used to calculate the estimates. These formulas define the **estimators.** The actual estimates vary from sample to sample, but the formulas generating these estimates stay the same. Everyone in your class uses the same estimators, whose formulas are programmed into your econometric software, but everyone calculates different estimates.

The estimators $\hat{\beta}_0$ and $\hat{\beta}_1$ are *random variables*. As such, they have probability distributions like other random variables. These distributions can be described by their means and standard deviations. If you know what these distributions look like, you can answer the question about how good your estimates are likely to be by computing confidence intervals.

What does the distribution for the estimator $\hat{\beta}_1$ look like? We could approach this question by generating numerous samples and computing $\hat{\beta}_1$ for each sample. Figure 1.2 shows the frequency distribution of 150 such computations for $\hat{\beta}_1$, which were generated by a computer program. If you did Exercise 1.1 150 times, you could draw such a distribution. The distribution has a mean of .801 and a standard deviation of .039. You could use the mean and standard deviation of this distribution of sample estimates to evaluate the goodness of your estimators.

Evaluating the Econometric Evaluations of Training Programs with Experimental Data

Econometricians intend their empirical studies to reproduce the results of experiments that use random assignment without incurring their costs. One way, then, to evaluate econometric methods is to compare them against experimentally determined results.

This paper undertakes such a comparison and suggests the means by which econometric analyses of employment and training programs may be evaluated. The paper compares the results from a field experiment, where individuals were randomly assigned to participate in a training program, against the array of estimates that an econometrician without experimental data might have produced. It examines the results likely to be reported by an econometrician using nonexperimental data and the most modern techniques, and . . . tests the extent to which the results are sensitive to alternative econometric specifications. The goal is to appraise the likely ability of several econometric methods to accurately assess the economic benefits of employment and training programs. . . .

Conclusion

This study shows that many of the econometric procedures and comparison groups used to evaluate employment and training programs would not have yielded accurate or precise estimates of the impact of the National Supported Work Program. The econometric estimates often differ significantly from the experimental results. Moreover, even when the econometric estimates pass conventional specification tests, they still fail to replicate the experimentally determined results. Even though I was unable to evaluate all nonexperimental methods, this evidence suggests that policymakers should be aware that the available nonexperimental evaluations of employment and training programs may contain large and unknown biases resulting from specification errors.

Source: LaLonde, R. J. "Evaluating the Econometric Evaluations of Training Programs with Experimental Data," *American Economic Review* 76 (September 1986), 604–620.

In the case of ordinary least-squares estimators, however, we can solve for the means and standard deviations analytically, using the **expectation operator.** We need not resort to the kind of exercise summarized in Figure 1.2. Such analytically derived information is always superior because it is exact information. The exercise summarized in Figure 1.2 has several associated difficulties. First, we could generate a distribution of sample estimates that is an inaccurate distribution. Improbable events do happen. Because we don't know the true random error term to begin with, we would also have to assume that our guesses about the true values are reasonable. Finally, we hardly want to go through such a laborious procedure to derive approximations for estimator distributions every time we compute a regression.

In advanced econometric work, there are times when it is impossible to analytically solve for the distribution of an estimator for small sample sizes. In these cases, econometricians proceed in the manner of Figure 1.2. They specify a set of parameters for an assumed model, generate a large number of samples of some explicit size, and calculate the various estimates. The distributions of the estimates are then analyzed. These empirical studies are called **Monte Carlo,** or **stochastic studies.**

Figure 1.2
Frequency Distribution for 150 Estimates of $\hat{\beta}_1$

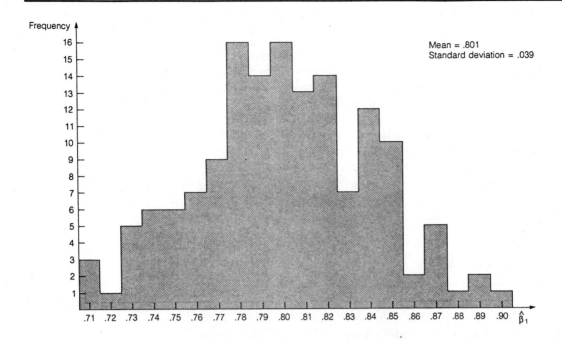

Your text explains the analytically derived properties of the distributions of the ordinary least-squares estimators. Because these derivations are so important, we go over some of the properties here. This is one case where a little repetition, if not good for the soul, is not likely to do any harm. (If you have trouble using the expectation operator, work through Lesson 2 before going further in this lesson.)

Assume a simple regression model obeying the **classical ordinary least-squares assumptions:**[3]

1. The dependent or explained variable Y is a linear specification of the independent or explanatory variable X and a random error term u:

    $$Y_i = \beta_0 + \beta_1 X_i + u_i, \qquad \text{for } i = 1, \dots, n$$

    For the classical ordinary least-squares model to be valid, Y (or some transformation of Y) must be a linear function of X (or some transformation of X). In other words, Y must be *linear in the parameters* of the specification. (The significance of the phrase "linear in the parameters" will become clear in Lesson 6.)

2. Each X_i is a fixed value that remains the same in repeated samples.

3. The expected value of the random error term is 0:

    $$E(u_i) = 0, \qquad \text{for } i = 1, \dots, n$$

4. The random error term has a constant variance:

    $$E(u_i u_j) = \sigma_u^2, \qquad \text{for } i = j; \, i,j = 1, \dots, n$$

5. The random error terms are uncorrelated:

    $$E(u_i u_j) = 0, \qquad \text{for } i \neq j; \, i,j = 1, \dots, n$$

A random error term that satisfies the classical assumptions is often described as being "well behaved."

Most demonstrations of the properties of ordinary least-squares estimators begin by rewriting the regression model in *deviation form* to make it easier to manipulate the calculations. To write the regression model in deviation form, each observation is expressed in terms of its distance from the means $\bar{X}$ and $\bar{Y}$. The observation (X_i, Y_i) is expressed in deviation form as $(X_i - \bar{X}, Y_i - \bar{Y})$ or (x_i, y_i), where $x_i = X_i - \bar{X}$ and $y_i = Y_i - \bar{Y}$. Generations of beginning econometric students have complained that it is difficult to distinguish a lowercase from an uppercase x in econometric formulas. We indicate the lowercase letters in italics to try and make the difference as clear as possible.

The regression line associated with a given data set always passes through the point of means $(\bar{X}, \bar{Y})$, as illustrated in Figure 1.3. When the data are written in deviation form, the new deviation axes must cross at the point of means. This has the effect of dropping the intercept term from the regression. In other words, the regression line in Figure 1.3 can be looked at with respect to the X and Y axes with the intercept $\hat{\beta}_0$, or with respect to the x and y axes with no intercept. *It is the same regression line.* The regression model in deviation form is written

$$y_i = \beta_1 x_i + u_i, \quad \text{for } i = 1, \dots, n \tag{1.7}$$

Notice that writing the model in deviation form is *not* the same as forcing the regression line to have a 0 intercept. A regression line forced to have a 0 intercept must pass through the point $(0,0)$ with respect to the X and Y axes. It is sometimes desirable to assume that a model's intercept is 0, and most econometric software allows regression models to be estimated with no intercept term. We turn our attention to forcing the parameters of regression models to obey such restrictions in Lesson 7.

The slope estimator associated with the model in deviation form can be shown to be

$$\hat{\beta}_1 = \frac{\Sigma x_i y_i}{\Sigma x_i^2} = \Sigma w_i y_i, \quad \text{where } w_i = \frac{x_i}{\Sigma x_i^2} \tag{1.8}$$

Because it is understood that values are being summed over the sample cases, the index of summation is dropped from below the summation sign. The w_i's are called **ordinary least-squares weights**. Because the x_i's are fixed values, the w_i's must also be fixed values.

Because any observed value y_i is assumed to be generated by Equation 1.7, Equation 1.7 can be substituted for y_i in Equation 1.8. This substitution gives

$$\hat{\beta}_1 = \Sigma w_i(\beta_1 x_i + u_i) \tag{1.9}$$

Using the rules of summation, Equation 1.9 can be rewritten as

$$\hat{\beta}_1 = \Sigma w_i \beta_1 x_i + \Sigma w_i u_i \quad \text{(distributive property of } \Sigma) \tag{1.10}$$

which becomes

$$\hat{\beta}_1 = \beta_1 \Sigma w_i x_i + \Sigma w_i u_i \quad \text{(because } \beta_1 \text{ is a constant)} \tag{1.11}$$

Equation 1.11 reduces to

$$\hat{\beta}_1 = \beta_1 + \Sigma w_i u_i \quad \text{(because } \Sigma w_i x_i = 1) \tag{1.12}$$

Taking the expected value of both sides of Equation 1.12 gives

$$E(\hat{\beta}_1) = E(\beta_1) + E(\Sigma w_i u_i) \quad \text{(distributive property of } E) \tag{1.13}$$

$$E(\hat{\beta}_1) = \beta_1 + E(\Sigma w_i u_i) \quad \text{(because } \beta_1 \text{ is a constant)} \tag{1.14}$$

Figure 1.3
The Regression Model in Deviation Form

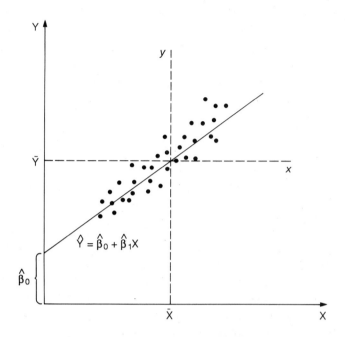

$$E(\hat{\beta}_1) = \beta_1 + \Sigma w_i E(u_i) \quad \text{(because each } w_i \text{ is a constant)} \tag{1.15}$$

$$E(\hat{\beta}_1) = \beta_1 \quad \text{(because } E(u_i) = 0) \tag{1.16}$$

Equation 1.16 shows that the expected value of the slope estimator is equal to the true parameter. Thus the ordinary least-squares slope estimator is *unbiased*. It can be shown in a similar manner that the ordinary least-squares intercept estimator $\hat{\beta}_0$ is unbiased.

EXERCISE 1.2

Calculate the ordinary least-squares weight for each data case in Exercise 1.1. Record your work in the blank columns.

Q_i	$q_i = Q_i - \bar{Q}$	q_i^2	$w_i = \dfrac{q_i}{\Sigma q_i^2}$
4,000	_____	_____	_____
5,000	_____	_____	_____
5,000	_____	_____	_____
5,000	_____	_____	_____
6,000	_____	_____	_____
7,000	_____	_____	_____

Q_i	$q_i = Q_i - \bar{Q}$	q_i^2	$w_i = \dfrac{q_i}{\Sigma q_i^2}$
12,000	_____	_____	_____
20,000	_____	_____	_____
25,000	_____	_____	_____
30,000	_____	_____	_____
$\Sigma Q_i =$		$\Sigma q_i^2 =$	

$$\bar{Q} = \frac{\Sigma Q_i}{10} =$$

Equation 1.8 shows that the ordinary least-squares slope estimator can be described as a weighted sum of the actual observations on the dependent variable. In other words, $\hat{\beta}_1$ is a *linear function* of the sample observations. Verify that Equation 1.8 is true for the estimate $\hat{\beta}_1$ you calculated in Exercise 1.1. (Rounding error may prevent you from getting an answer that is exactly the same as that generated in Exercise 1.1.) Show your work below.

_____

_____

_____

_____

_____

Next, solve for the variance of the slope estimator. Remember that $\text{var}(\hat{\beta}_1) = E(\hat{\beta}_1 - E(\hat{\beta}_1))^2$ by definition and that $E(\hat{\beta}_1) = \beta_1$. Begin by subtracting β_1 from both sides of Equation 1.12. This subtraction gives

$$(\hat{\beta}_1 - \beta_1) = \Sigma w_i u_i \qquad (1.17)$$

Squaring both sides of Equation 1.17 yields

$$(\hat{\beta}_1 - \beta_1)^2 = (\Sigma w_i u_i)^2 \qquad (1.18)$$

Taking the expected values of both sides of Equation 1.18 gives

$$E(\hat{\beta}_1 - \beta_1)^2 = E(w_1^2 u_1^2 + \ldots + w_n^2 u_n^2 + 2w_1 w_2 u_1 u_2 + \ldots + 2w_{n-1} w_n u_{n-1} u_n)$$

(writing out the summation elements) $\qquad (1.19)$

$$E(\hat{\beta}_1 - \beta_1)^2 = w_1^2 E(u_1^2) + \ldots + w_n^2 E(u_n^2) + 2w_1 w_2 E(u_1 u_2) + \ldots + w_{n-1} w_n E(u_{n-1} u_n)$$

(because w_i is a constant) $\qquad (1.20)$

$$E(\hat{\beta}_1 - \beta_1)^2 = w_1^2 E(u_1^2) + \dots + w_n^2 E(u_n^2) \qquad \text{(because } E(u_iu_j) = 0, \quad \text{for } i \neq j) \tag{1.21}$$

$$E(\hat{\beta}_1 - \beta_1)^2 = \sigma_u^2 \Sigma w_i^2 \qquad \text{(because each } E(u_i^2) = \sigma_u^2) \tag{1.22}$$

$$E(\hat{\beta}_1 - \beta_1)^2 = \frac{\sigma_u^2}{\Sigma x_i^2} \qquad \text{(because } \Sigma w_i^2 = \frac{1}{\Sigma x_i^2}) \tag{1.23}$$

The standard deviation of $\hat{\beta}_1$ ($\sigma_{\hat{\beta}_1}$) is then

$$\sigma_{\hat{\beta}_1} = \frac{\sigma_u}{\sqrt{\Sigma x_i^2}} \tag{1.24}$$

The standard deviation of the slope estimator is referred to as the **standard error of the estimator.**

In summary, the mean of the distribution of $\hat{\beta}_1$ is equal to the true parameter value. The standard deviation of the distribution of $\hat{\beta}_1$ is determined by the values of the independent variable and the standard deviation of the random error term. Additional properties are discussed in your text. Specifically, it can be shown that ordinary least-squares estimators are the **best linear unbiased estimators (BLUE).** An estimator is BLUE if (a) it is a linear function of the sample observations; (b) it is unbiased; and (c) it has a variance less than or equal to the variance of any other linear unbiased estimator. Equations 1.8 and 1.16 establish the first two results for ordinary least-squares estimators. The "best" in BLUE refers to the result that the estimator has minimum variance within the class of linear unbiased estimators. Such an estimator is said to be *efficient* within the class of linear unbiased estimators. This result is established for ordinary least-squares estimators by the **Gauss–Markov Theorem.**[4]

EXERCISE 1.3

Calculate the standard error of the estimator $\hat{\beta}_1$ for the consumption function in Exercise 1.1 using the *analytically derived* Equation 1.24. The values for this calculation can be found on pages 3 and 12.

_____

_____

What is the *analytically derived* mean of the distribution of $\hat{\beta}_1$ for the consumption function in Exercise 1.1? (HINT: Look at Equation 1.16.)

_____

_____

_____

_____

How do the *analytically derived* standard error and mean compare with those computed for the distribution shown in Figure 1.2?

_____

_____

_____

_____

A real-world econometrician would not know, of course, the true standard deviation of the random error term you used to answer Exercise 1.3. Like β_0 and β_1, σ_u is an unknown parameter. How is an estimate for this parameter derived? Go back to Exercise 1.1. Estimates of the error associated with each predicted value of consumption spending are shown in Column $\hat{u}_i$. It seems intuitively reasonable that the values in this column, the **regression residuals**, should provide the basic information for a good estimate of the random error term's standard deviation. These residuals are in fact used to arrive at the estimate. The formula for the estimate is

$$\hat{\sigma}_u = \sqrt{\frac{\Sigma \hat{u}_i^2}{(n-2)}}$$

(1.25)

This sample estimate of the true standard deviation of the random error term is called the **standard error of the regression** or the **standard error of the estimate**, depending on which text you are using. It is often indicated by the letter s.

EXERCISE 1.4

Using your econometric software, find the standard error of the regression for the consumption function in Exercise 1.1. How does your sample estimate compare with the true value?

_____

_____

_____

How will the analytically derived distribution for $\hat{\beta}_1$ change if the random error term associated with Equation 1.6 has a standard deviation of $500 instead of $1155?

_____

_____

_____

Justification for the Random Error Term

We have shown how the random error term affects the dependent variable in a regression model and the distributions of ordinary least-squares estimators. The inclusion of the random error term is clearly of critical importance to regression methodology. But is its inclusion really justified?

Econometricians usually have no second thoughts about including the random error term, feeling comfortable that its inclusion is justified. Indeed, convincing arguments can be made. Suppose that we know all the variables that cause consumption spending; consumption spending then is fully explained by these variables. For example, if we knew the values of these variables for each of the countries in Exercise 1.1, we could explain each level of observed consumption with no error. This last statement isn't completely correct because the sample of ten countries is much too small to allow valid statistical inferences about the relationships between a multiple of variables and consumption spending. We would need a much larger sample. But if we had a very large sample and included almost all the relevant variables in a multiple regression model instead of the single independent variable model, the random error term would be quite small. Even for a large sample, however, it would be difficult to account accurately for variables that have a very small effect on consumption spending. Some excluded variables would be difficult or impossible to quantify; others would have very small effects on consumption spending.

The random error term u can be thought of as capturing the net effect of such excluded variables. The excluded variables can be expected to work in opposite directions, some tending to increase consumption spending and others tending to decrease consumption spending. Thus, small values of u are more likely than large values, and it seems reasonable to expect the mean of u to be 0. This argument losses validity if a variable that is important in explaining consumption spending is contained in the set of excluded variables.

A second argument for including the random error term is that the term describes random measurement error in the dependent variables. This justification is a bit tricky. If the dependent variable contains measurement error, is it not likely that the independent variable contains measurement error? As you will see later in the course, measurement error in the independent variable can pose serious problems in interpreting ordinary least-squares estimators.

Finally, it is sometimes argued that there is a random, unpredictable element in human behavior, with the unpredictable element being captured by the random error term. This is really an argument based on psychological assumptions about human behavior, with which you may or may not agree. In any case, this last argument cannot be distinguished from the first argument in any empirically meaningful manner. Is the error between an observed and predicted value the result of a random element in human behavior or of our inability to identify the relevant variables?

EXERCISE 1.5

Make a list of all the variables you can think of that might influence a country's level of consumption spending.

We assumed a model and generated data in Exercise 1.1 to gain an understanding of how the random error term works. This in no way implies that Equation 1.5 is the proper specification to be used in actual empirical work. Look at your list of variables carefully. Do you see any difficulties with assuming the effects of these variables are captured by u? (HINT: Is wealth on your list?) Might these difficulties explain why econometricians seldom estimate the consumption function using a data set of countries, preferring instead to estimate the consumption function for a given country with income and consumption spending observed at different times?

_____

_____

_____

_____

We have seen that the estimators $\hat{\beta}_0$ and $\hat{\beta}_1$ are random variables. The **covariance** of a joint distribution of two random variables measures the extent to which the two random variables are linearly associated. (If you need to refresh your knowledge of covariance, read "Means, Variances, and Covariances" in Lesson 2.)

EXERCISE 1.6

Do you think $\hat{\beta}_0$ and $\hat{\beta}_1$ are linearly associated? That is, would you expect the covariance of their joint distribution to be 0, positive, or negative? If you knew you had overestimated β_0, would you expect your estimate for β_1 to be overestimated, underestimated, or not affected? Explain why.

_____

_____

_____

_____

Figure 1.4 shows a scattergram of estimates $\hat{\beta}_0$ and $\hat{\beta}_1$ computed from the 150 samples discussed earlier. Was your answer above in the right direction? The covariance of this scattergram is −19.305. This covariance is an empirical estimate of the true covariance of the joint distribution of $\hat{\beta}_0$ and $\hat{\beta}_1$. The covariance of the joint distribution can be solved for analytically using the expectation operator. The resulting formula is

$$\text{cov}(\hat{\beta}_0, \hat{\beta}_1) = \frac{-\bar{X}\sigma_u^2}{\Sigma x_i^2}$$

Figure 1.4
Scattergram for 150 Sample Estimates of β_0 and β_1

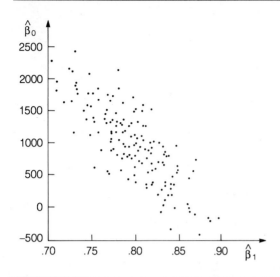

EXERCISE 1.7

Draw a sketch of the distribution of the random error term used to generate Table 1.1.

Does the fact that *u* is *not* normally distributed affect the *analytically derived* mean and variance of the sampling distribution for $\hat{\beta}_1$? What additional ordinary least-squares properties exist if *u* is assumed to be normally distributed? (You must consult your text to answer this question.)

_____

_____

_____

_____

_____

Expected Values

1. To review the algebra of expectations
2. To review selected statistical concepts
3. To provide practice in using the algebra of expectations

Most econometric texts present a set of rules for finding expected values. This set of rules, the **algebra of expectations**, derives the means and variances of expressions containing random variables. You will find many such applications in your text. An especially important application is the derivation of the means and variances of ordinary least-squares estimators. Students often have difficulty with these applications because they don't feel comfortable working with expected values. For many students, the simple statement of expected value rules doesn't convey enough understanding of the rules or provide facility in using the rules.

If you have trouble understanding expected values, work through this lesson. Because the algebra of expectations derives from the rules of summation, the first section reviews the rules of summation. The second section briefly discusses the features of probability distributions. The final section develops the algebra of expectations. After finishing the lesson, you will be able to solve for expected values and will have a better grasp of the general properties of random variables that are functions of other random variables.

Rules of Summation

Sigma Notation

Statisticians and mathematicians deal with sequences of summed numbers. To simplify their discussions, they use the Greek capital letter sigma (Σ) to describe the operation of summation. Capital sigma corresponds to our letter S and was the obvious Greek letter to use when mathematicians wanted a notation for summation. Always read the sigma sign as "the sum of." A general element of a summed sequence is written in terms of an **index of summation** and placed to the right of the sigma sign. The index of summation takes on a series of integer values, starting at some initial value and ending at some final value. The initial value is below the sigma sign; the final value is above the sigma sign.

To see how the sigma notation works, consider the following summation sequence:

$$1+2+3+4+5$$

Let i be the index of summation. The general element for the sequence is then $(1 + i)$, and the summed sequence is

$$\sum_{i=0}^{4} (1 + i)$$

A summed sequence does not have to be specific numbers, and the initial and final values for the index of summation do not have to be specific integers. For example, we write the sequence

$$(x_1 + a) + (x_2 + a) + \ldots + (x_n + a)$$

in sigma notation as

$$\sum_{i=1}^{n} (x_i + a)$$

To indicate the *i*th value of *x*, we use the index of summation as a subscript. The sequence is summed to the *n*th value of *i*. The sigma notation thus can be used to express general formulas.

The initial and final values of the index of summation sometimes are omitted if they are not necessary. For example, the mean of a **discrete random variable** X, μ_x, is usually written

$$\mu_x = \sum_{x} Xp(X)$$

The notation $\sum_{x}$ reads as "the sum over all values of X." Because the values of X are defined over the sample space of the probability experiment, a specific index of summation is not necessary.[1] The X is often dropped from below the sigma sign when the reader is assumed to know it is the index of summation. Thus, the mean of a discrete random variable is sometimes written

$$\mu_x = \sum Xp(X)$$

Econometric discussions frequently drop the index of summation when the definition of the index is clear from the context of the argument.

EXERCISE 2.1

Show the summation sequence associated with each of the following sigma notations. Notice that the index of summation is always below the sigma sign. While *i* is often indicated as the index of summation, any alphabetic character can be used.

$$\sum_{x=1}^{4} 5x =$$

$$\sum_{i=1}^{6} x_i =$$

$$\sum_{i=1}^{3} x^i =$$

$$\sum_{i=1}^{3} 2^i =$$

$$\sum_{i=0}^{3} 2^i =$$

$$\sum_{i=1}^{4} (x + 1 + i) =$$

$$\sum_{x=1}^{3} (x + xy^2) =$$

$$\sum_{i=1}^{n} ax_i =$$

$$\sum_{i=1}^{n} (x_i - b)^2 =$$

Three Rules of Summation

Most algebra texts discuss the three rules of summation. These rules derive the algebra of expectations. As you go over the rules, notice that constant c is defined as a term that does not contain the index of summation. It can, of course, contain other variables.

Rule 1: Let c be a constant and i the index of summation, then

$$\sum_{i=1}^{n} c = nc$$

Examples:

$$\sum_{i=1}^{5} 3 = 3 + 3 + 3 + 3 + 3 = 15$$

$$\sum_{i=1}^{3} x = x + x + x = 3x$$

If you have trouble with this rule, think for a moment about what the sigma sign means: Take the sum of the general element on its right a certain number of times. In the first example, the general element is 3. The sigma notation instructs you to sum the general element five times.

Rule 2: Let c be a constant and i the index of summation, then

$$\sum_{i=1}^{n} cx_i = c \sum_{i=1}^{n} x_i$$

Examples:

$$\sum_{i=1}^{3} 5i = 5 \cdot 1 + 5 \cdot 2 + 5 \cdot 3 = 5(1 + 2 + 3) = 5 \sum_{i=1}^{3} i$$

$$\sum_{x=1}^{3} (y + 5)x = (y + 5)1 + (y + 5)2 + (y + 5)3 = (y + 5) \sum_{x=1}^{3} x$$

Notice that $(y + 5)$ in the second example is a constant from the standpoint of the summation operation. It does not contain the index of summation.

Rule 3: Let i be the index of summation, then

$$\sum_{i=1}^{n} (x_i + y_i + z_i) = \sum_{i=1}^{n} x_i + \sum_{i=1}^{n} y_i + \sum_{i=1}^{n} z$$

Example:

$$\sum_{i=1}^{n} (x_i^2 + x_i) = \sum_{i=1}^{n} x_i^2 + \sum_{i=1}^{n} x_i$$

This is a very important rule. In mathematic terms, *the summation operation can be distributed when the only other operation to be carried out before the sum is taken is itself a sum or difference.*

The three rules used together can simplify many summation procedures. For example,

$$\sum_{x=1}^{3} (x^2 + 2x + 5) = \sum_{x=1}^{3} x^2 + \sum_{x=1}^{3} 2x + \sum_{x=1}^{3} 5 \quad \text{(by rule 3)}$$

$$= \sum_{x=1}^{3} x^2 + 2 \sum_{x=1}^{3} x + \sum_{x=1}^{3} 5 \quad \text{(by rule 2)}$$

$$= \sum_{x=1}^{3} x^2 + 2 \sum_{x=1}^{3} x + 3 \cdot 5 \quad \text{(by rule 1)}$$

$$= (1 + 4 + 9) + 2(1 + 2 + 3) + 15 = 41$$

EXERCISE 2.2

Evaluate the following summation sequences using the three rules of summation.

$$\sum_{i=1}^{10} 5 =$$

$$\sum_{i=1}^{6} 5x_i =$$

$$\sum_{i=5}^{8} (3i + 5) =$$

$$\sum_{x=1}^{4} (x + 3)^2 =$$

$$\sum_{x=1}^{3} (x^3 + 5x^2 + x) =$$

$$\sum_{x=1}^{4} \frac{x}{y} =$$

EXERCISE 2.3

The following formulas estimate the mean and variance of a variable from a data set:

$$\bar{x} = \frac{\Sigma x_i}{n} \quad \text{and} \quad s^2 = \frac{\Sigma(x_i - \bar{x})^2}{(n-1)}$$

Answer the following questions using the rules of summation:

1. A weather researcher finds an error in the recording of temperature data. All observations in a data set are 3 degrees too low because of a faulty temperature gauge. The researcher adds 3 degrees to each observation. How do the mean and variance for the corrected data differ from the mean and variance for the erroneous data?

_____

_____

_____

2. An economist is dealing with income data for a sample of consumers. The mean income for the sample is $15,000. The variance for income is $4000. The economist decides to change the data to hundreds of dollars to be directly comparable with other data measured in hundreds of dollars. For example, an income of $1000 becomes $10 when written in hundreds of dollars. Solve for the mean and variance of the transformed income data.

_____

_____

_____

Means, Variances, and Covariances

Two important characteristics of a probability distribution are the distribution's mean and variance. Table 2.1a shows the probability distribution for a discrete random variable X and shows how to compute the mean and variance of the distribution.[2] To compute the mean, multiply each value of X by its probability. The sum of these products is the mean.

$$\mu_x = \sum_x Xp(X) = E(x) \tag{2.1}$$

Table 2.1
The Mean and Variance of a Random Variable

(a)

X	$p(X)$	$Xp(X)$	$(X-\mu_x)^2\, p\,(X)$
2	.5	1	$(2-5)^2(.5)$
5	.2	1	$(5-5)^2(.2)$
10	.3	3	$(10-5)^2(.3)$
		$\mu_x = \Sigma Xp(X) = 5$	$\sigma_x^2 = \Sigma(X-\mu)^2p(X) = 12$

(b)

Y = 2X	$p(Y)$	$Yp(Y)$	$(Y-\mu_y)^2p(Y)$
4	____	____	____
10	____	____	____
20	____	____	____
	$\mu_y =$	$\sigma_y^2 =$	

(c)

Z = X + 2	$p(Z)$	$Zp(Z)$	$(Z-\mu_z)^2p(Z)$
4	____	____	____
7	____	____	____
12	____	____	____
	$\mu_z =$	$\sigma_z^2 =$	

To compute the variance of X, subtract the mean of X from each value of X. Square the resulting values. Finally, multiply each squared term by the probability of the relevant X. The sum of these product terms is the variance.

$$\sigma_x^2 = \sum_x (X-\mu_x)^2p(X) = E\,(x-\mu_x)^2 \tag{2.2}$$

EXERCISE 2.4

To make sure you understand how to compute the mean and variance of a probability distribution, compute the means and variances for the random variables Y and Z shown in Table 2.1b and 2.1c. Show your work by filling in the blank lines. Notice that both Y and Z are functions of X. For example, the probability of Y equal to 4 must be the same as the probability of X equal to 2.

Statisticians often deal with two random variables defined for the same sample space. In these cases, they want to know the joint occurrence of values for the two random variables. This information is given by the **joint probability distribution**. Table 2.2a shows a joint probability distribution. Read the probability of observing the joint occurrence of any two values of X and Y directly from the table. For example, the probability of observing X equal to 0 and Y equal to 2 is .4. The probabilities in a joint probability table must sum to 1.

Statisticians in general and econometricians in particular want to know the extent to which two jointly occurring random variables are *linearly associated*. You will remember from your statistics course that the answer to this question is found by computing the **covariance** of the joint probability distribution. Table 2.2b shows how the covariance is calculated for the distribution shown in part a. The formula for calculating the covariance is at the bottom of part b. First, compute the means of the two random variables. Next, determine the deviations from the means for jointly occurring values of the two variables. When X and Y both increase or decrease together, the product of the deviations is positive. When X and Y move inversely, the product of the deviations is negative. Finally, multiply each deviation product term by the joint probability of the two random variables values. The sum of all the product deviation terms multiplied by their joint probabilities gives a measure of the linear association between the two variables.

EXERCISE 2.5

Solve for the joint probability distribution of Y and Z by filling in the blank lines in Table 2.2c. Notice that Z is a function of X. Next, compute the covariance for the joint distribution shown in part c. Use the blank lines in part d to show your work.

When used directly as a measure of linear association, the covariance has an interpretation problem. The value of the covariance depends on the units in which X and Y are measured. If the units change, the covariance changes. A measure of linear association that fluctuates with measurement units obviously is not very easy to interpret. For this reason, the covariance is usually transformed into the **correlation coefficient** (ρ) by dividing through by the standard deviations of X and the standard deviation of Y. This transformation yields a unitless measure of linear association:

$$\rho = \frac{\sigma_{xy}}{\sigma_x \sigma_y}$$

(2.3)

The correlation coefficient is estimated from sample data using the following formula:

$$\hat{\rho} = \frac{\Sigma x_i y_i}{(n-1)\hat{\sigma}_x \hat{\sigma}_y}$$

(2.4)

Table 2.2
The Covariance of a Joint Probability Distribution

(a)

Y	X		
	0	1	2
0	.0	.0	.2
1	.0	.2	.2
2	.4	.0	.0

(b)

(X,Y)	$(X - \mu_x)(Y - \mu_y)p(X,Y)$		
(0,0)	$(0 - 1)(0 - 1.2)(.0)$	=	.0
(0,1)	$(0 - 1)(1 - 1.2)(.0)$	=	.0
(0,2)	$(0 - 1)(2 - 1.2)(.4)$	=	−.32
(1,0)	$(1 - 1)(0 - 1.2)(.0)$	=	.0
(1,1)	$(1 - 1)(1 - 1.2)(.2)$	=	.0
(1,2)	$(1 - 1)(2 - 1.2)(.0)$	=	.0
(2,0)	$(2 - 1)(0 - 1.2)(.2)$	=	−.24
(2,1)	$(2 - 1)(1 - 1.2)(.2)$	=	−.04
(2,2)	$(2 - 1)(2 - 1.2)(.0)$	=	.0

$$\sigma_{xy} = \sum_x \sum_y (X - \mu_x)(Y - \mu_y)p(X,Y) \quad = \quad -.60$$

(c)

Y	Z (Z = 3X)		
	0	3	6
0	___	___	___
1	___	___	___
2	___	___	___

(d)

(Z,Y)	$(Z - \mu_z)(Y - \mu_y)p(Z,Y)$		
___	_____	=	___
___	_____	=	___
___	_____	=	___
___	_____	=	___
___	_____	=	___
___	_____	=	___
___	_____	=	___
___	_____	=	___
___	_____	=	___
___	_____	=	___
	σ_{zy}	=	___

Compare Equation 2.4 with the formula for the regression slope estimator written in deviation form:

$$\hat{\beta}_1 = \frac{\Sigma x_i y_i}{\Sigma x_i^2}$$ (2.5)

Notice that both $\hat{\beta}_1$ and $\hat{\rho}$ contain the term $\Sigma x_i y_i$. Because their formulas look similar, the correlation coefficient and the slope estimator are sometimes confused. The two values, however, convey somewhat different information. The correlation coefficient is a measure of the extent to which X and Y are linearly associated. Ranging between −1 and +1, it measures the extent to which X and Y *cluster along a straight line*. A positive value for $\hat{\rho}$ indicates a positive linear association. When $\hat{\rho}$ = +1, all sample points lie along a positively sloped line. A negative value for $\hat{\rho}$ indicates a negative linear association. When $\hat{\rho}$ = −1, all sample points lie along a negatively sloped line. Finally, when $\hat{\rho}$ = 0, there is no linear association between X and Y. As $\hat{\rho}$ moves away from 0 toward −1 or +1 in a statistically significant manner, the strength of the linear association increases. In contrast, the slope estimator indicates the change in Y that follows from a one-unit change in X. It measures the *slope of an ordinary least-squares regression line* fitted to values of X and Y.

EXERCISE 2.6

How will the correlation coefficient and the ordinary least-squares slope estimate differ for the sample data shown in Figure 2.1?

_____

_____

_____

_____

_____

Will the correlation coefficient and the slope estimate always have the same sign?

_____

_____

_____

Will $\hat{\beta}_1$ always equal 0 when $\hat{\rho}$ equals 0?

_____

_____

_____

Figure 2.1
Sample Data Sets for Exercise 2.6

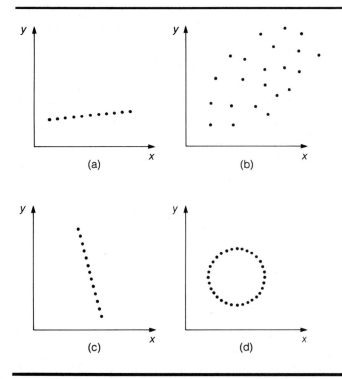

(a)

(b)

(c)

(d)

EXERCISE 2.7

Assume that a probability experiment consists of tossing two coins. Show the joint probability distribution for this experiment. A head is indicated by 1 and a tail by 5.

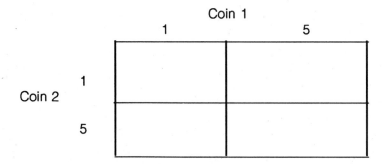

Solve for the joint distribution's covariance.

Two random variables X and Y are statistically *independent* if and only if $p(X|Y) = p(X)$ for all values of X and Y. (The notation I reads as "given.") If $p(X|Y) \neq p(X)$, the variables are statistically *dependent*. Show that the two random variables in this exercise are statistically independent.

When two random variables are statistically independent, $p(X,Y) = p(X)p(Y)$ for all values of X and Y. Verify that this is true for the joint probability distribution shown above.

Show that X and Y in Table 2.2a are statistically dependent.

Statistical independence implies a covariance of 0. But a covariance of 0 does not imply statistical independence. Random variables can be associated in a nonlinear manner. Compute the covariance for the following joint probability distribution in the space provided below.

		X		
		1	2	3
	1	.25	0	.25
Y	2	0	0	0
	3	.25	0	.25

The covariance is

Are the two random variables statistically independent?

Double Sigmas

If you have trouble working with the double-sigma operation in solving for covariances, work through the problems in this section. To see how the double-sigma notation is used, consider the following summation sequence:

$$X_{11} + X_{12} + X_{13} + X_{21} + X_{22} + X_{23}$$

This sequence, written using double sigmas, is

$$\sum_{i=1}^{2} \sum_{j=1}^{3} X_{ij}$$

The double-sigma signs read from left to right. The notation instructs first to set i equal to 1 and sum over all values of j. Next, set i equal to 2 and sum over all values of j.

EXERCISE 2.8

Statistical discussions often use two double-summation results. These results are indicated below. Show that these results are true for $n = 3$.

$$\sum_{i=1}^{n} \sum_{j=1}^{n} X_i Y_j = \left(\sum_{i=1}^{n} X_i \right) \left(\sum_{j=1}^{n} Y_j \right)$$

_____

_____

_____

_____

$$\sum_{i=1}^{n} \sum_{j=1}^{n} (X_{ij} + Y_{ij}) = \sum_{i=1}^{n} \sum_{j=1}^{n} X_{ij} + \sum_{i=1}^{n} \sum_{j=1}^{n} Y_{ij}$$

_____

_____

_____

_____

Also show that, in general, $\displaystyle\sum_{i=1}^{n} X_i Y_i \neq \left(\sum_{i=1}^{n} X_i \right) \left(\sum_{i=1}^{n} Y_i \right)$

_____

_____

_____

_____

Algebra of Expectations

The expected value of a random variable is simply the *mean* of the random variable. Thus, if X is a discrete random variable, its expected value by definition is

$$E(X) = \sum_x Xp(X) \qquad (2.6)$$

Why introduce a new term that is simply another way of referring to the mean? Knowledge of the mean of a random variable is a basic piece of information in many kinds of problems. In decision problems, the mean of a probability distribution shows the decision maker what he or she can expect to receive on average. Hence the term *expected value*. More significantly, statistical theory requires that we know the means and variances of estimators to develop the properties of estimators. A more general notation defined in terms of summation is thus useful.

To see the insights yielded by the general notation, consider the variance of the random variable X:

$$\sigma_x^2 = \sum_x (X - \mu_x)^2 p(X) \qquad (2.7)$$

Notice that the square of the deviations for X around its mean can be defined as a random variable. Let Z be this random variable. Then Equation 2.7 is equal to

$$\sigma_x^2 = \sum_z Zp(Z)$$

In other words, the variance of the random variable X can be thought of as being the mean or expected value of the random variable Z. *The variance of X is a weighted average, just as the mean of X is a weighted average.*

Using expected-value notation, the variance of X is defined as

$$E(X - E(X))^2 = \sum_x (X - \mu_x)^2 p(X) \qquad (2.8)$$

The covariance is also the mean of a random variable that is a function of two other random variables. Using expected-value notation, the covariance of X and Y is defined as

$$E[(X - E(X))(Y - E(Y))] = \sum_x \sum_y (X - \mu_x)(Y - \mu_y)p(X,Y) \qquad (2.9)$$

In looking at the probability distributions shown in Tables 2.1 and 2.2, it is obvious that general rules for finding the means and variances of random variables that are functions of other random variables would be extremely convenient. The summation formulas show how to calculate these values, but the formulas are tedious to apply to specific cases. The algebra of expectations provides such a set of rules.

Expected-Value Rules

The important point to grasp is that *an expected value is a sum of weighted values.* This means that we can find expected-value rules by using summation procedures. This section shows how several rules are derived and gives practice in using the rules. Symbol *E* is referred to as the **expectation operator.** Symbol *E* indicates that the operation of finding an expected value should be performed on the term shown in parentheses to its right.

Rule 1: The expected value of a constant is the constant:

$$E(a) = a$$

By definition, the expected value of a constant is equal to

$$E(a) = \sum_a a p(a)$$

Because a is a constant, the summation sign makes reference to only one element, $ap(a)$. The probability of a must equal 1. Thus, the expected value of a must equal a.

Rule 2: The expected value of a constant times a random variable is equal to the constant times the expected value of the random variable:

$$E(aX) = aE(X)$$

By definition the expected value of a constant times a random variable is

$$E(aX) = \sum_x aX p(aX)$$

The probability of aX must be the same as the probability of X for any value of X. It follows that

$$E(aX) = \sum_x aX p(X)$$

$$E(aX) = a\sum_x X p(X)$$

$$E(aX) = aE(X)$$

Rule 3: The expected value of a random variable plus a constant is equal to the expected value of the random variable plus the constant:

$$E(X + a) = E(X) + a$$

EXERCISE 2.9

Show how Rule 3 is derived using the rules of summation.

_____

_____

_____

_____

Rule 4: The expected value of the sum of two random variables is equal to the sum of their expected values:

$$E(X + Y) = E(X) + E(Y)$$

From the definition of expected value,

$$E(X + Y) = \sum_x \sum_y (X + Y)p(X,Y)$$

It follows that

$$E(X + Y) = \sum_x \sum_y (Xp(X,Y) + Yp(X,Y))$$

$$E(X + Y) = \sum_x \sum_y Xp(X,Y) + \sum_x \sum_y Yp(X,Y)$$

But for any value of X, $\sum_y p(X,Y) = p(X)$

And for any value of Y, $\sum_x p(X,Y) = p(Y)$

(If you have trouble seeing these last two statements, refer to Table 2.2a. Show that the statements are true for the values of X and Y shown in the joint probability table.)

Thus,

$$\sum_x \sum_y Xp(X) + \sum_x \sum_y Yp(Y) = \sum_x Xp(X) + \sum_y Yp(Y)$$

But by definition, this is

$$E(X) + E(Y)$$

Rule 4 allows the expectations operator to be *distributed over any summed expression*. It is an extremely important rule because it can be extended to any number of random variables. Suppose, for example, you want to find the expected value of $X + Y + Z$, where Y equals X^2 and Z equals 2X:

$$E(X + Y + Z) = E(X + X^2 + 2X)$$

Using Rule 4,

$$E(X + Y + Z) = E(X) + E(X^2) + E(2X)$$

Rule 5: If X and Y are two *independent* random variables, the expected value of X times Y is equal to the expected value of X times the expected value of Y:

$$E(XY) = E(X)E(Y)$$

By definition,

$$E(XY) = \sum_x \sum_y XYp(XY)$$

Because X and Y are independent random variables, $p(XY) = p(X)p(Y)$:

$$E(XY) = \sum_x \sum_y XYp(X)p(Y)$$

$$E(XY) = \sum_x \sum_y Xp(X)Yp(Y)$$

For any fixed value of X, $Yp(Y)$ is unrestricted. Thus,

$$E(XY) = \sum_x Xp(X) \sum_y Yp(Y)$$

$$E(XY) = E(X)E(Y)$$

Rule 5 can be generalized to any number of independent random variables.

Variances and Covariances

The five expected-value rules can be used to derive some useful results for variances and covariances of random variables. These results are shown next. Examine the derivation of each result carefully. Although many of the steps shown are just algebra, you will gain confidence in your use of the expectation operator if you work through the steps necessary to derive each result.

Result 1: The variance of a constant times a random variable is equal to the constant squared times the variance of the random variable:

$$\text{var}(aX) = a^2\text{var}(X)$$

Result 1 is derived as follows:

$$\text{var}(aX) = E[aX - E(aX)]^2 \quad \text{(by definition)}$$

$$\text{var}(aX) = E[aX - aE(X)]^2 \quad \text{(by Rule 2)}$$

$$\text{var}(aX) = E[a(X - E(X))]^2$$

$$\text{var}(aX) = E[a^2(X - E(X))^2]$$

$$\text{var}(aX) = a^2E(X - E(X))^2 \quad \text{(by Rule 2)}$$

$$\text{var}(aX) = a^2\text{var}(X)$$

Result 2: The variance of a random variable plus a constant is equal to the variance of the random variable:

$$\text{var}(X + a) = \text{var}(X)$$

Result 2 is derived as follows:

$$\text{var}(X + a) = E[(X + a) - E(X + a)]^2 \quad \text{(by definition)}$$

$$\text{var}(X + a) = E[X + a - E(X) - E(a)]^2 \quad \text{(by Rule 4)}$$

$$\text{var}(X + a) = E[X + a - E(X) - a]^2 \quad \text{(by Rule 1)}$$

$$\text{var}(X + a) = E[X - E(X)]^2$$

$$\text{var}(X + a) = \text{var}(X)$$

Result 3: The variance of the sum of two random variables is equal to the sum of their variances plus twice their covariance:

$$\text{var}(X + Y) = \text{var}(X) + \text{var}(Y) + 2\text{cov}(X,Y)$$

Result 3 is derived as follows:

$$\text{var}(X + Y) = E[(X + Y) - E(X + Y)]^2 \quad \text{(by definition)}$$

$$\text{var}(X + Y) = E[X + Y - E(X) - E(Y)]^2 \quad \text{(by Rule 4)}$$

$$\text{var}(X + Y) = E[(X - E(X)) + (Y - E(Y))]^2$$

$$\text{var}(X + Y) = E[(X - E(X))^2 + 2(X - E(X))(Y - E(Y)) + (Y - E(Y))^2]$$

$$\text{var}(X + Y) = E[X - E(X)]^2 + E[2(X - E(X))(Y - E(Y))] + E[Y - E(Y)]^2 \quad \text{(by Rule 4)}$$

$$\text{var}(X + Y) = E[X - E(X)]^2 + 2E[(X - E(X))(Y - E(Y))] + E[Y - E(Y)]^2 \quad \text{(by Rule 2)}$$

$$\text{var}(X + Y) = \text{var}(X) + 2\text{cov}(X,Y) + \text{var}(Y)$$

Similarly,

$$\text{var}(X - Y) = \text{var}(X) + \text{var}(Y) - 2\text{cov}(X,Y)$$

Result 4: The covariance of two independent random variables is equal to 0:

$$\text{cov}(X,Y) = 0$$

Result 4 is derived as follows:

$$\text{cov}(X,Y) = E[(X - E(X))(Y - E(Y))] \quad \text{(by definition)}$$

$$\text{cov}(X,Y) = E[XY - XE(Y) - YE(X) + E(X)E(Y)]$$

$$\text{cov}(X,Y) = E(XY) - E[XE(Y)] - E[YE(X)] + E[E(X)E(Y)] \quad \text{(by Rule 4)}$$
$$\text{cov}(X,Y) = E(XY) - E(X)E(Y) - E(Y)E(X) + E(X)E(Y) \quad \text{(by Rule 2)}$$

$$\text{cov}(X,Y) = E(XY) - E(X)E(Y)$$

$$\text{cov}(X,Y) = 0 \quad \text{(because X and Y are independent variables, } E(XY) = E(X)E(Y).\text{)}$$

EXERCISE 2.10

Answer the following questions:

1. Return to the probability distributions shown in Table 2.1. Given that you know $E(X) = 5$ and $E(X - E(X))^2 = 12$, solve for the following using the algebra of expectations.

$E(Y) =$

$E(Z) =$

var(Y) =

var(Z) =

2. Return to the probability distributions shown in Table 2.2. Given that you know $E[(X - E(X))(Y - E(Y))] = -.6$ and $Z = 3X$, solve for $E[(Z - E(Z))(Y - E(Y))]$ using the algebra of expectations.

3. Let X and Y be random variables. Which of the following statements are true? If a statement is false, write a correct statement in the space to the right of the statement.

$E(X + 5) = E(X) + 5$

$E(X^2 + X) = [E(X)]^2 + E(X)$

$E(XY) = E(X)E(Y)$

$E(3X + 4Y) = 3E(X) + 4E(Y)$

$E(2X + Y) = 4$

$E\left[\dfrac{X}{2Y}\right] = \dfrac{E(X)}{2E(Y)}$

$E(X^2 + 3Y^2)^2 = 4E(X^2 + 3Y^2)$

$E\left[\dfrac{X^2}{Y}\right] = \dfrac{4E(X)}{E(Y)}$

$E(X^2 + Y^2) = 2E(X + Y)$

$E(5X^2 + 7XY) = 5E(X^2) + 7E(XY)$

Specifying a Model

1. To gain an understanding of the basic issues involved in specifying a model

2. To learn to use the *Survey of Current Business*

Lesson 1 presented a simple consumption function to examine the effects of a random error term on a linear model. But econometricians seldom get a model to estimate. They must first *specify* a model based on discussions of how variables are related to each other. This is often not an easy task. Several different specifications may be consistent with the discussions, or there may be theoretical controversy over which specification is proper. Sometimes the theoretical discussions themselves are not clear.

This lesson deals with model specification for the consumption function. The story told in this lesson is just the beginning of the tale, which will turn out to be more interesting than you now suspect. We will return to issues surrounding consumption function estimation in several of the coming lessons. Before beginning our discussion of the consumption function, however, let's go over the questions involved in specifying a model.

Specifying a Model

To specify a model, an econometrician must answer the following questions:

1. What variables are in the model?
2. What is the functional form of the model?
3. What are the expected signs or values for the parameter estimates?
4. What error process is associated with the model?

The econometrician should also indicate how the variables in the model are to be measured.

Let's look at an example. A student in a macroeconomic principles course looks at the production possibilities curve P_oP_o shown in Figure 3.1. The principles text argues that the economy shown in the figure will grow faster if more investment goods are produced. Thus, if the economy moves from point a to point b, the production possibilities curve will shift out to P_bP_b instead of P_aP_a. While both the diagram and argument seem unambiguous, the student wonders if things *really* work out this way in the empirical world. The student is especially interested in knowing if the relationship is true for developing countries. The student decides to pursue the relationship between investment spending and growth by specifying and estimating a model.

Figure 3.1
Investment, Growth, and the Production Possibilities Curve

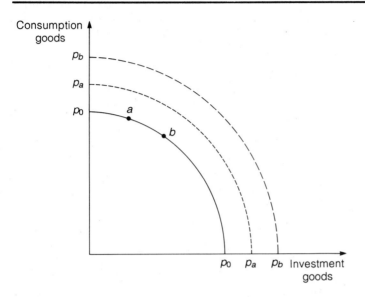

1. *What variables are in the model?* The student decides that the rate of growth in output (G) and some measure of the amount of investment spending (I) are the variables to include in the model.

2. *What is the functional form of the model?* The student decides that the relationship is linear:

    $$G = \beta_0 + \beta_1 I$$

    Why should the relationship be linear? The student decides that there is no reason to assume a nonlinear relationship, and specifying a linear relationship seems like a good starting point.

    (NOTE: Sometimes the problem *does* suggest a functional form. For example, assume that the student wants to specify the production function for the firm whose output and labor-hours data are shown in Figure 3.2. Some nonlinear function is required. In addition, production theory suggests that this nonlinear function be such that each additional labor-hour generates a smaller increase in output than the previous labor-hour. In other words, the production function must exhibit diminishing returns.)

3. *What are the expected signs or values for the parameter estimates?* This information, deduced from theoretical reasoning, is necessary to determine the correct null hypotheses and alternative hypotheses for the parameters. The student decides that if investment affects growth, the relationship will be positive: β_1 must be greater than 0 ($H_o : \beta_1 = 0$, and $H_a: \beta_1 > 0$). The student also decides that the sign of β_0 cannot be theoretically determined ($H_o: \beta_0 = 0$, and $H_a: \beta_0 \neq 0$).

    (NOTE: Although we usually indicate the expected signs of parameter estimates, there are times that we expect specific values. A good example of this is the *purchasing power parity theory* in international economics. The purchasing power parity theory states that exchange rates among currencies adjust such that the same product costs the same in both countries. For example, let an American wombat cost \$1 and a German wombat cost 4DM. According to the purchasing power parity theory, the exchange rate for the mark should be 25¢. Any other exchange rate would make the cost of the same good different between the two countries. This would

Figure 3.2
Production Data for a Firm

cause the exchange rate to adjust toward 25¢ as consumers in one country increase their purchases of the other country's wombats. The following model can be used to examine the validity of the purchasing power parity theory:

$$P = \beta_0 + \beta_1(eP^*)$$

where P is home prices, P^* is foreign prices, and e is the exchange rate. If the theory is valid, β_1 should equal 1 (H_o: $\beta_1 = 1$, and H_a: $\beta_1 \neq 1$).)

4. *What error process is associated with the model?* The student assumes the classical ordinary least-squares model error process. The student's answer to the fourth question may seem trivial. The student's assumption really begs the question: Are there any aspects of the modeling problem that suggest the specification for the error process? If there are, this information *must* be reflected in the model's specification. While this issue seems esoteric in a beginning econometric course, the proper specification of the error process becomes a significant question in advanced econometrics. We will see the significance of alternative specifications in Lesson 10.

The student now has specified a model. But to actually estimate the model, additional questions must be answered, the most significant of which is how to measure the variables. The student decides that the measure of output should be output per capita, feeling that the production possibilities curve is more meaningful when it is expressed in per-capita terms. The student also decides that the percent of a country's output used in capital formulation is the appropriate measure of the investment variable. With these measurements decided, the student needs a data set to estimate the model. In this case, the student could use time-series data for a given country or cross-sectional data for several countries. The student refers to the *United Nations Statistical Yearbook* and collects the necessary data for a cross-sectional sample of developing countries. The student is now ready to estimate the model. (If you are curious about the estimation results, the student's data, along with several other variables, are included in the data bank, under the heading "World Bank and United Nations Data.")

Keynes and the Consumption Function

To understand the difficulties an econometrician faces in specifying a model, read the following passages taken from John Maynard Keynes's *The General Theory of Interest, Employment, and Money*.[1] Examine the last two paragraphs carefully. The passages are drawn from Keynes's discussion of the consumption function, which he calls the propensity to consume. Minor editing changes have been made to make the passages easier to read. *The General Theory* revolutionized the way economists thought about aggregate economic activity. Many still consider the formulation of the aggregate consumption function to be one of Keynes's major contributions. After *The General Theory* was published, economists turned their attention to estimating the consumption function, but they first had to specify the model.

We will therefore define what we shall call the propensity to consume as the functional relationship f between Q, a given level of income, ... and C, consumption out of that level of income, so that

$$C = f(Q)$$

... in a given situation the propensity to consume may be considered a fairly stable function. Windfall changes in capital-values will be capable of changing the propensity to consume, and substantial changes in the rate of interest and in fiscal policy may make some difference; but the other objective factors which might affect it, whilst they must not be overlooked, are not likely to be important in ordinary circumstances.

The fact that, given the general economic situation, the expenditure on consumption depends in the main, on the volume of output and employment is the justification for summing up the other factors in the portmanteau function "propensity to consume." For whilst the other factors are capable of varying (and this must not be forgotten), the aggregate income is, as a rule, the principle variable upon which the consumption–constituent of the aggregate demand function will depend. ...

Granted, then, that the propensity to consume is a fairly stable function so that, as a rule, the amount of aggregate consumption depends on the amount of aggregate income, changes in the propensity itself being treated as a secondary influence, what is the normal shape of this function?

The fundamental psychological law, upon which we are entitled to depend with great confidence both a priori *from our knowledge of human nature and from the detailed facts of experience, is that men are disposed, as a rule and on the average, to increase their consumption as their income increases, but not by as much as the increase in their income. That is to say, if C is the amount of consumption and Q is income,... ΔC has the same sign as ΔQ but is smaller in amount, i.e., $\dfrac{\Delta C}{\Delta Y}$ is positive and less than unity.*

This is especially the case where we have short periods in view, as in the case of the so-called cyclical fluctuations of employment during which habits, as distinct from more permanent psychological propensities, are not given time enough to adapt themselves to changed objective circumstances. For a man's habitual standard of life usually has the first claim on his income, and he is apt to save the difference which discovers itself between his actual income and the expense of his habitual standard; or, if he does adjust his expenditures to changes in his income, he will over short periods do so imperfectly. Thus a rising income will often be accompanied by increased saving, and a falling income by decreased saving, on a greater scale at first than subsequently.

But, apart from short-period changes in the level of income, it is also obvious that a higher absolute level of income will tend, as a rule, to widen the gap between income and consumption. For the satisfaction of the immediate primary needs of a man and his family is usually a stronger motive than the motives towards accumulation, which only acquire effective sway when a margin of comfort has been attained. These reasons will lead, as a rule, to a greater proportion of income being saved as real income increases. But whether or not a greater proportion is saved, we take it as a fundamental psychological rule of any modern community that, when its real income is increased, it will not increase its consumption by an equal absolute amount, so that a greater absolute amount must be saved, unless a large and unusual change is occurring at the same time in other factors.

Think for a moment about what model you would specify on the basis of the passage. Don't feel uneasy if you have trouble specifying a consumption function; econometricians also had difficulty developing a specification. Keynes does little more than speculate. His fundamental psychological law seems to materialize out of thin air and certainly does not derive from any explicit theory of consumer behavior. What is the meaning of a "habitual standard of life"? How could one measure such a standard for purposes of estimating a consumption function? Is there really an important empirical difference between long-run and short-run consumption behavior? Is wealth an important variable in the aggregate function, or can it be ignored? These questions puzzled the economists who read and reread (and reread) *The General Theory*. Economists initially resolved these questions by turning to the empirical evidence. They found that a simple, short-run function of the form $C = \beta_0 + \beta_1 Q$ fit past data remarkably well.

We begin our examination of the consumption function by estimating this simple consumption function. Besides specification questions, there are measurement questions that must be answered before estimating the model.

EXERCISE 3.1

Examine the data on consumption expenditures and income in a recent issue of the *Survey of Current Business*. If you have never used the *Survey*, read Lesson Note 3.1. Which variables should be used to measure consumption and income for the model $C = \beta_0 + \beta_1 Q$? Explain your choices. (HINT: Do consumers purchase the same kind of commodity when they buy a nondurable good or service as when they buy a durable good? Should all three kinds of consumption expenditures be added together to form the consumption variable?)

_____

_____

_____

_____

Many times economists assume that their readers will know certain features of a model specification or a measurement, and they do not state these features explicitly. The passage does not indicate whether the variables should be measured in constant dollars or current dollars. Do you think Keynes assumed that his reader should know this? Should the variables be measured in constant or current dollars? Why?

_____

_____

_____

EXERCISE 3.2

Estimate the simple linear consumption function using your econometric software. You will find the variables you selected in Exercise 3.1 in the data bank. Write your estimated function below. *Follow the format for presenting regression results used in your text. Use this format to present your regression results for all the problems in the* Sourcebook.

How well does the model fit the data?

_____

_____

_____

_____

_____

Examine the residuals. Are there any years the model seems to perform poorly? Do these years have anything in common? (CAUTION: Residuals, as we will see in later lessons, must be looked at very carefully. Specifically, the residuals for this problem indicate that one of the common assumptions used to specify the general regression model may not be valid ($E(u_i u_j) = 0$, for $i \neq j$). We avoid consideration of these issues in this lesson.)

_____

_____

_____

_____

_____

Is Keynes's reasoning in the last paragraph of the passage correct?

_____

_____

_____

_____

_____

_____

Problems with the Simple Consumption Function

The short-run consumption function of the form $C = \beta_0 + \beta_1 Q$ seemed to fit the data. The existence of Keynes's fundamental law seemed confirmed. But problems with the simple consumption function quickly became apparent. The function turned out to be a poor forecaster. In the late 1940s, the simple consumption function predicted levels of consumption far below those that actually occurred. The forecasts were so poor that some economists argued that the Keynesian consumption function, which they interpreted to be $C = \beta_0 + \beta_1 Q$, did not explain consumption behavior.

The simple consumption function also had a positive intercept term ($\beta_0 > 0$). This meant that as an economy's income grew, the ratio of consumption to income, called the average propensity to consume, should decrease. But when Kuznets and Goldsmith examined long-run data, they found that the C/Q ratio was essentially constant over a time period when income increased by a factor of 4.[2] The long-run consumption function thus had to have a 0, not a positive, intercept. In addition, when the short-run C/Q ratio was examined in more detail, economists found that it varied with the business cycle. Consumption fell proportionately much less than income during recessions. As the postwar quarters began to accumulate, cases of consumption and income moving in opposite directions were occasionally observed.

A final puzzle developed when economists compared two different types of data, time-series data and cross-sectional data. When estimating the consumption function in the first part of this lesson, you used variables measured at different times. Your data cases were periods of time. Consumption spending and income were measured for each data case. Kuznets and Goldsmith also used time-series data in developing their estimates. Other researchers examined budgets for individual families; the data cases were individual families observed for the same time period (or cross section of time). The cross-sectional studies found that the C/Q ratio decreased as family income increased. These studies also found that the marginal propensity to consume, the change in consumption accompanying a change in income, tended to decline as family income increased. Yet the simple consumption function had a constant marginal propensity to consume, with the marginal propensity to consume being equal to the slope of the function (β_1).

Something was seriously wrong with the simple consumption function. One of the first attempts to explain the contradictory evidence was made by Duesenberry.[3] Duesenberry's reconciliation, known as the *relative income hypothesis*, is an excellent example of how a model specification is tailored from empirical cloth and threads of economic reasoning. Duesenberry's final garment is no longer accepted by most economists, but it remains a brilliant solution in model specification. Going over Duesenberry's reasoning will give you practice in manipulating a model specification and will provide the foundation for explaining the econometric estimation of modern theories of the consumption function, to which we will turn our attention in coming lessons.

Duesenberry argued that an individual's consumption does not depend on the individual's current level of disposable income. Instead, consumption is determined by the individual's "percentile position in the income distribution." He further argued that an individual would consume a smaller portion of income as the individual moved to higher percentiles in the income distribution in a manner consistent with cross-sectional data. But if individuals stayed at the same percentile, they would continue to consume the same proportion of their income, even though their income might increase dramatically. While some individuals might move up in the income distribution, they would be balanced by others moving down. The aggregate C/Q ratio would remain unchanged. The relative income hypothesis was thus able to reconcile the short-term and long-term time-series data.

EXERCISE 3.3

To see how the relative income hypothesis works, consider the following hypothetical community of five consumers. Columns Q and C show each consumer's income and consumption expenditures. Double each individual's income and record the new income in Column New Q. Using Duesenberry's argument, solve for the new consumption level for each consumer and record this value in Column New C. Compare the aggregate ratio of consumption to income before and after the doubling of income for the community.

Q	C	New Q	New C
10,000	9,000	_____	_____
20,000	17,500	_____	_____
30,000	25,000	_____	_____
40,000	32,000	_____	_____
50,000	38,000	_____	_____

Average Propensity to Consume for Q

Average Propensity to Consume for New Q

Duesenberry next argued that consumer standards are irreversible. If consumers' incomes increase and then decrease, the decrease in income is not accompanied by a return to the initial level of consumption. Consumers continue to base their consumption decisions on the higher level of income, their previous peak income. This irreversibility explains why the C/Q ratio varies systematically over the business cycle.

The relative income hypothesis is specified by the following function form:

$$\frac{C_t}{Q_t} = a + b\left[\frac{Q_t}{Q_o}\right] \quad b < 0 \qquad\qquad (3.1)$$

where Q_o is previous peak income.

EXERCISE 3.4

Let's see how this specification captures Duesenberry's arguments. First, assume that the economy is growing so that $Q_o = Q_{t-1}$ and Q_t /Q_{t-1} is equal to the constant $(1 + r)$, where r is the rate of income growth. These assumptions describe a long-run growth path for the economy. What happens to the long-run C/Q ratio under these assumptions?

_____

_____

_____

_____

Now assume that the economy slips into a recession with Q_t being less than Q_o. What happens to the C/Q ratio?

_____

_____

_____

_____

Duesenberry estimated his function using econometric techniques and found that $\hat{a} = 1.2$ and $\hat{b} = -.25$. With these parameter estimates, consumption and income must always move in the same direction. Thus, he was not able to reconcile all the empirical paradoxes.

Despite the power of Duesenberry's arguments, many economists were troubled by some of his model's implications. The functional representation did not differentiate the effects of large and small changes in income on consumption. Increases in consumption were always proportional to an increase in income, regardless of whether the change in income was large or small. It seemed more reasonable to many economists that a large increase in income might be accompanied, at least initially, by a less-than-proportionate increase in consumption. Consumer behavior was "sticky," with consumers adjusting very slowly to income changes. Extending this stickiness to decreases in income, some argued that consumer behavior was not truly irreversible. Consumers simply responded slowly over a long period of time. Such a lagging response might also explain why income and consumption occasionally moved in opposite directions.

Speculation about the lagging response of consumption spending ultimately led to new theories of the consumption function. But now, we must leave the story. The new specifications resulting from these theories require a better understanding of the regression model than does the simple consumption function you estimated in the first part of this lesson. We will return to problems of estimating the consumption function after you have worked through the complexities of ordinary least-squares estimation in more detail.

Lesson Note 3.1

Using the *Survey of Current Business*

Exercise 3.1 refers you to a recent issue of the *Survey of Current Business* to select the variables needed to estimate your consumption function. You will notice that the *Survey* includes several articles (white pages) and economic statistics (blue pages). To find the variables you need, turn to the inside back cover of the *Survey*. Here you will see an index to the statistical section. Table 3.1 shows the index from a recent issue. Notice that information on consumption and income is found on pages 1 and 2. Table 3.2 shows page 1 of the statistical section from the same issue. You should select your consumption and income variables from the measures reported on this page.

The *Survey of Current Business* is *the* authoritative source on the National Income and Product Accounts (NIPA) of the United States. Its primary purpose is to ensure the accuracy of published NIPA data. Because the *Survey's* major concern is NIPA data, it is not a good source for monthly economic statistics. Most of the data reported in the *Survey* are published much earlier in other sources. And, although the *Survey* gives some industry data, these data are not systematically organized or consistently reported in the monthly issues.

When using the *Survey* as a data source, always remember that the national income accounts are constantly being revised. Make sure

that you are using the numbers that reflect the most recent revisions. Every July, the *Survey* reports all the yearly revisions and additions to the national income accounts. Some years this issue is published late because the laborious task of completing the revision runs behind schedule. Look through last July's issue to see the extensiveness of the scope and the procedures required to maintain accurate national income data. When using the *Survey*, you should also read any footnotes or other references associated with the data you are examining. These footnotes are located in a statistical data reference section. This reference section shows important information about selected variables, such as lack of seasonal adjustment, deflation procedure, and the like.

Finally, the government publishes a biennial supplement, *Business Statistics*. The supplement presents historical data on the approximately 2100 data series reported in the *Survey* and in a much more organized manner than does the *Survey* itself. *Business Statistics* is an excellent data reference when it is first released. But, as time goes by, the constant revision activity required to maintain the accuracy of the national accounts makes it a less useful reference.

Table 3.1
Index to Current Business Statistics, Pages S1–S36

SECTIONS

General:

Business indicators 1-5
Commodity prices 5, 6
Construction and real estate 7, 8
Domestic trade 8, 9
Labor force, employment, and
    earnings 9–13
Finance 13–16
Foreign trade of the United States 16–18
Transportation and
    communication 18, 19

Industry:

Chemicals and allied products 19, 20
Electric power and gas 20
Food and kindred products;
    tobacco 20–23
Leather and products 23
Lumber and products 23, 24
Metals and manufacturers 24–27
Petroleum, coal, and products 27, 28
Pulp, paper, and paper products 28, 29
Rubber and rubber products 29
Stone, clay, and glass products 30
Textile products 30–32
Transportation equipment 32

Footnotes 33–35

INDIVIDUAL SERIES

Advertising 8, 12
Aerospace vehicles 32
Agricultural loans 13
Air carrier operations 18
Air conditioners (room) 27
Aircraft and parts 4, 32
Alcohol, denatured and ethyl 19
Alcoholic beverages 8, 20
Aluminum 25
Apparel 2, 4–6, 8–12, 31, 32
Asphalt.. 28
Automobiles, etc. 2–4, 6, 8, 9, 14, 15, 17, 32

Banking 13, 14
Barley 21
Battery shipments 27
Beef and veal 22
Beverages 8, 17, 20
Blast furnaces, steel mills 3–5
Bonds, prices, sales, yields 15, 16
Brick 30
Building and construction materials 2, 4, 5
Building costs 7
Building permits 7
Business incorporation (new), failures ... 5
Business sales and inventories 2, 3
Butter 21

Carpets 31
Cattle and calves 22
Cement 30
Chain-store sales, firms with 11 or more
    stores (retail trade) 9
Cheese 21
Chemicals 2–4, 10–12, 15, 17, 19, 20
Cigarettes and cigars 23
Clay products 2–4, 30
Clothing (see apparel)
Coal 2, 27
Cocoa 22
Coffee 22
Coke 27

Combustion, atmosphere, heating
    equipment 26
Communication 15, 19
Construction:
    Contracts 7
    Costs 7
    Employment, unemployment, hours,
        earnings 10–12
    Housing starts 7
    New construction put in place 7
Consumer credit 14
Consumer goods output, index 1, 2
Consumer Price Index 5, 6
Copper and copper products 25, 26
Corn 21
Cost of living (see Consumer Price
    Index) 5, 6
Cotton, raw and manufactures 5, 30, 31
Credit, commercial bank, consumer 14
Crops 5, 21, 23, 30
Crude oil 3, 27
Currency in circulation 15

Dairy products 5, 21
Debt, U.S. Government 14
Deflator, PCE.................................... 1
Department stores, sales, inventories.... 9
Deposits, bank................................... 13, 15
Dishwashers and disposers.................. 27
Disposition of personal income............ 1
Distilled spirits 20
Dividend payments............................. 1, 15
Drugstores, sales................................ 8, 9

Earnings, weekly and hourly................ 12
Eating and drinking places.................. 8, 9
Eggs and poultry................................ 5, 22
Electric power.................................... 2, 20
Electrical machinery and
    equipment.................... 2–5, 10–12, 15, 27
Employee-hours, aggregate, and
    indexes.. 11
Employment and employment cost 10–12
Explosives... 20
Exports (see also individual
    commodities)................................. 16–18

Failures, industrial and commercial....... 5
Farm prices 5, 6
Fats and oils 17
Federal Government finance 14
Federal Reserve banks, large
    commercial 13
Federal Reserve member banks 13
Fertilizers 19
Fish 22
Flooring, hardwood 24
Flour, wheat 22
Food products 2–6, 8, 10–12, 15, 17, 20–23
Foreign trade (see also individual
    commod.) 16–18
Freight cars (equipment) 32
Fruits and vegetables 5
Fuel oil 6, 28
Fuels 2, 6, 17, 27, 28
Furnaces 27
Furniture 2, 6, 8–12

Gas, output, prices, sales, revenues 2, 6, 20
Gasoline 28
Glass and products 30
Glycerin 19
Gold 14

Table 3.1 (continued)
Index to Current Business Statistics, Pages S1–S-36

Grains and products 5, 21, 22
Grocery stores 9
Gypsum products 30

Hardware stores 8
Heating equipment 26
Help-wanted advertising index 12
Hides and skins 6
Hogs 22
Home loan banks, outstanding
   advances 8
Home mortgages 8
Hotels, motor hotels, and economy
   hotels 18
Hours, average weekly 11
Housefurnishings 2, 4, 6, 8, 9
Household appliances, radios, and television
   sets 27
Housing starts and permits 7

Imports (see also individual
   commodities) 17, 18
Income, personal 1
Income and employment tax receipts 14
Industrial production indexes:
   By industry 1, 2
   By market grouping 1, 2
Installment credit 14
Instruments and related products ... 2–4, 10–12
Interest and money rates 14
Inventories, manufacturers' and trade .. 3, 4, 9
Inventory-sales rates 3
Iron and steel 2, 15, 24, 25

Labor force 9, 10
Lamb and mutton 22
Lead 26
Leather and products 2, 6, 10–12, 23
Livestock 5, 22
Loans, real estate, agricultural, bank
   (see also Consumer credit) 8, 13
Lubricants 28
Lumber and products 2, 6, 10–12, 23, 24

Machine tools 26
Machinery 2–6, 10–12, 15, 17, 26, 27
Manufacturers' sales (or shipments),
   inventories, orders 3–5
Manufacturing employment, unemployment,
   production workers, hours,
   earnings 10–12
Manufacturing production indexes 1, 2
Meat animals and meats 5, 22
Medical care 6
Metals 2–6, 10–12, 15, 24–26
Milk 21
Mining 2, 10–12
Mobile homes, shipments, installment
   credit 7, 14
Monetary statistics 15
Money and interest rates 14
Money supply 15
Mortgage applications, loans,
   rates 8, 13, 14
Motor carriers 18
Motor vehicles 2–4, 6, 8, 9, 15, 17, 32

National parks, visits 18
Newsprint 29
New York Stock Exchange, selected
   data 16
Nonferrous metals 2, 4, 5, 15, 25, 26

Oats 21
Oils and fats 17

Orders, new and unfilled,
   manufacturers' 4, 5
Outlays, U.S. Government 14

Paint and paint materials 20
Paper and products and
   pulp 2–4, 6, 10–12, 15, 28, 29
Parity ratio 5
Passenger cars 2–4, 6, 8, 9, 15, 17, 32
Passports issued 18
Personal consumption expenditures 1
Personal income 1
Personal outlays 1
Petroleum and
   products 2–4, 10–12, 15, 17, 27, 28
Pig iron 24
Plastics and resin materials 20
Population 9
Pork 22
Poultry and eggs 5, 22
Price deflator, implicit (PCE) 1
Prices (see also individual
   commodities) 5, 6
Printing and publishing 2, 10–12
Private sector employment, hours,
   earnings 10–12
Producer Price Indexes (see also individual
   commodities) 6
Profits, corporate 15
Public utilities 1, 2, 7, 15, 20
Pulp and pulpwood 28
Purchasing power of the dollar 6

Radio and television 8, 27
Railroads 13, 18, 32
Ranges and microwave ovens 27
Real estate 8, 13
Receipts, U.S. Government 14
Refrigerators and freezers 27
Registrations (new vehicles) 32
Rent (housing) 6
Retail trade 2, 3, 5, 8–12, 32
Rice 21
Rubber and products (incl.
   plastics) 2–4, 6, 10–12, 29

Saving, personal 1
Savings and loan associations 8, 14
Savings deposits 13, 15
Securities issued 15
Security markets 15, 16
Services 6, 10–12
Sheep and lambs 22
Shoes and other footwear 23
Silver 14
Spindle activity, cotton 31
Steel and steel manufactures 24, 25
Stock market customer financing 15
Stock prices, yields, sales, etc. 16
Stone, clay, glass
   products 2–4, 10–12, 15, 30
Sugar 23
Sulfur 19
Sulfuric acid 19
Superphosphate 19
Synthetic textile products 31

Tea imports 23
Telephone and telegraph carriers 19
Textiles and
   products 2–4, 6, 10–12, 15, 30, 31
Tin 26
Tires and inner tubes 29
Tobacco and manufactures 2–4, 10–12, 23
Tractors 27

Table 3.1 (continued)
Index to Current Business Statistics, Pages S1–S-36

Trade (retail and wholesale) 2, 3, 5, 8–12, 32
Transit lines, urban 18
Transportation 6, 10–12, 15, 18
Transportation
  equipment 2–6, 10–12, 15, 17, 32
Travel 18
Truck trailers 32
Trucks 2, 32

Unemployment and insurance 9, 10, 13
U.S. Government bonds 16
U.S. Government finance 14
Utilities 2, 6, 7, 15, 20

Vacuum cleaners 27
Variety stores 9
Vegetables and fruits 5

Wages and salaries 1, 12
Washers and dryers 27
Water heaters 27
Wheat and wheat flour 21, 22
Wholesale trade 2, 3, 5, 8, 10–12
Wood pulp 28
Wool and wool manufactures 31

Zinc 26

Table 3.2
Current Business Statistics

The statistics here update series published in *Business Statistics: 1984*, a statistical supplement to the *Survey of Current Business*. That volume (available from the Superintendent of Documents for $13.00, stock no. 003-010-00160-7) provides a description of each series, references to sources of earlier figures, and historical data as follows: For all series, monthly or quarterly, 1981 through 1984, annually, 1961–84; for selected series, monthly or quarterly, 1961–84 (where available).

The sources of the series are given in *Business Statistics: 1984*; they appear in the main methodological note for each series, and are also listed alphabetically on pages 143–144. Series originating in Government agencies are not copyrighted and may be reprinted freely. Series from private sources are provided through the courtesy of the compilers, and are subject to their copyrights.

Unless otherwise stated in footnotes below, data through 1984 and methodological notes are as shown in *Business Statistics, 1984*	Units	Annual		1985										1986			
		1984	1985	Mar.	Apr.	May	June	July	Aug.	Sept.	Oct.	Nov.	Dec.	Jan.	Feb.	Mar.	Apr.
PERSONAL INCOME BY SOURCE																	
Seasonally adjusted, at annual rates:																	
Total personal income	bil. $	3,111.9	3,293.5	3,258.2	3,288.6	3,271.2	3,280.5	3,290.0	3,295.5	3,309.9	3,330.8	3,347.9	3,384.3	3,386.3	3,401.7	3,407.5	3,446.9
Wage and salary disbursements, total	do	1,834.9	1,960.5	1,930.9	1,940.5	1,946.8	1,958.5	1,959.6	1,969.3	1,981.2	1,991.5	2,003.6	2,022.2	2,027.0	2,034.4	2,043.9	2,048.1
Commodity-producing industries, total	do	577.9	607.3	602.6	603.2	605.1	605.8	605.0	608.0	609.9	614.8	614.7	621.0	622.9	619.0	619.6	619.8
Manufacturing	do	438.9	457.6	455.0	453.9	455.0	455.8	455.5	457.6	458.3	463.2	463.1	467.9	466.9	464.9	466.4	465.3
Distributive industries	do	441.6	468.8	463.9	463.8	467.3	471.0	469.1	470.6	473.9	473.9	476.8	479.7	480.2	483.4	485.2	486.0
Service industries	do	469.4	513.6	500.2	504.5	506.9	512.8	514.9	518.0	523.1	526.9	531.8	538.4	540.8	547.1	552.5	554.0
Govt. and govt. enterprises	do	346.1	370.8	364.2	369.0	367.4	369.0	370.8	372.7	374.3	375.8	380.3	383.0	383.2	384.8	386.6	388.4
Other labor income	do	193.4	206.4	202.2	203.5	204.8	206.1	207.3	208.5	209.5	210.5	211.5	212.4	213.3	214.3	215.3	216.2
Proprietors' income:																	
Farm	do	32.1	21.2	23.8	40.4	14.4	13.8	12.2	11.6	12.9	17.5	21.0	31.4	15.7	19.1	12.0	44.4
Nonfarm	do	201.6	221.0	215.2	216.9	218.6	218.8	222.1	224.8	228.9	227.2	226.9	228.7	233.8	236.4	236.9	237.6
Rental income of persons with capital consumption adjustment	bil. $	10.8	13.8	11.7	12.8	13.9	14.9	15.5	16.2	11.7	16.0	13.9	17.8	18.3	18.9	19.6	20.3
Dividends	do	74.6	78.9	78.3	78.6	78.7	78.8	78.9	79.1	79.2	79.4	79.9	80.1	80.9	82.3	83.1	84.0
Personal interest income	do	442.2	456.3	463.8	462.7	461.0	457.9	453.3	449.8	448.6	450.1	451.7	452.4	452.5	451.7	450.7	449.7
Transfer payments	do	454.7	484.5	479.5	480.9	481.2	480.9	490.0	486.0	488.4	489.8	491.4	492.5	501.8	502.1	503.8	504.7
Less: Personal contributions for social insurance	do	132.4	149.1	147.2	147.6	148.1	149.1	149.1	149.7	150.4	151.1	151.9	153.1	157.0	157.4	157.9	158.1
Total nonfarm income	do	3,053.3	3,246.1	3,208.2	3,221.9	3,230.5	3,240.5	3,251.9	3,258.1	3,271.2	3,287.5	3,301.0	3,326.9	3,344.5	3,356.5	3,369.2	3,376.1
GENERAL BUSINESS INDICATORS																	
DISPOSITION OF PERSONAL INCOME																	
Seasonally adjusted, at annual rates:																	
Total personal income	bil. $	3,111.9	3,293.5	3,258.2	3,288.6	3,271.2	3,280.5	3,290.0	3,295.5	3,309.9	3,380.8	3,347.9	3,384.3	3,386.3	3,401.7	3,407.5	3,446.9
Less: Personal tax and nontax payments	do	441.8	492.7	533.1	479.8	413.7	493.6	494.1	498.0	502.6	504.8	508.2	512.5	504.2	504.6	503.2	505.0
Equals: Disposable personal income	do	2,670.2	2,800.8	2,725.1	2,808.8	2,857.5	2,786.9	2,795.9	2,797.5	2,807.3	2,826.0	2,839.7	2,871.8	2,882.2	2,897.1	2,904.3	2,941.9
Less: Personal outlays	do	2,497.7	2,671.8	2,615.0	2,630.0	2,663.0	2,658.7	2,665.6	2,697.4	2,729.9	2,706.0	2,719.3	2,766.5	2,757.8	2,772.1	2,774.6	2,782.9
Personal consumption expenditures	do	2,423.0	2,582.3	2,530.2	2,544.0	2,575.5	2,570.4	2,575.5	2,606.2	2,636.6	2,611.1	2,623.6	2,669.8	2,659.4	2,673.0	2,674.8	2,682.5
Durable goods	do	331.1	361.5	356.4	347.1	369.2	353.2	355.3	378.3	394.3	355.7	357.2	373.0	368.8	367.6	355.9	369.5
Nondurable goods	do	872.4	912.2	895.8	912.5	909.5	908.6	909.2	912.9	921.6	926.0	925.3	933.5	933.9	933.8	940.3	930.9
Services	do	1,219.6	1,308.6	1,278.1	1,284.4	1,296.8	1,308.6	1,311.0	1,315.0	1,320.7	1,329.3	1,341.1	1,363.3	1,356.8	1,371.6	1,378.7	1,382.0
Interest paid by consumers to business	do	73.3	87.4	82.7	84.1	85.6	86.5	87.9	89.0	91.0	92.7	93.6	94.5	96.2	97.0	97.6	98.2
Personal transfer payments to foreigners (net)	do	1.3	2.1	2.1	1.8	1.8	1.8	2.2	2.2	2.2	2.2	2.2	2.2	2.2	2.2	2.2	2.2
Equals: personal saving	do	172.5	129.0	110.1	178.8	194.5	128.2	130.3	100.1	77.4	120.0	120.4	105.3	124.4	124.9	129.7	159.0
Personal saving as percentage of disposable personal income	percent	6.5	4.6	5.0	5.8	5.9	5.4	4.3	3.7	3.5	3.8	4.0	4.1	4.1	4.4	4.7	...

	Units	Annual		1985										1986			
		1984	1985	Mar.	Apr.	May	June	July	Aug.	Sept.	Oct.	Nov.	Dec.	Jan.	Feb.	Mar.	Apr.
Disposable personal income in constant (1982) dollars	bil. $	2,468.4	2,508.8	2,459.4	2,530.9	2,567.1	2,498.5	2,504.0	2,501.4	2,504.2	2,510.9	2,510.3	2,530.1	2,532.7	2,555.3	2,571.5	...
Personal consumption expenditures in constant (1982) dollars	do	2,239.9	2,313.0	2,283.5	2,292.3	2,313.8	2,304.4	2,306.6	2,330.3	2,351.9	2,319.9	2,319.2	2,352.1	2,336.9	2,357.6	2,368.3	...
Durable goods	do	318.6	345.3	337.9	332.3	350.9	337.6	340.2	360.9	376.8	341.1	342.2	356.8	351.6	349.4	339.7	...
Nondurable goods	do	828.0	846.9	835.8	848.8	846.4	845.0	845.6	849.2	854.7	854.9	847.9	850.5	850.7	864.3	881.1	...
Services	do	1,093.3	1,120.8	1,109.9	1,111.2	1,116.5	1,121.8	1,120.7	1,120.2	1,120.4	1,123.9	1,129.0	1,144.8	1,134.6	1,143.9	1,147.4	...
Implicit price deflator for personal consumption expenditures	index, 1982 = 100	108.2	111.6	110.8	111.0	111.3	111.5	111.7	111.8	112.1	112.5	113.1	113.5	113.8	113.4	112.9	...
INDUSTRIAL PRODUCTION *Federal Reserve Board Index of Quantity Output* Not Seasonally Adjusted																	
Total index	1977 = 100	121.8	124.5	124.1	122.9	123.3	127.1	122.2	127.4	129.2	127.0	124.9	122.2	123.2	125.5	124.9	124.0
By industry groupings:																	
Mining and utilities	do	110.9	110.7	111.8	107.6	106.7	110.6	108.4	111.6	111.4	108.7	108.1	111.8	113.2	112.5	107.0	103.3
Manufacturing	do	123.9	127.1	126.4	125.8	126.5	130.2	124.5	130.4	132.6	130.3	128.2	124.1	125.3	128.2	127.9	127.8
Nondurable manufactures	do	122.5	125.6	122.5	122.4	123.7	128.7	124.6	131.7	134.1	130.6	127.2	122.3	122.7	126.6	126.5	126.5
Durable manufactures	do	124.8	128.2	129.2	128.2	128.5	131.2	124.4	129.4	131.4	130.1	128.8	125.3	127.1	129.3	128.9	128.7
Seasonally Adjusted																	
Total index	do	121.8	124.5	124.0	124.1	124.1	124.3	124.1	125.2	125.1	124.4	125.4	126.4	126.7	125.7	124.9	125.1
By market groupings:																	
Products, total	do	127.1	131.7	130.3	130.8	131.4	131.6	131.6	133.0	133.1	131.8	133.5	134.1	134.4	133.2	132.2	132.6
Final products	do	127.8	132.0	130.8	131.3	131.7	131.6	131.8	133.3	133.3	131.9	133.7	134.4	134.4	132.9	131.6	132.1
Consumer goods	do	118.2	120.7	119.8	119.5	120.0	120.4	120.1	121.5	121.8	120.8	122.7	124.2	123.9	123.2	122.2	123.0

Single-Equation Models

1. To practice specifying and estimating models
2. To learn to transform variables and add to a data base using your econometric software
3. To learn to use the *Business Conditions Digest*

In this lesson, you will formulate models to examine two basic relationships suggested by economic theory. You will examine the relationship between the growth rate of the money supply and the inflation rate and the relationship between changes in Gross National Product (GNP) and changes in productivity. The variables needed to estimate the models are in the data bank. But in most cases, these variables will not be used as they are given. They will need to be transformed in some fashion.

Transforming Variables

Most econometric models require some data transformation before they can be estimated. Let's look at a few examples.

1. Deciding that the independent variable (X) affects the dependent variable (Y) with a one-period lag, your model becomes

   $$Y_t = \beta_0 + \beta_1 X_{t-1} + u_t$$

   To estimate the model, X must be lagged one period. Notice that the earliest data case is lost when X is lagged. Some software require that you "reset" the sample cases to reflect the lost data case.

2. Deciding that you need the percentage change in the independent variable rather than the variable itself, your model becomes

   $$Y_t = \beta_0 + \beta_1 \left[\frac{X_t - X_{t-1}}{X_{t-1}} \right] + u_t$$

   A new independent variable, the percentage change in X, must be computed from the original data for X before the model can be estimated. This is also the case for the next three examples.

3. Deciding that the independent variable should be a long-run measure, calculated as a four-period moving average, your model becomes

$$Y_t = \beta_0 + \beta_1 \left[\frac{X_t + X_{t-1} + X_{t-2} + X_{t-3}}{4} \right] + u_t$$

4. Deciding that the independent variable should be the sum of the last three periods change in X, your model becomes

$$Y_t = \beta_0 + \beta_1 [(X_t - X_{t-1}) + (X_{t-1} - X_{t-2}) + (X_{t-2} - X_{t-3})] + u_t$$

5. Deciding that both the independent and dependent variables should be the *logarithms* of X and Y, your model becomes

$$\log Y_t = \beta_0 + \beta_1 \log X_t + u_t$$

(Lesson 6 contains reasons why you might want to use logarithms.)

EXERCISE 4.1

The ability to transform old variables quickly and to compute new ones is one of the more important features of econometric software. Show how you would instruct your econometric software to transform or compute variables in each of the previous five examples.

1. _____

2. _____

3. _____

4. _____

5. _____

Inflation and Money Supply Growth

Virtually all macroeconomic models show a *long-run* relationship between the growth rate of the money supply and the inflation rate. The *short-run* relationship between the two variables continues to be controversial. The strongest statement of the short-run relationship follows from the strict (sometimes termed *old*) statement of the quantity theory. The short-run relationship develops as follows: The income velocity of money (V) times the money stock (M) is equal to nominal income. Nominal income is in turn equal to real income (Q) times the price level (P):

$$MV = PQ$$

Solving for the price level gives

$$P = M \left[\frac{V}{Q} \right]$$

The strict quantity theory assumes that velocity is constant and income is at the full employment level. Given these assumptions, the price level must be proportional to the stock of money. Changes in the money stock cause proportionate changes in the price level. Another statement of the quantity theory, not our concern in this lesson, changes the quantity theory into a theory of nominal aggregate demand, PQ.

Most macroeconomists argue that the proportionate results indicated by the price-level quantity theory are correct but only in the long run. They recognize that the strict proportionate results must be modified somewhat because the full employment level of output must be assumed to grow in the long run. Controversy centers on the variability of velocity in the short run and fluctuations in short-run real income.

EXERCISE 4.2

Using the strict quantity theory argument, specify a regression model to test the validity of the short-run relationship between the inflation rate and the growth rate in the money supply. You will have to formulate an empirically meaningful definition of the short run and will have to derive this relationship from the quantity theory argument, which is not directly written in terms of the inflation rate or the growth rate of the money supply. Inflation is the growth rate of the price level. Remember to answer all four model-specification questions. Pay special attention to the null hypothesis for the money-supply growth-rate coefficient.

(HINT: The growth rate of the *product* of two variables is equal to the *sum* of the separate growth rates of the two variables. The growth rate of the *quotient* of two variables is equal to the *difference* between the growth rate of the variable in the numerator and the growth rate of the variable in the denominator. For example, nominal GNP (Q^*) is equal to real GNP (Q) times the price level (P), $Q^* = QP$. If real GNP growth is 3 percent and price-level growth (inflation) is 4 percent, then nominal GNP growth is 7 percent. For another example, per-capita real GNP ($\hat{Q}$) is equal to real GNP (Q) divided by population (N), $\hat{Q} = Q/N$. If real GNP growth is 2 percent and population growth is 3 percent, then per-capita GNP growth is –1 percent.) Using this information, a student derived the following model for this exercise.

$$\frac{P_t - P_{t-1}}{P_{t-1}} = \beta_0 + \beta_1 \left[\frac{M_t - M_{t-1}}{M_{t-1}} \right]$$

Look at the data bank. How will you measure the short-run inflation rate and the short-run growth rate of the money supply? Which measure of the money supply should you use? Should the growth rate of the money supply be measured in real or nominal terms?

EXERCISE 4.3

Estimate your model and write the estimated equation below.

Are the suggested economic relationships confirmed? Do parameter estimates have the expected signs or values? Are the null hypotheses rejected? (Read Lesson Note 4.1 before reporting your *t*-test results. The Lesson Note discusses the economic meaning of hypothesis testing using the purchasing power parity model. Some issues noted in the reading may be relevant to interpreting your results for this exercise and Exercise 4.4.)

_____

_____

_____

_____

_____

EXERCISE 4.4

Specify a model to examine the long-run relationship between the inflation rate and the growth rate of the money supply.

How will you measure the long-run inflation rate and the long-run growth rate of the money supply? (HINT: To find the hypothesized relationship requires that both the long-run inflation rate and the long-run growth rate of the money supply be measured with moving averages computed over at least three to four years.)

_____

_____

_____

Estimate your long-run model and write the estimated equation below.

Are the suggested economic relationships confirmed? Do parameter estimates have the expected signs or values? Are the null hypotheses rejected?

_____

_____

_____

_____

Lesson Note 4.1

A Comment on Statistical Significance

The usual test of purchasing power parity ... fits prices at home (P) to prices abroad (P^*), allowing for the exchange rate (e): $P = \alpha + \beta(eP^*)$ + error term. The equation can be in levels or rates of change. If the coefficient b is statistically significantly different from 1.0, the hypothesis of purchasing power parity is rejected; if not, not. The test seems to tell about substantive significance without any tiresome inquiry into how true a hypothesis must be in order to be true. The table of t will tell.

But a number is large or small relative only to some standard. Forty degrees of frost is paralyzing cold by the standard of Virginia, a normal day by the standard of Saskatoon in January, and a heat wave by the standard of most interstellar gas. A *New Yorker* magazine cartoon shows water faucets labeled "Hot (A Relative Concept)" and "Cold (A Relative Concept)." Nothing is large-in-itself. It is large (or yellow, rich, cold, stable, well-integrated, selfish, free, rising, monopolistic) relative to something with which it can be interestingly compared. The remark "But how large is large?" is one of those seminar standbys, applying to any paper, like "Have you considered simultaneity bias?" or "Are there unexploited opportunities for entry?" It's usually a good question, inheriting some of its excellence from

its father in thought, the mind-stunning "So What?" (and its Jewish mother: "So What Else Is New?"). You say the coefficient is 0.85 with a standard error of 0.07? So?

The literature does not discuss how near the slope has to be to 1.0 to be able to say that purchasing power parity succeeds or fails. It does not answer how large is large. The only standard offered is statistical significance, that is, how surprising it would be to get the observed sample if the hypothesis of $\beta = 1.0$ were in fact exactly true.

But "exactly" true is not relevant for most economic purposes. What is relevant is merely that β is in the neighborhood of 1.0, where "the neighborhood" is defined by *why* it is relevant—for policy, for academic reputation, for the progress of knowledge. The question requires thought about the loss function. One begins to think that the neighborhood of small loss might be large. And even outside it, one begins to think that $\beta = .10$, say, would still be economically significant, were the fit tight enough to constrain prices at home; or that even a coefficient of -7854.86 would belie closed economy models of inflation.

The usual test does not discuss standards. It gives them up in favor of irrelevant talk about the probability of a type I error in view of the logic of random sampling. Most economists appear to have forgotten how narrow is the question that a statistical test of significance answers. It tells the intrepid investigator how likely it is that, *because of the small size of the sample he has*, he will make a mistake of excessive skepticism in rejecting a true hypothesis (in this case, $\beta = 1.0$). Though not to be scorned, it isn't much. It warns him about a certain narrow kind of foolishness.

The elementary but neglected point is that statistical tests of significance are merely about one sort of unbiased errors in *sampling*. The standard error, after all, is $(s^2/N)^{1/2}$. Except in the limiting case of literally zero correlation, if the sample were large enough all the coefficients would be significantly different from everything. The inverse of the square root of an extremely large number is very small. Any social scientist with large samples has had such logic impressed on him by events. A psychologist, Paul Meehl, for instance, reports a sample of 55,000 Minnesota high school seniors which "reveal statistically significant relationships in 91 percent of pairwise associations among a congeries of 45 miscellaneous variables such as sex, birth order, religious preference, ..., dancing, interest in woodworking. ... The majority of variables exhibited significant relationships with *all but three of the others*, often at a very high confidence level." ...

The large-sample case makes clear the irrelevance of statistical significance to the main question: So what? In the usual test of purchasing power parity, a sample size of a million yielding a very tight estimate that $\beta = 0.999$, "significantly" different from 1.0, could be produced under the usual procedures as evidence that the theory had "failed." Common sense, presumably, would rescue the investigator from asserting that if $\beta = 0.999$, with a standard error of .00000001, we should abandon purchasing power parity, or run our models of the American economy without the world price level. Similar common sense should be applied to findings that $\beta = .80$ or 1.30 with sample sizes of 30. It is not.

The point can be put most sharply by supposing that we *knew* the coefficient to be, say, 0.85. Suppose God told us. God does not play dice with the universe, and His is no mere probabilistic assurance. Would the scientific task be finished? No, it would not. We would still need to decide, by some criterion of why it matters (a human, not a divine, concern), whether 0.85 is high enough to affirm the theory. No mechanical procedure can relieve us of this responsibility. Nor is it a decision that should be made privately, as a matter of "mere opinion." It is the most important scientific decision, and it should be made out in the open. The test of significance doesn't make it.

Source: McCloskey, D. N. "The Loss Function Has Been Mislaid: The Rhetoric of Significance Tests," *American Economic Review* 75 (May 1985): 201–205.

Productivity and GNP

Figure 4.1 shows an aggregate production function. An aggregate production function describes how an economy's labor, capital, and other inputs are transformed into aggregate output. The production function shown in Figure 4.1 assumes that labor is the only variable input. All other inputs are assumed to be fixed. The production function is also drawn to exhibit diminishing returns. This means that each one-unit increase in labor causes output to rise by a smaller increment than does the previous one-unit increase in labor. The increment in output is called the marginal product of labor and can be represented by the slope of the production function ($\Delta Q/\Delta L$). Because the slope of the production function becomes flatter as more and more labor is employed, the production function shows diminishing returns.

In contrast, the average product of a given amount of labor L_o is equal to the output produced by L_o units of labor divided by L_o units of labor (Q_o/L_o). The average product is represented by the slope of a ray drawn from the origin

Figure 4.1
The Aggregate Production Function

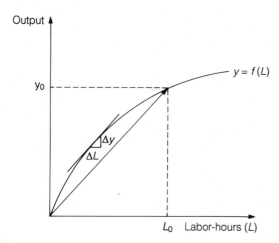

Marginal product of labor = $\frac{\Delta y}{\Delta L}$, shown by the slope of the production function

Average product of labor = $\frac{y_0}{L_0}$, shown by the slope of a ray from the origin

to the relevant output level on the production function. When the ray becomes flatter, average product is falling. Notice that average product declines continuously for the production function shown in Figure 4.1 as labor-hours increase.

Before estimating any regression, you *must* understand the data. What exactly is represented by a variable? Is it the right measure to include in the model? For example, it is easy to forget how to measure an industry's output. GNP is a measure of *aggregate* production. Most goods flow through a number of intermediate production stages before they are ready in their final form. If we add up the sales at every stage, we will overcount actual productive activity. For example, if we add together the wheat sold by the farmer, the flour sold by the miller, and the bread sold by the baker, we will count the same wheat three times. Aggregate productive activity thus can be measured by calculating the value of all final goods and services, the value added at each stage of production, or the gross income generated by the productive process.

But what is the correct measure of production for an industry? The value added by the industry is usually the correct measure. Table 4.1 shows how value added is calculated for a hypothetical firm. The table also shows how personal income is derived. The industry data needed for such calculations can be obtained from the *Census of Manufacturing* published by the U.S. Bureau of the Census. When economists talk about the contribution of an industry to GNP, they mean the value added generated by the industry. We end this lesson with exercises focusing on aggregate production.

Table 4.1
Calculating Value Added and Personal Income for a Hypothetical Firm

Income Statement		Contribution to GNP and Personal Income	
Sales	$5,256,000	Sales	$5,256,000
Costs		Plus: net increase in inventory	–$132,000
Materials and supplies		Less: intermediate products	–$1,388,000
Products and services	$1,388,000	Value added (contribution to GNP)	$3,736,000
Net withdrawal from inventory	$132,000	Less: capital consumption allowances	–$302,000
Employment costs		Contribution to net national product	$3,434,000
Wages and salaries	$1,723,000	Less: indirect business taxes	–$111,000
Employee benefits (Social Security,		Contribution to national income	$3,323,000
pension contributions, etc.)	$262,000	Less: corporate profits	–$1,305,000
Allowance for depreciation	$302,000	Plus: dividends	+$170,000
Interest on debt	$33,000	Contribution to personal income	$2,188,000
State and local taxes	$111,000		
Total cost	$3,951,000	Employee compensation	$1,985,000
Profits before U.S. corporate income tax	$1,305,000	Interest	$33,000
U.S. corporate income tax	$372,000	Dividends	$170,000
Profits after taxes	$933,000		$2,188,000
Dividends	$170,000		
Retained earnings	$763,000		

EXERCISE 4.5

Assume that productivity is measured by the amount of GNP produced in the nonfarm-business sector per labor-hour. This measure is usually referred to as output per hour. Does this measure reflect the average or marginal product of labor in Figure 4.1?

_____

_____

_____

Using Figure 4.1, develop a hypothesis to explain how changes in quarterly GNP are related to changes in quarterly productivity. Use your argument to answer the following questions:

1. Do you expect changes in productivity and GNP to increase together and decrease together, or do you expect them to move inversely?

_____

_____

_____

_____

2. Do you expect the two variables to change at the same time, or do you expect one to change before the other? That is, is one variable a depen-

dent variable, caused by the other, or do both reflect the current level of economic activity?

_____

_____

_____

Structure your answers to Questions 1 and 2 into hypotheses that can be tested by a regression model (or models). Write your model(s) below and explain how your hypotheses can be tested.

_____

_____

_____

_____

_____

_____

_____

_____

_____

_____

EXERCISE 4.6

Estimate your model(s) formulated in Exercise 4.5. Before conducting your regression analysis for GNP and productivity changes, update the data bank to include the most recent quarters. Follow the directions on how to use the data editor to add the updated values. The new data can be quickly obtained from the *Business Conditions Digest*. If you have never used the *Digest* before, read Lesson Note 4.2. Write your estimated model(s) in the following space.

Are the suggested economic relationships confirmed? Do the parameters have the expected signs? Are the null hypotheses rejected?

_____

_____

_____

If a suggested economic relationship is not supported by your analysis, explain why you feel the relationship is not supported. Is the relationship wrong? Are the variable measures valid? Have you given the model enough time to find the relationship?

_____

_____

_____

_____

_____

_____

_____

_____

Lesson Note 4.2

Using the *Business Conditions Digest*

The *Business Conditions Digest* (BCD) is published monthly by the Bureau of Economic Analysis (BEA) of the U.S. Department of Commerce. When looking up recent economic data, you will usually first turn to the *Digest*. It is much easier to use than the *Survey of Current Business*, although the *Survey* does report some variables not reported by the *Digest*.

The *Digest* was first published in 1961 under the name *Business Cycle Developments*. The variables included in the publication were largely determined by the leading, coincident, and lagging indicators developed by the National Bureau of Economic Research (NBER). The "cyclical indicators approach" to analyzing economic activity heavily relies on these variables. Table 4.2, taken from a recent issue, shows the indicator series reported in the *Digest*. Even though the major focus of the *Digest* is still on cyclical indicators, the *Digest* was expanded in 1968 to include other important economic variables, notably national income variables and sample survey variables of business and consumer intentions.

To find the productivity series needed to update the data bank, turn to the Alphabetical Index—Series Finding Guide at the back of the current issue of the *Digest*. Table 4.3 shows a section of the Index from a recent issue. Find output per hour in the nonfarm-business sector in the table. Notice that several items of information are given in the guide. Information on output per hour in the nonfarm-business sector is found on pages 50 and 88. A number (370) has been assigned to identify the series. This number can be extremely useful in using different government documents; it eliminates any ambiguity about what data series is being considered. Also notice that the historical series for the variable is reported in the January, 1985, issue. Each issue of the *Digest* gives several such historical updates. Thumb through this section in the current issue to see how the historical data are presented. Finally, the guide indicates that a complete description of the series begins on page 52 of the *Handbook of Cyclical Indicators*. The *Handbook of Cyclical Indicators* describes all the series reported by the *Digest*. Figure 4.2 reproduces the productivity and GNP discussions from the *Handbook*. The *Handbook* is clearly in need of revision.

Table 4.2
Cross Classification of Cyclical Indicators Reported in the *BCD* by Economic Process and Cyclical Timing

A. Timing at Business Cycle Peaks

Cyclical Timing \ Economic Process	I. EMPLOYMENT AND UNEMPLOYMENT (15 series)	II. PRODUCTION AND INCOME (10 series)	III. CONSUMPTION, TRADE, ORDERS, AND DELIVERIES (13 series)	IV. FIXED CAPITAL INVESTMENT (19 series)	V. INVENTORIES AND INVENTORY INVESTMENT (9 series)	VI. PRICES, COSTS, AND PROFITS (18 series)	VII. MONEY AND CREDIT (28 series)
LEADING (L) INDICATORS (61 series)	Marginal employment adjustments (3 series); Job vacancies (2 series); Comprehensive employment (1 series); Comprehensive unemployment (3 series)	Capacity utilization (2 series)	Orders and deliveries (6 series); Consumption and trade (2 series)	Formation of business enterprises (2 series); Business investment commitments (5 series); Residential construction (3 series)	Inventory investment (4 series); Inventories on hand and on order (1 series)	Stock prices (1 series); Sensitive commodity prices (2 series); Profits and profit margins (7 series); Cash flows (2 series)	Money (5 series); Credit flows (5 series); Credit difficulties (2 series); Bank reserves (2 series); Interest rates (1 series)
ROUGHLY COINCIDENT (C) INDICATORS (24 series)	Comprehensive employment (1 series)	Comprehensive output and income (4 series); Industrial production (4 series)	Consumption and trade (4 series)	Business investment commitments (1 series); Business investment expenditures (6 series)			Velocity of money (2 series); Interest rates (2 series)
LAGGING (Lg) INDICATORS (19 series)	Comprehensive unemployment (2 series)			Business investment expenditures (1 series)	Inventories on hand and on order (4 series)	Unit labor costs and labor share (4 series)	Interest rates (4 series); Outstanding debt (4 series)
TIMING UNCLASSIFIED (U) (8 series)	Comprehensive employment (3 series)		Consumption and trade (1 series)	Business investment commitments (1 series)		Sensitive commodity prices (1 series); Profits and profit margins (1 series)	Interest rates (1 series)

B. Timing at Business Cycle Troughs

Economic Process / Cyclical Timing	I. EMPLOYMENT AND UNEMPLOYMENT (15 series)	II. PRODUCTION AND INCOME (10 series)	III. CONSUMPTION, TRADE, ORDERS, AND DELIVERIES (13 series)	IV. FIXED CAPITAL INVESTMENT (19 series)	V. INVENTORIES AND INVENTORY INVESTMENT (9 series)	VI. PRICES, COSTS, AND PROFITS (18 series)	VII. MONEY AND CREDIT (28 series)
LEADING (L) INDICATORS (47 series)	Marginal employment adjustments (1 series)	Industrial production (1 series)	Orders and deliveries (5 series) Consumption and trade (4 series)	Formation of business enterprises (2 series) Business investment commitments (4 series) Residential construction (3 series)	Inventory investment (4 series)	Stock prices (1 series) Sensitive commodity prices (3 series) Profits and profit margins (6 series) Cash flows (2 series)	Money (4 series) Credit flows (5 series) Credit difficulties (2 series)
ROUGHLY COINCIDENT (C) INDICATORS (23 series)	Marginal employment adjustments (2 series) Comprehensive employment (4 series)	Comprehensive output and income (4 series) Industrial production (3 series) Capacity utilization (2 series)	Consumption and trade (3 series)	Business investment commitments (1 series)		Profits and profit margins (2 series)	Money (1 series) Velocity of money (1 series)
LAGGING (Lg) INDICATORS (41 series)	Job vacancies (2 series) Comprehensive employment (1 series) Comprehensive unemployment (5 series)		Orders and deliveries (1 series)	Business investment commitments (2 series) Business investment expenditures (7 series)	Inventories on hand and on order (5 series)	Unit labor costs and labor share (4 series)	Velocity of money (1 series) Bank reserves (1 series) Interest rates (8 series) Outstanding debt (4 series)
TIMING UNCLASSIFIED (U) (1 series)							Bank reserves (1 series)

Table 4.3
Alphabetical Index—Series Finding Guide—Continued

Series title (See complete titles in "Titles and Sources of Series," following this index)	Series number	Current issue (page numbers) Charts	Tables	Historical data (issue date)	Series description (*)
Plant and equipment—See also investment, capital					
Contracts and orders, constant dollars.............20		12.23	66	5/86	21
Contracts and orders, current dollars...............10		23	66	5/86	21
Expenditures by business, constant dollars...... 100		24	67	5/86	...
Expenditures by business, current dollars........ 61		24	67	5/86	23
Expenditures by business, DI.........................970		38	76	11/85	23
Population, civilian employment as percent of......90		17	62	4/86	9
Price indexes					
Consumer prices—See also International comparisons					
All items..320		49	84.95	8/86	49
Food...322		49	84	8/86	49
Deflators					
Fixed-weighted, gross domestic business product..311		48	84	5/86	49
Implicit price deflator, GNP...................310		48	84	5/86	38
Labor cost, price per unit of, nonfarm business.. 26		29	70	8/86	28
Producer prices					
All commodities....................................330		48	85	7/86	50
Capital equipment.................................333		48	86	7/86	51
Crude materials....................................331		48	85	7/86	50
Finished consumer goods.....................334		48	86	7/86	51
Industrial commodities.........................335		48	85	7/86	51
Intermediate materials..........................332		48	86	7/86	50
Sensitive crude and intermediate materials...98		28	69	6/86	51
Raw industrials, spot market prices					
Components....................................... ...		...	79	...	...
Diffusion index.....................................967		37	75	1/86	25
Spot market index...................................23		28	69	1/86	25
Sensitive crude and intermediate materials, change in producer prices.......98		28	69	6/86	51
Sensitive materials prices, percent change..... 99		13.28	69	6/86	25
Stock prices—See also International comparisons					
500 common stocks................................19		13.28	69	11/85	25
500 common stocks, DI...........................968		37	75	7/85	25
Price to unit labor cost, nonfarm business...............26		29	70	8/86	28
Prices, selling					
Manufacturing, DI................................976		38	76	12/85	37
Retail trade, DI....................................978		38	76	12/85	37
Wholesale trade, DI...............................977		38	76	12/85	37
Prime contract awards, Defense Department.......525		53	90	12/85	55
Prime rate charged by banks..............................109		35	73	6/85	35
Producer prices—See Price indexes					
Producers' durable equipment, nonresidential, GPDI...88		25	67	2/86	40
Production—See Gross national product and Industrial production					
Productivity					
Output per hour, business sector.....................370		50	88	1/85	52
Output per hour, nonfarm business sector........358		50	88	1/85	52
Profitability, CI...916		11	60	1/86	5

NOTE: CCAdj, capital consumption adjustment; CI, composite index; GNP, gross national product; GPDI, gross private domestic investment; IVA, inventory valuation adjustment.
*The number shown is the page of the *Handbook of Cyclical Indicators* (1984) on which the series description appears.

Figure 4.2
Handbook of Cyclical Indicators Sample Sections

GROSS NATIONAL PRODUCT

Series 200.	Gross National Product in Current Dollars
Series 200b.	Change in Gross National Product in Current Dollars
Series 200c.	Percent Change in Gross National Product in Current Dollars
Series 50.	Gross National Product in 1972 Dollars
Series 50b.	Change in Gross National Product in 1972 Dollars
Series 50c.	Percent Change in Gross National Product in 1972 Dollars
Series 310.	Implicit Price Deflator for Gross National Product
Series 310c.	Percent Change in the Implicit Price Deflator for Gross National Product
Series 217.	Per Capita Gross National Product in 1972 Dollars
Series 213.	Final Sales in 1972 Dollars

Source: U.S. Department of Commerce, Bureau of Economic Analysis and Bureau of the Census

(Data contained in these series are seasonally adjusted.)

Gross National Product (GNP) is the most widely used measure of the Nation's production. It measures the market value of the goods and services produced by the labor and property supplied by residents of the United States. More specifically, it is the market value of "final" sales of goods and services plus inventory change; purchases by one producing unit from another of "intermediate" products are not included, but depreciation charges and other allowances for business and institutional consumption of fixed capital goods have not been deducted in deriving it.

GNP is measured as the sum of products: Personal consumption expenditures (series 230), gross private domestic investment (including the change in business inventories) (series 240), net exports (exports less imports) of goods and services (series 250), and government purchases of goods and services (series 260). (For a detailed description of each of these categories, see the appropriate sections in this *Handbook*.) GNP can also be measured as the sum of the costs incurred and the profits earned in production of GNP. By this approach, the incomes of labor and property are summed, in the forms in which they accrue to residents and before the deduction of taxes on the incomes, to national income (series 220), and to national income is added the other charges that must be included to arrive at the total market value of goods and services. (For a detailed description of national income, see the *National Income* section in this *Handbook*.) The two measures of GNP—that is, as the sum of products and as the sum of incomes and other charges—differ by a statistical discrepancy, which reflects measurement error.

Estimates of GNP now cover the 50 States and the District of Columbia; prior to 1960, they did not cover Alaska and Hawaii.

GNP in 1972 dollars, or real GNP, is derived principally by dividing components of the current-dollar GNP by appropriate price indexes in as fine a breakdown as possible.

SERIES 200 measures the current-dollar value of GNP, as described above.

Series 200b measures the quarter-to-quarter amount of change in series 200.

Series 200c measures the quarter-to-quarter percent change in series 200.

In *BCD*, series 200, 200b, and 200c appear under the category "GNP and personal income."

SERIES 50 measures the value of GNP in 1972 dollars.

Series 50b measures the quarter-to-quarter amount of change in series 50.

Series 50c measures the quarter-to-quarter percent change in series 50.

In *BCD*, series 50, 50b, and 50c appear under the category "GNP and personal income." Series 50 also appears under the economic process "production and income."

SERIES 310, the implicit price deflator for GNP, is a current-weighted price index (1972 = 100) and is derived by dividing the current-dollar GNP by the constant-dollar GNP for each period. It is a weighted average of the detailed price indexes used in the deflation of GNP with the composition of the constant-dollar output in each quarter as weights. In other words, the price indexes for each quarter are weighted by the ratio of the quantity of the item valued in 1972 prices to the total output for the corresponding quarter in 1972 prices. Therefore, changes in the implicit price deflator reflect both changes in prices and changes in the composition of output.

Series 310c measures the quarter-to-quarter perecnt change in series 310.

In *BCD*, series 310 and 310c appear under the category "price movements."

SERIES 217 measures the per capita GNP in constant (1972) dollars. It is computed by dividing series 50 by the U.S. population. The U.S. population includes residents of the 50 States and the District of Columbia, and members of the U.S. Armed Forces stationed in foreign countries and in the outlying areas, but not dependents living with them. It excludes residents of Puerto Rico, residents of the outlying areas under U.S. sovereignty or jurisdiction, and other American citizens living overseas. Population estimates for the first of each month are published by the Bureau of the Census. A quarterly population estimate is computed by the Bureau of Economic Analysis by taking 2-month averages of the beginning-of-month estimates to represent monthly averages and averaging the monthly averages for the quarter. The quarterly population estimate is then divided into the GNP estimate for the quarter to obtain series 217.

In *BCD*, series 217 appears under the category "GNP and personal income."

SERIES 213 measures that part of GNP that is sold to final users. It consists of personal consumption expenditures, gross private domestic fixed investment, government purchases, and net exports. It equals GNP less the change in business inventories.

In *BCD*, series 213 appears under the category "GNP and personal income."

OUTPUT PER HOUR

Series 370.	Index of Output Per Hour, All Persons, Business Sector
Series 370c.	Percent Change in Output Per Hour, All Persons, Business Sector
Series 358.	Index of Output Per Hour, All Persons, Nonfarm Business Sector

Source: U.S. Department of Labor, Bureau of Labor Statistics

(Data contained in these series are seasonally adjusted.)

The index (1977 = 100) of output per hour is a productivity measure based on changes in the ratio of output to labor input. Productivity is defined as the constant-dollar value of final goods and services produced within a certain period in relation to paid hours, including hours paid for holidays, vacation, and sick leave. Hours of employees, proprietors, and unpaid family workers are included. Index changes through time reflect the joint effects of many influences, such as changes in technology, capital investment, layout and flow of materials, capacity utilization, energy use, managerial skills, and skills and efforts of the work force.

Real gross domestic product, compiled by the U.S. Department of Commerce, Bureau of Economic Analysis (BEA), is used as the output measure. It is the market value, in 1972 dollars, of the goods and services produced by labor and property located in the United States. Labor input data are based primarily on the hours and employment series compiled by the Bureau of Labor Statistics from monthly reports submitted by nonagricultural establishments to State employment security agencies. Estimates are computed separately for each industry and are then aggregated. (For a more detailed description of these series, see the *Employment, Hours, and Earnings* section in this *Handbook.*) For proprietors, unpaid family workers, and persons engaged in the farm sector, where establishment data are not available, data from the national income and product accounts

compiled by BEA, or data from the current population survey (CPS) compiled by the U.S. Department of Commerce, Bureau of the Census are used to develop hours and employment estimates. Weekly hours data from the CPS are adjusted to eliminate distortions due to holidays.

In *BCD*, series 370, 370c, and 358 appear under the category "wages and productivity."

SERIES 370 is an index (1977 = 100) that is a productivity measure for the business sector. The business sector includes agriculture, forestry, and fisheries; mining; construction; manufacturing; transportation and public utilities; wholesale and retail trade; finance, insurance, and real estate; services; and government enterprises. It excludes government, private households, gross housing product of owner-occupied dwellings, nonprofit institutions, and rest of the world.

Series 370c measures the percent change in series 370 over 1- and 4-quarter spans.

SERIES 358 is an index (1977 = 100) that is a productivity measure of the nonfarm business sector. In addition to the exclusions listed under series 370, series 358 excludes farms.

Suggested Reading

You will undoubtedly be startled by your results for the GNP–productivity relationship. A brief discussion of how economists explain the empirical behavior of productivity over the business cycle can be found on pages 64–69 in A. S. Blinder's *Economic Policy and the Great Stagflation* (New York: Academic Press, 1979). This reading also discusses controversies concerning changes in the trend for productivity. The empirical relationship you observed in the lesson played an historic role in modern macroeconomics, when economists discovered the short-run demand for labor could not be directly derived from a production function like that shown in Figure 4.1. This issue is discussed in most intermediate macroeconomic texts.

If you would like a better understanding of the National Income Accounting System, read Chapter 1 in A. T. Sommers, *The U.S. Economy Demystified: What Major Economic Statistics Mean and Their Significance for Business* (Lexington, Mass.: D.C. Heath, 1985). This lucid paperback book discusses a variety of economic measures besides national income measures and provides an excellent introduction to the U.S. statistical system.

More Single-Equation Models

1. To practice specifying and estimating models

2. To learn about some of the issues involved in using price indices

3. To learn to use the *Economic Report of the President*

In Lesson 4, you constructed single-equation models to examine hypothesized economic relationships. This lesson gives you more practice in developing single-equation models. In answering the questions posed by the various problems, strive for clarity when developing your arguments and explaining how you expect variables to be related. These arguments provide the foundation for your models. Two of these models will be extended in subsequent lessons.

Okun's Law

In the early 1960s, Arthur Okun formulated an empirical relationship between the unemployment rate and lost output in the economy.[1] Lost output was defined as the difference between potential GNP and actual GNP. The difference was referred to as the GNP gap. Potential GNP was defined as that level of GNP that would be produced *if* the economy were operating at full employment. Okun examined the data and concluded that every 1-percent increase in unemployment above the full employment–unemployment rate was associated with a 3-percent loss in real output. This relationship came to be known as Okun's Law and was used by the Council of Economic Advisors to dramatize the loss in output associated with the stagnant economy of the early 1960s.

EXERCISE 5.1

Specify a model to test the validity of Okun's Law. Assume the full employment–unemployment rate is 4 percent. Write your model below:

Estimate the model for annual data through 1963 using the appropriate variables in the data bank. Transform the variables in the data bank to percentages before using them in your model. Write your estimated model in the following space:

Do you agree with Okun's interpretation of the data?

_____

_____

_____

_____

_____

Use your estimated model and data from 1964–1980 to predict values for the model's dependent variable. Plot the predicted and actual values in Figure 5.1. If your econometric software does the plot for you, attach the plot to the figure. How well do the predicted values fit the actual values? What do you conclude about the usefulness of Okun's Law in more recent years?

_____

_____

_____

_____

_____

If Okun's Law seems to be less exact in more recent years, can you explain why? To answer this question, think about output as being equal to the number of labor-hours employed multiplied by the average productivity of each labor-hour. Decompose the number of labor-hours employed further. Let N be the number of people in the labor force, u the unemployment rate, and h the average number of hours worked per worker. The number of labor-hours employed is then equal to $h(1 - u)N$. Let π be productivity. Thus, GNP can be written as

$$GNP = \pi h(1 - u)N \tag{5.1}$$

Equation 5.1 shows that, in the short run, increases in GNP can be explained by four variables. In other words, Equation 5.1 indicates the short-run determinants of GNP. Okun assumed that the four variables move together in a stable, consistent manner. In formulating his relationship, he used the unemployment rate as an inclusive measure, assuming that the effects of all four variables were captured by the unemployment rate.

Figure 5.1
Actual and Fitted Values for Okun's Law

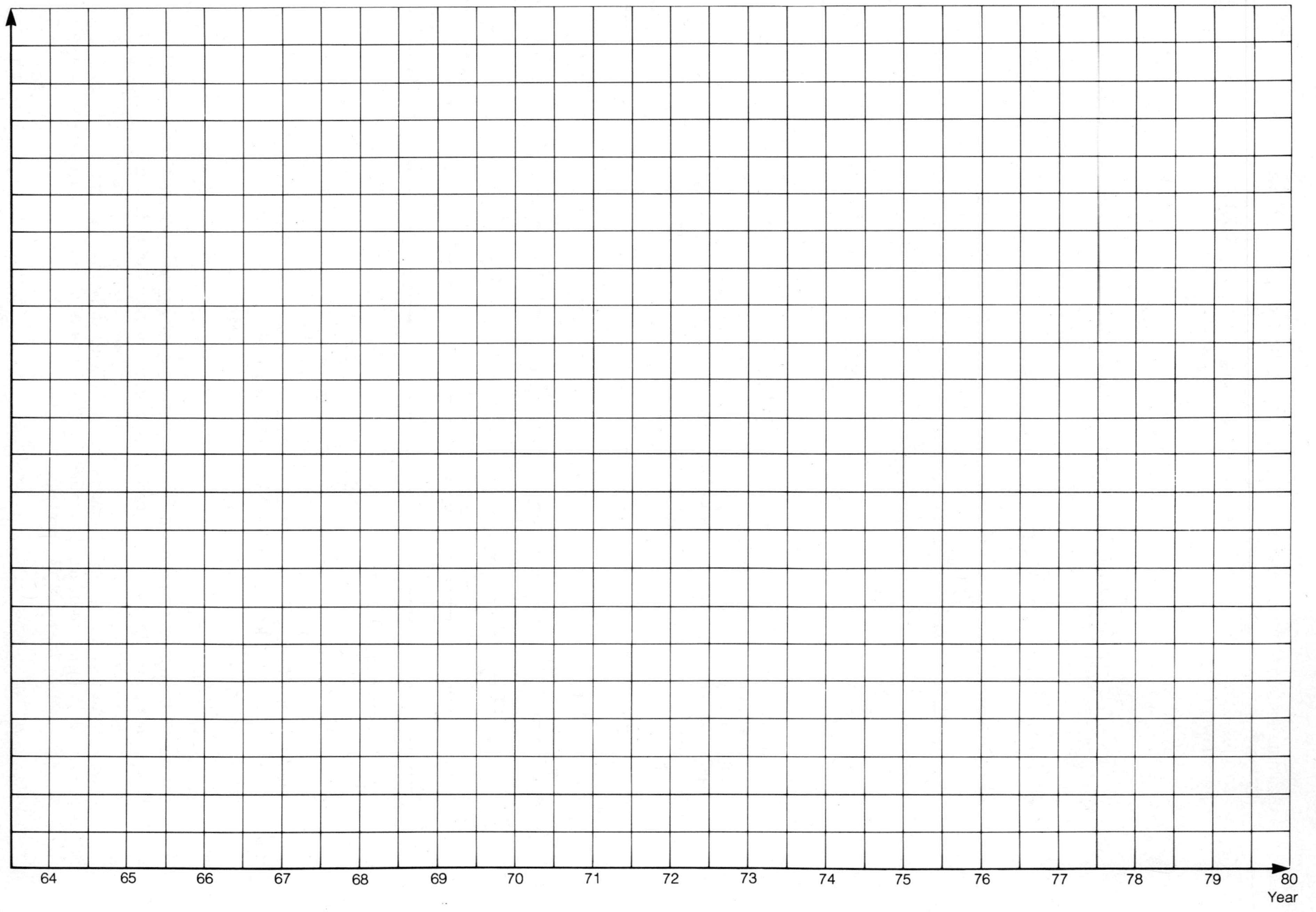

Year

64 65 66 67 68 69 70 71 72 73 74 75 76 77 78 79 80

EXERCISE 5.2

Using the appropriate variables in the data bank (OKUN series), examine the validity of Okun's assumption concerning the four variables.[2] Discuss your conclusions. (HINT: Treat Equation 5.1 as isolating the four components of the growth rate of GNP. Refer to page 53.)

_____

_____

_____

_____

_____

_____

_____

_____

_____

EXERCISE 5.3

Explain how government economists computed the potential GNP figures used in your model. You will find the construction of potential GNP explained in the 1982 _Economic Report of the President_, the last year the Council of Economic Advisors calculated potential GNP.

_____

_____

_____

_____

_____

_____

_____

Are there problems with using 4 percent as the full employment–unemployment rate in the second part of your analysis?

_____

_____

_____

_____

When you use the *Economic Report of the President* to answer the question on potential GNP, spend a little time looking through the document. Among other things, the 1946 Full Employment Act created the Council of Economic Advisors in the Executive Office of the President. Every February, the Council sends the current administration's report to Congress. The traditional indicators of fiscal policy, along with the administration's assumptions about future economic activity, are discussed in the *Report*. If you are interested in a systematic statement of an administration's economic policies and goals, the *Report* is usually the first place to look. The *Report* also includes an extensive statistical appendix on many different aspects of economic activity.

Fixed Business Investment

Exercise 5.4 asks you to formulate a model for nonresidential fixed business investment (structures and producers' durable equipment). Be aware that explaining fixed business investment is a difficult problem. Sir John Hicks, a noted British economist, once referred to investment spending as a "flighty bird." Most econometricians feel that Hicks was being much too polite in his description. We will return to the problems of estimating fixed investment in later lessons.

EXERCISE 5.4

How do you think business firms go about deciding to invest or not invest in new plants and equipment? (This discussion should allow you to isolate the variables in your model and decide if any should be lagged.)

_____

_____

_____

_____

_____

_____

Use the general arguments you developed to specify a linear model of investment that can be estimated using ordinary least-squares. Specify your model below:

Estimate your model for quarterly data using the variables in the data bank. Write the estimated model below:

Are you satisfied with the results? If not, explain why the model is not satisfactory.

_____

_____

_____

_____

_____

_____

The Demand for New Autos

Your assignment for this section is to develop a model to explain the demand for new autos in the United States.

EXERCISE 5.5

Discuss a consumer's decision to buy or not buy a new auto. What variables should you include in your model?

_____

_____

_____

_____

Use your arguments to specify a linear model that can be estimated using ordinary least-squares. Specify your model below:

Estimate your model using quarterly data from the data bank. Write your estimated model below:

Discuss the estimation results. Are you satisfied with the results? If not, explain why the model is not satisfactory.

_____

_____

_____

_____

_____

Because of the importance of the automobile industry in the economy, explaining the demand for autos is an important topic in applied econometrics. Economists devote much effort to developing models of auto demand to include in macroeconomic forecasting models, and all major auto companies employ economists to predict future demand and changing market conditions for their product. Modeling demand for a durable good like autos raises a significant estimation issue. In terms of economic theory, consumers do not consume a durable good like autos; they consume a flow of services provided by the durable good. Estimating demand for a good like autos thus requires some formulation of the flow of services consumers receive from autos. Purchasing new autos adds to the stock of existing autos, with consumers receiving automobile services from the total stock. We will return to this issue in later lessons.

In examining the time-series data for new autos, another problem may have occurred to you. The data reflect quarterly auto purchases for several decades. Yet the auto purchased in 1989 is hardly the same auto as was purchased in 1950. There have been marked improvements in the quality of autos over the decades. Doesn't this improvement in quality invalidate the observed market price of autos as a measure of price in the demand function? After all, a rise in price from one year to the next might indicate a higher-quality product, not a rise in the price of a constant-quality product. There is no way to tell.

If the price index for autos in the data bank were based on observed sales prices, the price index would be an invalid measure. But the variable you should have selected from the data bank is the Consumer Price Index (CPI) component for new autos. The CPI reflects prices for a constant quality–market basket of goods. In other words, government statisticians adjust the prices for autos reflected in the CPI to reflect quality changes in autos. When an improvement in auto quality takes place, the quoted market price is adjusted downward to maintain an equivalent price for the auto "as if" it were not improved.

How do government statisticians go about making these price adjustments? Usually the adjustment is made on the basis of cost data provided by the producer. In the case of the catalytic converter, for example, the production cost of the converter was deducted from the price of new autos equipped with the converter. Many economists have suspected that the CPI contains an upward bias because they doubt changes in quality are fully reflected in the cost-based adjustments. It should be noted that this suspicion, while perhaps justified for a few items, has never been convincingly proven for the overall index.

In a more general sense, price indices are frequently used to measure inflation and deflate nominal values in applied econometric analysis. Lesson Notes 5.1 and 5.2 discuss selected measurement problems associated with inflation measures for consumption goods and the significance of the "base period" for a price index.[3]

Lesson Note 5.1

Some Issues in Measuring Inflation

Rapid inflation usually brings with it greater disparity in the rates of advance of different prices. During periods of rough stability in the general price level, some prices go up and some come down but the divergence as a rule is not very large. Double-digit inflation, on the other hand, is characterized by enormous advances in some prices and much smaller advances in others. One of the consequences of the divergence is that the actual extent of inflation becomes more difficult to measure, and measurement becomes more affected by the decisions about how to do it. In short, measures of inflation become more controversial.

Index numbers such as the consumer price index are affected by the sample of prices that go into them, by the quantities that are assumed to be bought at those prices, and by the conceptual framework that determines what the index measures and how it is done. Obviously, if all prices went up 10 percent, these things would not matter. The index would go up 10 percent. It is the variation that makes them matter, and the more variation, the more they

matter. [Table 5.1] makes a simple comparison between 1967–1968, when the consumer price index was going up at a 4 percent rate, and 1978–1979, when it went up at an 11 percent rate. In the first period prices in some of the major expenditure categories rose about 3 percent, whereas others rose as much as 6 percent. The overall index, which rose 4 percent, was quite representative, because there was a close consensus among the seven categories. In 1978–1979 the situation was very different. The increases were spread across a range running from 4 percent for apparel to 14 percent for transportation. The 11 percent increase in the overall index was far less representative, because there was little or no consensus among the price increases in the seven categories. Similar figures for the intervening years show that, as a rule, as the overall rate of inflation increased, the variation among the price increases in the different categories also increased (as shown in [Figure 5.1]).

This phenomenon opens the way for criticism of the price indexes. One of the more elementary lines of commentary that it provokes focuses upon the areas that are rising fastest and shows what the index would do if they were omitted. Naturally the index then rises less rapidly. The lower rate is sometimes called the basic or underlying rate of inflation. The consequence of removing prices that are at the other end of the spectrum, rising least rapidly or declining, is usually disregarded. Sometimes the argument is more sophisticated, based on the special circumstances that affect the high-rising prices or upon the reasons for believing that the measurement of the high-rising prices is defective. Yet it is curious that the special circumstances or the measurement difficulties that are stressed always pertain to the high-risers rather than the low-risers. Also, the "special circumstances" argument, usually applied to food or energy, ignores the question of whether the behavior of those prices affects the others. If food or energy prices had not risen so fast, would other prices have risen faster, because money not spent on food or energy might then have been directed to driving up prices of other goods and services?

The measurement problems are more fundamental. Those that have surfaced in recent months mostly pertain to the differences between the consumer price index and the deflator for personal consumption expenditures. The latter is derived in the process of constructing the estimates of gross national product and represents the value of consumption expenditures in current prices divided by their value in constant (1972) prices. There are a very large number of differences between the two indexes, but perhaps the three most important are the following:

1. The CPI refers to the urban population (or, alternatively, to urban wage earners and clerical workers), whereas the PCE covers the entire population including, of course, the rural and farm population. The PCE also covers the expenditures of private nonprofit institutions, such as hospitals, universities, and churches.

2. The CPI refers to a fixed market basket of goods and services, determined by a survey of consumer expenditures in 1972–1973. Hence the movements in the CPI are determined solely by price changes, not by changes in quantities purchased. The PCE refers to a constantly changing market basket, determined by what consumers are buying currently. Hence it is influenced both by changes in prices and by changes in quantities. Some of the quantity changes may be in response to efforts by consumers to buy less of goods that are rising rapidly in price and more

of goods that have become relatively cheap, but other shifts in expenditure patterns may reflect changes in tastes, in the availability of goods, in affluence, or other factors.

3. The CPI treats the cost of owner-occupied housing as an expense consisting of the net amount spent for new houses in 1972–1973 by the small fraction of the urban population that bought houses then, the amount committed to be spent on mortgage interest payments for these new houses, and the amounts spent by all homeowners for repairs and maintenance, property taxes, and property insurance. The PCE treats the cost of owner-occupied housing as an expense to be estimated by the rent that might be paid for such housing, using the rent index from the CPI for this purpose.

The difference in the population coverage of the two indexes means that the PCE is influenced by prices and expenditures that are not included in the CPI, notably prices paid by rural families and by nonprofit institutions. For some purposes, such as deflating total personal income or disposable income, the broader coverage of the PCE is desirable. For other purposes, such as measuring real wages of urban workers, the narrower coverage of the CPI is desirable. The CPI also is available for different areas of the country, while the PCE is not.

The issue of the fixed or changing market basket is complicated. One argument is that the use in the CPI of quantity weights pertaining to 1972–1973, before the sharp increase in oil prices began, means that cost-saving shifts in fuel consumption and in types of automobiles purchased are not allowed for. The result, so the argument goes, is that the CPI exaggerates the effective increase in prices, whereas the PCE, by using current quantity weights, avoids this bias.

In measuring the change in prices between a base period, say 1972, and the current period, an index using quantity weights pertaining to the base period will usually show a larger increase than an index using quantity weights pertaining to the current period. That is, the cost of the base period's market basket will ordinarily increase faster than the cost of the current period's market basket. Neither index, however, shows the increase in cost of a market basket that is best adapted to the price situation in *each* period. The use of base period quantities generally overestimates this increase, whereas the use of current period quantities generally underestimates it.

Hence this factor alone tends to give the

PCE a downward bias, whereas it gives the CPI an upward bias. This tendency, however, pertains only to comparisons with the base period. Much of the time these are not the comparisons of interest. Attention is usually focused on the rate of inflation over short periods, such as a month, or six months, or a year. The base period is not involved (directly), and it becomes impossible to say, on theoretical grounds, which type of index will show higher rates of increase. All that is clear, in this case, is that the PCE does not measure price change alone, since the quantities change (in an undefined way) as well as the prices, whereas the CPI measures only the change in prices, because the market basket stays fixed in all periods.

Table 5.1
Changes in Consumer Prices, by Major Expenditure Classes (*percent*)

Expenditure Class and Relative Importance December 1979[a]	1967–1968	1978–1979
Food and beverages (19)	3.6	10.8
Housing (45)	4.0	12.2
Apparel and upkeep (5)	5.4	4.4
Transportation (18)	3.2	14.3
Medical care (5)	6.1	9.3
Entertainment (4)	5.7	6.7
Other goods and services (4)	5.2	7.3
All items (100)	4.2	11.3
Smallest change	3.2	4.4
Largest change	6.1	14.3
Range	2.9	9.9
Average deviation[b]	1.1	3.1
Standard deviation[b]	1.2	3.8

[a]Figures in parentheses are percentages of the total cost of the CPI market basket at December 1979 prices.
[b]Computed from the all-items figure rather than from the simple arithmetic mean of the seven group figures.
Source: U.S. Bureau of Labor Statistics.

Figure 5.2
Variability of Price Changes and the Rate of Inflation, 1967–1979

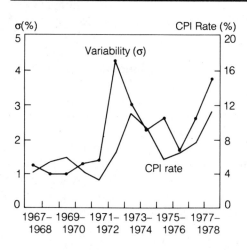

Note: The CPI rate is the percentage change between annual averages of the all-items index. The variability measure is the root-mean-square deviation of the year-to-year percentage changes in the seven major component indexes from the CPI rate. The seven components are listed in [Table 5.1]. *Source:* U.S. Bureau of Labor Statistics.

Source: Moore, G. H. "Inflation and Statistics," in *Essays in Contemporary Problems 1980.* (Washington, D.C.: American Enterprise Institute for Public Policy Research, 1980).

Lesson Note 5.2

Different Base Periods for Price Indices

The Base Period

The selection of an appropriate base is fundamental to the development of index numbers. If a price index is to serve as a stable basis for comparison of price movements over time, a period of time must be selected and held as the base long enough to generate a series of indexes for subsequent periods that will be useful in comparing those periods not only with the base but also with each other.

In devising an aggregate index for general-purpose use, the selection of the base period is necessarily somewhat arbitrary. Under ideal conditions, however, the base period chosen would be one in which sharp fluctuations in prices in underlying economic conditions would be minimal. Such "normal" periods are difficult to find, since prices of hundreds of items must be taken into account. If the index is of the special-purpose variety, however, the selection of an appropriate base is somewhat easier. For example, the earliest concern with index numbers involved an attempt to measure changes in the purchasing power of money (i.e., the reciprocal of the price index) resulting from the importation of silver into Europe after the discovery of America. This first price index, developed by Carli in 1764, covered a 250-year time span with the year 1500 as its base.

Base periods of price indexes are occasionally updated for convenience. Also, as spending patterns change and as technological change occurs, particular selections of goods and services in the "market basket" become obsolete as standards for comparison. Items purchased in the current period either may not have been available or may have undergone substantial quality changes since the base period. A revision of the sample of items in the "market basket" is required to account for these changes, and a sample revision is often accompanied by a shift of the base period to one that better represents the revised sample of goods and services.

Although sometimes desirable, it is not necessary that both of the above changes be made at the same time. An updating of the "market basket" can be accomplished without shifting the base, if the revised selection of items is worked into the sample without distorting the continuity of the index. This type of adjustment is discussed later in connection with other statistical problems. A straightforward shift of the base period without changing the sample of goods and services is also possible and quite simple to accomplish. For example, if the index of 1970 prices for a particular sample of items on a 1960 base is 120.0 and the index on the same base was 105.0 in 1965, then 1970 prices can be expressed on a 1965 base as 114.3, or 120.0/105.0.* This kind of linkage, while frequently used, does nothing to improve the quality of the index. This procedure was used by the Bureau of Labor Statistics in 1971 to rebase its indexes of wholesale and consumer prices to 1967 from their former 1957–1959 base period. The revised number gave the same information as the original index and in no way allowed for changes in quality of goods and services or changes in spending patterns. Thus, the most crucial test of an index is whether its market basket continues to be representative. If it is, revisions of the base period may be convenient but not essential.

*It is common practice to express index numbers as ratios multiplied by 100 and rounded to one decimal place (e.g., the index 114.3 is the ratio 1.143).

Source: Wallace, W. H. and Cullison, W. E. *Measuring Price Changes: A Study of the Price Indexes,* 4th ed. (Richmond, Va.: Federal Reserve Bank of Richmond, 1981).

Suggested Reading

If you want to know more about the CPI, you should read: "The Consumer Price Index: Concepts and Content over the Years," Bureau of Labor Statistics Report 517, May 1978 (revised). A good discussion of the problems involved in assessing the accuracy of price adjustments for quality changes is in J. E. Triplett, "The Measurement of Inflation: A Survey of Research on the Accuracy of Price Indexes," ed. P. H. Earl, *Analysis of Inflation* (Lexington, Mass.: Lexington Books, 1975). Finally, if you are interested in the calculation of potential GNP or the high-employment budget, read: F. deLeeuw et al., "The High Employment Budget: New Estimates," *Survey of Current Business* (November 1980).

Making Nonlinear Functions Linear

1. To learn how to estimate a variety of functional forms using ordinary least-squares and econometric software
2. To understand the issues involved in matching a functional form to an economic problem
3. To learn how to write a research report explaining econometric results

The functional form used to model a relationship reflects the expected value of the dependent variable. We wish to model the average response of the dependent variable to a set of independent variables. Many of the relationships discussed in economic courses are not linear. Potential GNP growth is exponential. Total cost is S-shaped. Average total cost and marginal cost are U-shaped. Specifying any of these relationships with a linear function clearly distorts the underlying model. Such a distortion is called a **misspecification of the model's functional form**. Functional misspecification is one of the most serious errors that can be made in conducting empirical research.

But the ordinary least-squares regression model can be used to estimate a variety of nonlinear functions. The regression model is thus more widely applicable than it might first appear. A function need not be linear in the *variables* to apply ordinary least-squares. A function need only be linear in the *parameters*. Any function that can be transformed such that the dependent variable is equal to a weighted sum of the parameters can be estimated with ordinary least-squares. This lesson shows you how to estimate a variety of such nonlinear functions. Sometimes a little algebraic manipulation is all that is needed. Other times, more complex transformations are required. The rules of logarithms are very helpful in making these transformations. Consequently, the next section reviews logarithms. You will also need to know how to work with logarithms to solve some of the problems in Lesson 7.

Logarithms

A logarithm is an *exponent* defined in terms of some *base number*. It is the exponent (or power) to which the base must be raised to give a specific number. For example, 2 is the logarithm of 9 to the base 3. Base 3 must be raised to the exponent 2 to obtain 9. We write this as

$$\log_3 9 = 2$$

In general terms, if $y = b^n$, then $n = \log_b y$.

Two bases are widely used, the number 10 and the irrational number e, equal to approximately 2.718. When 10 is the base, the exponent is called the **common logarithm**. When e is the base, the exponent is called the **natural logarithm**. Common logarithms convey an unambiguous order of magnitude, as can be seen by examining the following sequence:

$$\log_{10}10,000 = 4$$
$$\log_{10}1000 = 3$$
$$\log_{10}100 = 2$$
$$\log_{10}10 = 1$$
$$\log_{10}1 = 0$$
$$\log_{10}.1 = -1$$

The common logarithm of a number between 10 and 100 must be between 1 and 2. The common logarithm of a number between 100 and 1000 must be between 2 and 3, and so on. Every one-unit increment in the logarithm is associated with a tenfold increase in magnitude.

Base 10 is often used for scientific measurement, but base e is much more convenient for analytical analysis. Many analytical arguments contain the term e^n, where n is a real number. These arguments are easier to manipulate when written in terms of natural logarithms. For example, using e as the base reduces the $\log_e e^n$ to n, a most convenient result. For the remainder of this book, we assume natural logarithms and omit the notation e in the log statement. This follows the convention used in most economic writing.

Three Rules of Logarithms

Three rules of logarithms are particularly useful for transforming variables for estimation purposes.

Rule 1 (Log of a Product): $\log xz = \log x + \log z$

Examples:
$$\log 10x = \log 10 + \log x$$
$$\log xzq = \log x + \log z + \log q$$

Rule 2 (Log of a Quotient): $\log\left[\dfrac{x}{y}\right] = \log x - \log z$

Examples:
$$\log\left[\frac{5}{x}\right] = \log 5 - \log x$$

$$\log\left[\frac{xz}{w}\right] = \log xz - \log w$$

Rule 3 (Log of a Power): $\log x^n = n \log x$

Examples:
$$\log x^5 = 5\log x$$
$$\log e^{10} = 10 \log e = 10$$

It is easy to see why these rules are so useful. Rule 1 transforms a multiplication operation into an addition operation. Rule 2 transforms a division operation into a subtraction operation. Rule 3 reduces a power term to a multiplication term.

EXERCISE 6.1

To gain some familiarity using the three rules, indicate which of the following statements are correct. If the statement is incorrect, write a correct statement when possible.

$\log 6z = \log 6 + \log z$

$\log x = \log 5 + \log x$

$\log(6 + z) = \log 6 + \log z$

$\log 6^z = z \log 6$

$\log xy^5 = \log x + 5 \log y$

$\log 2y = \log 2 - \log y$

$\log\left[\dfrac{z}{10}\right] = \log z - \log 10$

$\log(x + y) = \log x + \log y$

$\log e^4 x = 4 + \log x$

$\log(ex)^4 = 4(1 + \log x)$

Exponential Function

An exponential function is written

$$y = \beta_0 b^{\beta_1 x}, \quad \text{for } b > 1 \tag{6.1}$$

where β_0 and β_1 are the parameters and b is the base of the function. It can be shown that β_1 is the proportionate rate of change in y with respect to a one-unit change in x. In most econometric applications, the base is e, and x is time. Parameter β_1 then indicates the growth rate of y with respect to time. Equation 6.1 becomes

$$y_t = \beta_0 e^{\beta_1 t} \tag{6.2}$$

Notice that t is used as both a variable and a subscript to indicate the value of y at time t. Figure 6.1 shows the shape of the exponential function for $\beta_1 > 0$ and for $\beta_1 < 0$.

The exponential function is clearly not linear. But by applying the rules of logarithms, the function can be transformed into an equation that can be estimated by ordinary least-squares. Let the base be e and x be time, as in Equation 6.2. Taking the logarithms of both sides of Equation 6.2 gives

$\log y_t = \log \beta_0 + \log e^{\beta_1 t}$ (by logarithm Rule 1)

$\log y_t = \log \beta_0 + \beta_1 t$ (by logarithm Rule 3)

The ordinary least-squares estimators give unbiased estimates of β_1 and $\log \beta_0$. The estimate for β_0 is found by taking the antilog of $\log \beta_0$. The antilog estimate is biased, however, despite the fact that the estimate for $\log \beta_0$ is unbiased.

Figure 6.1
The Exponential Function

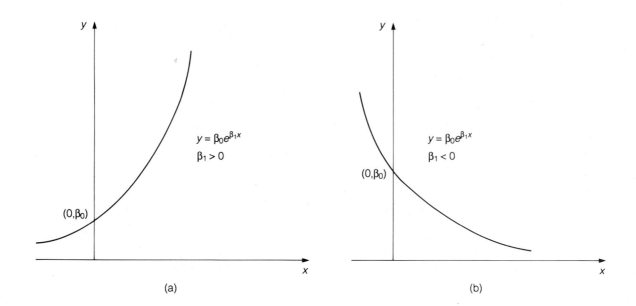

(a)

(b)

Before any function can be estimated, some assumption must be made about how the random error term enters the function. Assume that u is a well-behaved random error term. There are many ways this term can be included in Equation 6.2. Examples are

$$y_t = \beta_0 e^{\beta_1 t} e^{u_t} \qquad (6.3)$$

$$y_t = \beta_0 e^{\beta_1 t} u_t \qquad (6.4)$$

$$y_t = \beta_0 e^{\beta_1 t} + u_t \qquad (6.5)$$

$$y_t = \beta_0 e^{\beta_1 t} + e^{u_t} \qquad (6.6)$$

EXERCISE 6.2

Is there any reason to prefer one of the specifications indicated in Equations 6.3 through 6.6 on strictly logical grounds?

_____

_____

_____

_____

Use the rules of logarithms to transform each of the specifications, where such transformation is possible. Which is the most convenient to use? Can ordinary least-squares be used to estimate all four equations?

_____

_____

_____

_____

_____

Econometricians are seldom able to decide on a random error specification by deducing how errors *should* enter a particular function. It has become standard research practice to use the most convenient specification, unless there are compelling reasons not to do so.

_____

The exponential function is a continuous growth model; it assumes that growth takes place continuously over time. What if the underlying model for some problem is not continuous but discrete, with change taking place once per time period? Annual interest compounding is an example of such a discrete change. Consider the following pattern of growth for a savings account, with interest compounded annually. Let S_0 be the initial deposit, i the interest rate, and S_t the amount of savings after the tth year. The amount of savings after one year is

$$S_1 = S_0(1 + i)$$

The amount of savings after two years is

$$S_2 = S_1(1 + i) = S_0(1 + i)^2$$

The amount of savings after three years is

$$S_3 = S_2(1 + i) = S_0(1 + i)^3$$

The general function for the amount of savings in the tth year is thus

$$S_t = S_0(1 + i)^t \qquad \text{(6.7)}$$

Including a well-behaved random error term in Equation 6.7 gives

$$S_t = S_0(1 + i)^t e^{u_t} \qquad \text{(6.8)}$$

_____

EXERCISE 6.3

Using the rules of logarithms, transform Equation 6.8 into an equation that can be estimated by ordinary least-squares.

_____

_____

_____

_____

While a discrete growth model can be estimated directly, econometricians usually assume a continuous model. This is because any discrete growth process can be described by an exponential growth process. Examine the general formula Equation 6.8 for savings account growth. If $(1 + i)$ is considered as the base of the function, Equation 6.8 is equivalent to the exponential form

$$S_t = S_0 b^t e^{u_t} \qquad (6.9)$$

with t being restricted to integer values. As long as b is a positive number, b can always be expressed as the power of any real number greater than 1. Because e is a real number greater than 1, there is some value β_1 such that

$$(1 + i) = b = e^{\beta_1} \qquad (6.10)$$

The discrete growth process can thus be modeled by an exponential process

$$S_t = S_0(1 + i)^t e^{u_t} = S_0 e^{\beta_1 t} e^{u_t} \qquad (6.11)$$

EXERCISE 6.4

Using the data for real quarterly GNP in the Data Bank, estimate the growth rate for real GNP assuming the growth process is continuous. You must transform the GNP variable to a logarithm before running your regression. The instructions on how to use your econometric software show how to make this transformation. Your econometric software may or may not create a time variable. If the software does not create a time variable, use the variable QTIME in the Data Bank.

Discuss your results in the form of a brief paper, not to exceed two typewritten pages. Your paper should be organized around the following headings:

I. *GNP Growth as a Continuous Process:* This section explains how GNP growth is modeled as a continuous process. The specification of your model should be clearly developed.

II. *Regression Results:* This section evaluates your regression results. What is the quarterly growth rate of GNP? Is your estimated growth rate statistically significant?

III. *The Usefulness of the Continuous Growth Model:* How well does the continuous growth model fit the behavior of real GNP? Of what predictive use is your estimated growth rate?

Double-Logarithmic Function

The double-logarithmic function is written

$$y = \beta_0 x^{\beta_1} \qquad (6.12)$$

where β_0 and β_1 are parameters. Figure 6.2 shows the general shape of the function for different values of β_1.

Figure 6.2
The Double-Logarithmic Function

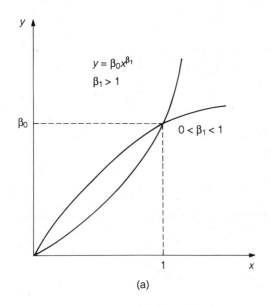

(a)

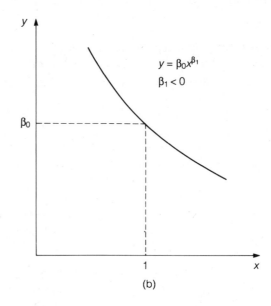

(b)

EXERCISE 6.5

What does Equation 6.12 look like when $\beta_1 = 1$? Sketch the shape of the function when $\beta_1 = 1$.

The double-logarithmic function has a very important property from the standpoint of economic theory. It can be shown that

$$\beta_1 = \left[\frac{\Delta y}{\Delta x}\right]\left[\frac{x}{y}\right]$$

(6.13)

If y is the quantity demanded for some commodity and x is the commodity's price, β_1 is the price elasticity of demand. This property holds when more than one independent variable is included in the function. For example, assume that you are given data for a set of consumers. You are asked to estimate a demand function for commodity Q as a function of its own price P, consumer income Y, and the price of a substitute commodity S. Given the elasticity property of the double-logarithm's function, it is convenient for estimation purposes to write the demand function as

$$Q = \beta_0 P^{\beta_1} Y^{\beta_2} S^{\beta_3}$$

(6.14)

Parameter β_1 is the own-price elasticity of demand, β_2 is the income elasticity of demand, and β_3 is the cross-price elasticity of demand. You can see why the double-logarithmic function is sometimes referred to as a **constant elasticity function** and is often used to model demand relationships.

EXERCISE 6.6

Using the rules of logarithms and adding a random error term, show how Equation 6.14 can be transformed such that β_1, β_2, and β_3 can be estimated using ordinary least-squares.

The double-log function is also used to model production relationships. Let Q be output, K capital, L labor, and β_0 a technological constant. The double-logarithmic production function is then

$$Q = \beta_0 K^{\beta_1} L^{\beta_2}$$

(6.15)

This double-logarithmic production function is better known as the **Cobb–Douglas production function**. We will return to the Cobb–Douglas production function in Lesson 7; although it may seem that the production function (Equation 6.15) can be estimated in the same straightforward manner as the demand function (Equation 6.14), there are important theoretical complications. Labor and capital *jointly* produce output. In econometric terms, this means that all three variables are *simultaneously* determined and capital is not independent of the random error term. This lack of independence violates one of the basic assumptions of the ordinary least-squares model. Consequently, the Cobb–Douglas production function is seldom estimated directly. Functional forms cannot be considered apart from the problem to which they are applied.

EXERCISE 6.7

How would you estimate the demand for beef in the United States? Write a brief paper, not exceeding four typewritten pages, on estimating the demand for beef. The first section of the paper, titled "Beef-Demand Model," should specify your initial model and should discuss and explain each parameter estimate you expect to observe. After you write this section, turn to the Data Bank. Under the heading "MEATS DATA," you will find variables related to beef consumption. Estimate your model using this and any other data you feel is relevant.

Discuss your estimation results in the second section of your paper, titled "Regression Results." If some variable in your initial specification is not included in the "MEATS DATA," see if you can add the variable to the Data Bank from some other source or approximate the variable with one of the variables in the Data Bank. If you can't find a measure of one or more of your variables, discuss the likely impact of the exclusion on your estimated function. If you are not satisfied with your model, or feel it can be improved, try other specifications. Discuss your results in a third section, titled "An Evaluation of Alternative Models."

Reciprocal Function

A reciprocal function is written

$$y = \beta_0 + \beta_1 \left[\frac{1}{x} \right] \tag{6.16}$$

Figure 6.3 shows the shape of the reciprocal function. Notice that the slope of the function flattens as x increases in both representations. The function asymptotically approaches β_0 as x becomes very large. Equation 6.16 is transformed into a linear equation by simply defining $1/x$ as a new variable. Ordinary least-squares can then be used to estimate the function.

The reciprocal function is used in a variety of economic applications. The Phillips curve, the subject of Lesson 15, is often estimated as a reciprocal function. Investigators regress the rate of wage change on the reciprocal of the unemployment rate. The reciprocal function is also used to model consumer expenditure relationships, with x being consumer income and y being consumer expenditures on some commodity.

Figure 6.3
The Reciprocal Function

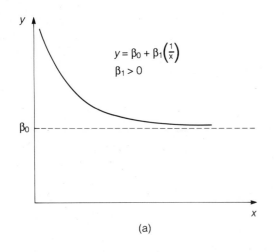
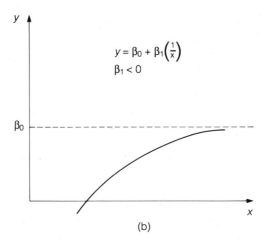

(a)

(b)

Do you see any problems with using the reciprocal function to model consumer expenditures? Can the function be used equally well for commodities that are luxuries and necessities? Inferior goods and normal goods?

_____

_____

_____

_____

_____

How do you interpret the constant term β_0 from the standpoint of consumer expenditures?

_____

_____

_____

_____

Polynomial Function

The general form of the polynomial function is written

$$y = \beta_0 + \beta_1 x + \beta_2 x^2 + \dots + \beta_n x^n \qquad (6.17)$$

Integer exponent n indicates the highest power of x in a polynomial function. Polynomial functions are usually grouped according to n:

A zero-degree polynomial or constant function:

$$n = 0; \; y = \beta_0$$

A first-degree polynomial or linear function:

$$n = 1; \; y = \beta_0 + \beta_1 x$$

A second-degree polynomial or quadratic function:

$$n = 2; \; y = \beta_0 + \beta_1 x + \beta_2 x^2$$

A third-degree polynomial or cubic function:

$$n = 3; \; y = \beta_0 + \beta_1 x + \beta_2 x^2 + \beta_3 x^3$$

Figure 6.4 shows two examples of polynomial functions. The polynomial function is, by definition, linear in the parameters. The fact that the independent variables are related to each other does not violate ordinary least-squares assumptions. If the independent variables were a direct linear function of each other, it would be impossible to obtain parameter estimates. This is the case of extreme or perfect multicollinearity. It is clear, however, that x, x^2, x^3, and so on, although related, are not linear functions of each other. Nevertheless, multicollinearity can still pose serious problems in estimating polynomial functions. Figure 6.5 shows the relationship between x and x^2. Consider the data set shown in the figure. Although x^2 is not a linear function of x, any measure of linear association computed for the data will show a strong linear association. Multicollinearity is not extreme, but it is likely to be a significant problem as the number of polynomial terms increases.

Polynomial functions are estimated by ordinary least-squares by simply letting x to some power form a new variable ($x^2 = z$, $x^3 = w$, and so on). There are, however, some things to remember when using polynomial functions. As a general rule, use a polynomial function suggested by the underlying theoretical structure of the problem whenever possible. A polynomial with as many terms as observations fits a sample perfectly. The estimated equation passes through all data points, and $R^2 = 1.0$. But such an estimated function is impossible to interpret in any economically meaningful way. How, for example, would you make sense of a twenty-fifth-degree polynomial model of total cost estimated for a data set of twenty-six firms in an industry? Would you expect the model to predict the total cost of a new firm entering the industry? If not, the twenty-fifth-degree function is a distortion of our ability to explain variation in the total cost data. Also, there are no degrees of freedom associated with the estimated function.

All this suggests that a lower-order polynomial derived from a discussion of what cost curves *should* look like is a far better function to model total cost. A polynomial function of degree three is the simplest polynomial function that can be used to model the S-shaped total cost relationship shown in microeconomic principles texts. The parameter estimates associated with this form have clear economic meaning when the function is subjected to economic analysis. Letting Q be output and TC be total cost, the third-degree polynomial is

$$TC = \beta_0 + \beta_1 Q + \beta_2 Q^2 + \beta_3 Q^3 \tag{6.18}$$

Figure 6.4
Polynomial Examples

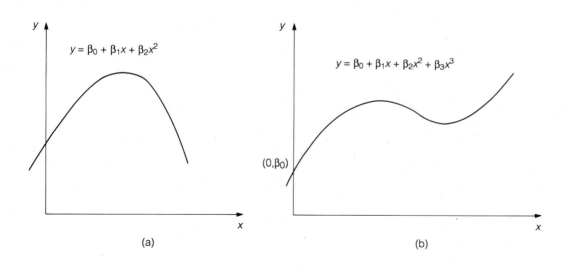

$y = \beta_0 + \beta_1 x + \beta_2 x^2$

$y = \beta_0 + \beta_1 x + \beta_2 x^2 + \beta_3 x^3$

$(0, \beta_0)$

(a)

(b)

Figure 6.5
Relationship Between x and x^2

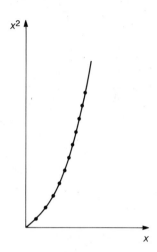

EXERCISE 6.9

What if you want to estimate the average cost function associated with Equation 6.18 directly? That is, you want to estimate the average cost function, given data on total cost and quantity. What function would you estimate? Does it matter that the transformed average cost function is not a polynomial function for estimation purposes?

Logistic Function

Not all functions can be transformed into an equation that is linear in the parameters. The logistic curve is a good example of such a function. A logistic function is written

$$y = \frac{\beta_0}{1 + \beta_2 e^{-\beta_1 x}}$$
(6.19)

The function's parameters are β_0, β_1, and β_2. As x gets very large, the function approaches β_0, referred to as the saturation level. Figure 6.6 shows the shape of the logistic function.

The logistic function is used frequently to model growth processes, where the rate of change of a variable with respect to time is assumed to be proportional to the current level of the variable and to the current distance from the

Figure 6.6
The Logistic Function

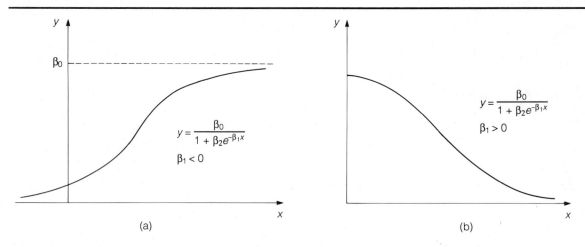

(a)

(b)

saturation level. Examine Figure 6.6a. When y starts to grow, the size of the variable is small, and the distance to the saturation level is large. The formula for the logistics curve is such that the distance to the saturation level is the strongest initial argument, causing y to increase rapidly. But at some point, which can be shown to equal $\beta_0/2$ on the y axis, the distance to the saturation level becomes such that the growth rate decreases steadily as y rises toward β_0. The logistic function is also used to model decay processes, as shown in Figure 6.6b.

The logistic function is used widely in economic analyses. The growth in market share of a new product often is modeled by a logistic function. At first, sales for the new product rise dramatically. Then, sales growth slows, and sales eventually reach a constant market share. The logistic function is used in resource economics, where it models the growth of many renewable resources like fish, and the growth in professional income over an individual's lifetime often follows a logistic growth path. The logistic function also has been shown to model the acceptance of technologic innovation. A classic example of this use of the logistic function is given in Lesson Note 6.1.[1]

Lesson Note 6.1

Hybrid Corn and the Economics of Innovation

The idea that a cross between plants that are genetically unlike can produce a plant of greater vigor and yield than either of the parental lines dates back to Darwin and earlier. Serious research on hybrid corn, however, did not begin until the first years of this century, and the first application of research results on a substantial commercial scale was not begun until the early 1930s. During the last twenty-five years, the change from open pollination to hybrid seeds has spread rapidly through the Corn Belt, and from the Corn Belt to the rest of the nation. The pattern of diffusion of hybrid corn, however, has been characterized by marked geographic differences. As shown in [Figure 6.7], some regions began to use hybrid corn much earlier than others, and some regions, once the shift began, made the transition much more rapidly than others. For example, Iowa farmers began planting hybrid corn earlier than did Alabama farmers, and Iowa farmers increased their acreage in hybrid corn from 10 to 90 percent more rapidly than did Alabama farmers.

Although the explanation of area differences in the pattern of diffusion of hybrid corn constitutes the main contribution of the study reported here,* it is worth drawing attention first to the striking similarity in the general pattern of diffusion of hybrid seed in the various areas. Almost everywhere the development followed an S-shaped growth curve. As illustrated in [Figure 6.7], the rate of change is slow at first, accelerating until it reaches its peak, at approximately the mid-point of development, and then slowing down again as the development approaches its final level.[†]

Interestingly enough, this pattern of development also applies to increases in the use of farm equipment—combines, corn pickers, pickup balers, and field forage harvesters, as illustrated in [Figure 6.8]. Similar patterns occur in the use of new drugs by doctors and in the diffusion of other new items or ideas.[‡]

Thus, the data on hybrid corn and other technical changes in U.S. agriculture support the general finding that the pattern of technical change is S-shaped.

Although the finding that technical change follows this pattern is not very surprising or new,[§] it is very useful. It allows us to summarize large bodies of data on the basis of three major characteristics (parameters) of a diffusion pattern: the date of beginning (origin), relative speed (slope), and final level (ceiling). The interesting question then is, given this general S-shape, what determines the differences among areas in the origin, slope, and ceiling? Why were some areas ahead of others in first using hybrid corn? Why did hybrid corn spread faster in some areas than in others? Why did some areas reach higher levels of equilibrium than others? . . .

Summary and an Implication

. . . The use of hybrid seed in an area depends, in part, upon the date at which superior

---

*A more detailed and technical account of this study can be found in Z. Griliches, "Hybrid Corn: An Exploration in the Economics of Technological Change," *Econometrica* (Oct. 1957). See also my "Research Costs and Social Returns: Hybrid Corn and Related Innovations," *Political Econ.* (Oct. 1958). This study was supported by the Social Science Research Council and the National Science Foundation.

†In my article in *Econometrica* I show that the data fit the logistic growth curve very well. Unpublished data by small subdivisions—country and crop-reporting districts—give essentially the same picture, though the development is somewhat more irregular in the marginal corn areas.

‡See J. Coleman, E. Katz, H. Menzel, "The Diffusion of an Innovation Among Physicians," *Sociometry* (Dec. 1957).

§See, for example, A. Lotka, *Elements of Physical Biology* (1925) and S. Kuznets, *Secular Movements in Production and Prices* (1930).

hybrids become available. This date, in turn, depends upon the activities of seed producers guided by their expectations of profits, and upon the contributions of the various experimental stations. Thus, the South was late in getting hybrids because the market for seed was substantially poorer there than in other areas and because southern experiment stations produced few hybrids of importance until the middle 1940s. The use of hybrid seed in an area also depends upon the rate at which hybrids are accepted by farmers. This rate, in turn, depends upon the profit farmers expect to realize from the shift to hybrids. Thus, farmers in the Corn Belt accepted hybrids at a faster rate than farmers in the South because the absolute magnitude of profit was higher in the Corn Belt than in the South. Similarly, the fraction of acreage ultimately planted to hybrid seed depends upon expectations of profits to be realized from the change and the distribution of these expectations around their mean.

When uncertainty and the fact that the spread of knowledge is not instantaneous are taken into account, it appears that American seed producers and American farmers have behaved, on the whole, in a fashion consistent with the idea of profit maximization. Where the evidence appears to indicate the contrary, I predict that a closer examination of the relevant economic variables will show that the change was not as profitable as it appeared to be.*

This study of hybrid corn has at least one interesting implication. Hybrid corn was an innovation which was more profitable in the "good" areas than in the "poor" areas. This, probably, is also a characteristic of many other innovations. Obviously, tractors contribute more on large than on small farms, and so forth. Hence, there may be a tendency for technological change to accentuate regional disparities in levels of income and rates of growth. Moreover, this tendency is reinforced by the economics of the innovation process, which results in the new techniques being supplied to the "good" areas before they are supplied to the "poorer" areas, and also in the more rapid acceptance of these techniques in the "good" areas. A lag of this sort can by itself cause long-run regional differences in levels of income. The kinds of inventions we get, and the process by which they are distributed, may lead to aggravation of the already serious problem of regional differentials in levels of income and growth.

Source: Shughart, W. F. II, and Tollison, R. "Corporate Chartering: An Exploration in the Economics of Legal Change," *Economic Inquiry* 23 (October 1985), 585–599.

*That these findings are not restricted to hybrid corn has been confirmed by a recent study of the spread of a series of industrial innovations (diesel locomotives, continuous mining machines, and so on) within particular industries. It was found there that (i) the logistic growth curve summarized the data well, and (ii) most of the variability in the rate of acceptance of different innovations can be explained on the basis of the relative profit to be realized from the innovation and the size of the required initial investment. See E. Mansfield, "Technological Change and the Rate of Imitation," a paper that was read at the 1959 winter meetings of the Econometric Society in Washington, D.C.

Figure 6.7
Percentage of All Corn Acreage Planted to Hybrid Seed

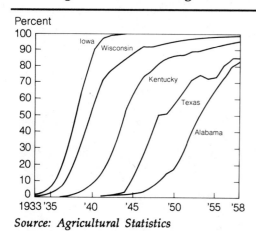

Source: Agricultural Statistics

Figure 6.8
Machines in Use on Farms in the United States, 1940–1959

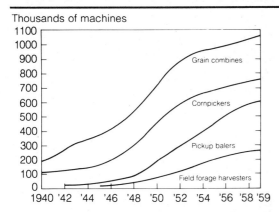

Source: U.S. Dept. Agr. Statist. Bull. No. 233 (1959)
Note the resemblance to Figure 6.7.

The logistic function cannot be transformed into an equation that is linear in the parameters. Because the logistic function fits the behavior of many economic variables, how can it be estimated? While some linear approximations have been suggested, the only really valid solution is to apply methods of nonlinear estimation, which are discussed in advanced econometric texts. Another option is to find a function that both approximates the behavior modeled by the logistic function and is linear in its parameters.

The logarithmic reciprocal function satisfies both criteria and is often estimated in place of the logistic function. The logarithmic reciprocal function is written

$$y = e^{\beta_0 - \beta_1/x} \tag{6.20}$$

EXERCISE 6.10

Using the rules of logarithms and adding a random error term, transform Equation 6.20 into an equation that can be estimated by ordinary least-squares.

_____

_____

_____

Both the logarithmic reciprocal function and the logistic function show an S-shaped growth path, but the rate of growth for the logarithmic reciprocal model begins to slow at a relatively low value of x. In other words, the logistic function is more symmetric. The seriousness of this distortion must be weighed against the ease of estimating a logarithmic reciprocal function.

EXERCISE 6.11

It has been argued that a legal innovation is a kind of technologic innovation. It thus should be possible to model the acceptance of a legal innovation with a logistic function. In a recent article, Shughart and Tollison explore the deregulation of corporate charters that took place in the United States in the nineteenth and twentieth centuries.[2] Over this period of time, states replaced special chartering with incorporation statutes. These statutes provided a superior organizational structure. Shughart and Tollison argue that the acceptance of this legal innovation can be described by an economic cost–benefit calculus: "The empirical results show that legal change tended to occur first in states where the stake in deregulation was greatest, and where the costs of lobbying for 'liberal' corporation codes were low."

The data shown in Table 6.1 were collected by Shughart and Tollison. Model the acceptance of incorporation statutes using the reciprocal logarithmic function. Use a dependent variable like that used in Figures 6.7 and 6.8 in Lesson Note 6.1. Estimate and write your estimated model below.

Does the acceptance of this legal innovation follow an S-shaped acceptance path?

_____

_____

_____

_____

Discuss the appropriateness of using the reciprocal logarithmic model instead of the logistic model. Is the reciprocal model a good approximation?

_____

_____

_____

_____

_____

Table 6.1
Chronology of Adoption by States of Incorporation Under General Laws

State	Year Adopted	State	Year Adopted
Connecticut	1837[a]	New Jersey	1875
Louisiana	1845	Maine	1875
Iowa	1846[b]	Texas	1876
New York	1846	Colorado	1876[b]
Illinois	1848	Georgia	1877
Wisconsin	1848[b]	North Dakota	1889[b]
California	1849[b]	South Dakota	1889[b]
Michigan	1850	Montana	1889[b]
Maryland	1851	Washington	1889[b]
Ohio	1851	Idaho	1889[b]
Indiana	1851	Wyoming	1889[b]
Massachusetts	1851[a]	Mississippi	1890
Minnesota	1857[b]	Kentucky	1891
Oregon	1857[b]	Utah	1895[b]
Kansas	1859[b]	South Carolina	1895
West Virginia	1862[b]	Delaware	1897
Nevada	1864[b]	Florida	1900
Missouri	1865	New Hampshire	1901[a]
Nebraska	1866[b]	Virginia	1902
Alabama	1867	Oklahoma	1907[b]
North Carolina	1868	New Mexico	1911[b]
Arkansas	1868	Arizona	1911[b]
Tennessee	1870	Vermont	1913
Pennsylvania	1873		

Source: Shughart, W. F. II and Tollison, R. "Corporate Chartering: An Exploration in the Economics of Legal Change," *Economic Inquiry* 23 (October 1985), 585–599.

[a] Enacted by statute rather than by constitutional amendment.

[b] Coincided with statehood.

Suggested Reading

An advanced discussion of the topics presented in this lesson is found in J. Johnston, *Econometric Methods*, 3d ed. (New York: McGraw-Hill, 1984), 61–74.

Parameter Constraints

1. To learn how to specify models subject to linear constraints

2. To learn how to estimate constrained models using econometric software

3. To review some of the general issues posed by estimating Cobb–Douglas production functions

Economic theory often requires that parameters in a model satisfy linear constraints. A parameter may be thought to equal a constant value, another parameter, or the sum of other parameters. What do you do when confronting such a case? There are two different ways to proceed. First, the model can be estimated without taking account of the constraint. The validity of the constraint then can be evaluated using standard hypothesis-testing concepts. Second, the model can be estimated under the assumption that the constraint is true. In other words, the regression equation can be *forced* to assume the constraint is true.

The second approach often bothers students. Isn't it always better to estimate an unconstrained model and evaluate the validity of a constraint? Isn't econometric research based on testing the validity of economic relationships and suggested parameter values? Unfortunately, things are often not so simple. Sometimes models cannot be estimated without assuming parameter constraints. At other times, problems such as multicollinearity or simultaneous equation bias can be solved by specifying a parameter-constrained model. Further, if there is widespread agreement that the parameter constraint is valid, the second approach is defensible. In fact, some econometricians feel that strongly held beliefs on constraints should be incorporated into a model. There is, of course, no way to evaluate the actual validity of a constraint when the second approach is used.

The first and second sections of this lesson show how to deal with linear constraints by working through some examples for demand functions and production functions. These sections focus on estimating double-logarithmic demand functions and Cobb–Douglas production functions subject to simple linear constraints. The third section is more general, discussing conceptual issues posed by the estimation of constrained and unconstrained Cobb–Douglas production functions. The fourth and final section is still more general, addressing econometric procedures that in some sense use the actual data to arrive at the "correct" model specification.

A Simple Constraint

Consider the following market-demand function for good X:

$$X = \beta_0 Y^{\beta_1} P_x^{\beta_2} P_y^{\beta_3} \qquad (7.1)$$

where Y is community income, P_x the price of good X, and P_y the price of a substitute good Y. Assume that you read an article that argues that the income elasticity of demand for X is 1.2. You can estimate the demand function and test the null hypothesis that $\beta_1 = 1.2$. But what if you want to estimate the demand function *assuming* that $\beta_1 = 1.2$? What regression will you run? The new demand function reflecting the constraint is

$$X = \beta_0 Y^{1.2} P_x^{\beta_2} P_z^{\beta_3} \qquad (7.2)$$

which can be estimated by ordinary least-squares in the log-linear form

$$\log\left[\frac{X}{Y^{1.2}}\right] = \log\beta_0 + \beta_2 \log P_x + \beta_3 \log P_z \qquad (7.3)$$

Notice that a new dependent variable must be computed for the data set before the model can be estimated. For each data case, the value of community income must be taken to the exponent 1.2 and divided into value of X. The logarithm of this quotient is the new dependent variable.

EXERCISE 7.1

Using the demand function for beef that you estimated in Lesson 6 (Exercise 6.7), test the hypothesis that the income elasticity of the demand for beef is 1.2.

_____

_____

_____

Reestimate the demand model *forcing* the regression model to assume that the income elasticity of demand is 1.2. Write your estimated model below.

How do the estimation results change when compared with the original model?

_____

_____

Should the sum of the squared residuals for the reestimated model be larger or smaller than for the original model? Explain your reasoning. Is your answer supported by the estimation results?

_____

_____

_____

_____

_____

_____

Testing Hypotheses About Constraints

Now consider a more complex linear constraint on the demand function (Equation 7.1). Assume that you read an article arguing that goods X and Y are very close substitutes. The article further argues that the cross-price elasticity for good X with respect to good Y is equal in magnitude to the own-price elasticity but opposite in sign. In other words, the author of the article alleges that

$$\beta_2 = -\beta_3 \tag{7.4}$$

How can the validity of this argument be tested? Specifically, how can the constraint be structured in the form of the testable null hypothesis $\beta_2 + \beta_3 = 0$? A test statistic that reflects constraint (Equation 7.4) is needed. This test statistic can be constructed as follows: First, define a new random variable $\hat{\theta}$, which is equal to $\hat{\beta}_2 + \hat{\beta}_3$.

$$\hat{\theta} = \hat{\beta}_2 + \hat{\beta}_3 \tag{7.5}$$

Because $\hat{\theta}$ is the sum of two random variables, it must also be a random variable. Next, solve for the mean of the distribution of $\hat{\theta}$. The mean of the distribution of $\hat{\theta}$ is

$$E(\hat{\theta}) = E(\hat{\beta}_2 + \hat{\beta}_3) = \beta_2 + \beta_3 \tag{7.6}$$

Notice that when constraint (Equation 7.4) is true, $E(\hat{\theta}) = 0$. There is, of course, a population parameter θ equal to $\beta_2 + \beta_3$.

But is an observed sample value of $\hat{\theta}$ significantly different from 0? To answer this question, we must also solve for the variance of the distribution of $\hat{\theta}$. Recall from Lesson 2 that when two random variables are added together the variance of the resulting new random variable is equal to the sum of the variances of the two original random variables plus twice their covariance. Thus, the variance of $\hat{\theta}$ is

$$\sigma_{\hat{\theta}}^2 = \sigma_{\hat{\beta}_2}^2 + \sigma_{\hat{\beta}_3}^2 + 2\sigma_{\hat{\beta}_2\hat{\beta}_3} \qquad (7.7)$$

Econometric software computes estimates for $\sigma_{\hat{\beta}_2}^2$ and $\sigma_{\hat{\beta}_3}^2$ in solving for the ordinary least-squares estimates $\hat{\beta}_2$ and $\hat{\beta}_3$. You have been using the square roots of such variances throughout the course to generate t-distributed statistics to evaluate regression coefficients. An estimate of the covariance $\sigma_{\hat{\beta}_2\hat{\beta}_3}$ is also calculated by the software.

Using the estimates for the variances and covariances of the regression coefficients, an estimate of the standard deviation of $\hat{\theta}$ can be computed. If the null hypothesis $\theta = 0$ is true, then a t-distributed test statistic is defined. The test statistic is

$$t = \frac{\hat{\theta} - 0}{\sigma_{\hat{\theta}}} \qquad (7.8)$$

EXERCISE 7.2

Assume that regression results are computed for demand function (Equation 7.1). The sample size is 30. The regression results are

$$\hat{\beta}_2 = .91 \qquad \hat{\sigma}_{\hat{\beta}_2}^2 = .25 \qquad \hat{\sigma}_{\hat{\beta}_2\hat{\beta}_3} = -.15$$

$$\hat{\beta}_3 = -.72 \qquad \hat{\sigma}_{\hat{\beta}_3}^2 = .20$$

Test the null hypothesis that $\theta = 0$.

You can now see why the computer output you have been using shows the variances and covariances for the ordinary least-squares estimators. This information is used to test hypotheses about linear relationships among parameters, a very common problem in econometric analysis. Make sure that you don't confuse the variances and covariances for the *estimators* with the variances and covariances for the *variables* when you record regression results to test a hypothesis about a linear constraint.

What if your econometric software did *not* compute the covariances of the estimators? This may cause you to do a little more work, but it really presents no great difficulty in testing hypotheses about linear parameter constraints. It is always possible to structure a model so that the regression solution computes the needed information. Let's show how this can be done for the problem discussed above. The linear constraint (Equation 7.4) can be rewritten as

$$\beta_2 = \theta - \beta_3 \qquad\qquad (7.9)$$

Substituting Equation 7.9 into demand function (Equation 7.1) gives

$$X = \beta_0 Y^{\beta_1} P_x^{(\theta - \beta_3)} P_z^{\beta_3} \qquad\qquad (7.10)$$

which can be written as

$$X = \beta_0 Y^{\beta_1} P_x^{\theta} \left[\frac{P_z}{P_x}\right]^{\beta_3} \qquad\qquad (7.11)$$

Equation 7.11 can be estimated by ordinary least-squares in the log-linear form

$$\log X = \log\beta_0 + \beta_1 \log Y + \theta \log P_x + \beta_3 \log\left[\frac{P_z}{P_x}\right] \qquad\qquad (7.12)$$

The null hypothesis $\theta = 0$ can be tested directly by using the regression coefficient for $\log P_x$.

Assume for the rest of this section that it is valid to estimate a Cobb–Douglas production function directly by expressing the variables in logarithmic form. You are given the following Cobb–Douglas production function for firms in a hypothetical industry.

$$Q = \beta_0 K^{\beta_1} L^{\beta_2} \qquad\qquad (7.13)$$

The sum of parameters β_1 and β_2 has special economic significance. The sum indicates the returns to scale associated with the production function. When the sum is greater than 1, the production function is said to exhibit **increasing returns to scale**. This means that a proportionate increase in inputs is associated with a more-than-proportionate increase in output. If all inputs are doubled, output more than doubles. When the sum is less than 1, the production function exhibits **decreasing returns to scale**. A proportionate increase in inputs generates a less-than-proportionate increase in output. When the sum equals 1, **constant returns to scale** exist. A proportionate increase in inputs generates a proportionate increase in output. If all inputs are doubled, output doubles.

EXERCISE 7.3

Discuss how you would test the hypothesis of constant returns to scale ($\beta_1 + \beta_2 = 1$) using computer output for estimator variances and covariances of the logarithmic form of Equation 7.13.

_____

_____

_____

_____

Show the regression equation you would use to estimate Equation 7.13 under the assumption that constant returns to scale is true. That is, you want to *force* the production function to assume constant returns to scale; you want to estimate a *restricted model*.

Finally, assume that your econometric software does not calculate the co-variances of the estimators. Show how Equation 7.13 can be restructured so that the regression results will give the information needed to test the hypothesis of constant returns to scale.

_____

_____

_____

One of the linear restrictions that emerges from consumer-demand theory is that the sum of all elasticities for a commodity (income elasticity, own-price elasticity, and cross-price elasticities) must be equal to 0. The demand function for beef that you estimated in Lesson 6 does not represent the complete specification of the demand function for beef in the economy. It represents a *partial* function. A complete specification would require that the demand function be treated as one equation in the set of all demand functions for the economy. Econometricians have tried to estimate sets and subsets of demand functions, with mixed results. The econometric theory needed to compute estimates for a set of equations is obviously quite complex. Nevertheless, to give you some practice in dealing with linear constraints, assume the "sum of the elasticities" condition holds for your demand function for beef for purposes of answering Exercise 7.4.

EXERCISE 7.4

Reestimate the demand function for beef assuming the "sum-of-the-elasticities" condition is true. First, explain how you derive the new restricted regression model subject to the linear constraint.

_____

_____

_____

_____

Write your estimated, restricted model below.

Discuss how your estimation results for the restricted model differ from those for the unrestricted, Lesson 6 model.

_____

_____

_____

_____

_____

The procedure of restricting regression models with linear constraints is referred to as **restricted least-squares**. Although a t test can be used to assess the statistical significance of a linear restriction, an F test is usually applied to the restricted and unrestricted model in the econometric literature. The F test allows us to examine the significance of a model with many independent variables and several linear constraints. The F test can be expressed in terms of R^2 or in terms of the sum of the squared residuals. Let

SSR_u be the sum of the squared residuals in the unrestricted model

SSR_r be the sum of the squared residuals in the restricted model

R_u^2 R^2 for the unrestricted model

R_r^2 R^2 for the restricted model

n be the number of observations

k be the number of parameters in the unrestricted model

j be the number of linear restrictions

The F test is then,

$$F_{(j,n-k)} = \frac{(SSR_r - SSR_u)/j}{SSR_u/(n-k)} \quad \text{or} \quad F_{(j,n-k)} = \frac{(R_u^2 - R_r^2)/j}{(1 - R_u^2)/(n-k)}$$

In estimating a Cobb–Douglas production function forced to assume constant returns to scale, one linear restriction is imposed ($\beta_1 + \beta_2 = 1$). One linear restriction is also imposed if independent variable Z is dropped from a regression model to form a restricted model ($\beta_z = 0$), and so forth. The definition of the F test is quite general. The F test can be used to compare two regressions when one regression is a restricted form of the other.

EXERCISE 7.5

Using an F test, evaluate the statistical significance of your restricted beef-demand model.

After reading Lesson Note 7.1, return to this exercise and verify the comments about the F test for the second equation.

Conceptual Difficulties in Estimating Production Functions

In Exercise 7.3, you showed how the Cobb–Douglas production function can be estimated assuming constant returns to scale. The equation you derived is known as the **intensive form** of the production function. A production function in intensive form relates output-per-labor hour to the capital–labor ratio. The equation derived is

$$\log\left[\frac{Q}{L}\right] = \log\beta_0 + (1 - \beta_2)\log\left[\frac{K}{L}\right] \tag{7.14}$$

This form has the advantage of reducing the problem of multicollinearity between capital and labor, which is often present when the unconstrained form of the Cobb–Douglas function is estimated. Capital and labor are used together in the productive process, and they can be expected to increase and decrease together as production fluctuates. Because Equation 7.14 is written in terms of the *ratio* of capital to labor, problems of multicollinearity are limited.

But, as was noted briefly in Lesson 6, another estimation problem remains because of the simultaneous choice of capital and labor in the firm's production decisions. A consumer treats price and income as given variables, or exogenous variables, in the utility-maximizing decision. In contrast, a firm must choose a combination of both inputs to maximize profits. In other words, capital and labor are endogenous variables in the production decision. This raises the possibility that capital and labor may be correlated with the random error term, causing ordinary least-squares estimators to be biased and inconsistent. Your text (and Lesson 14) discusses the general issue of what happens when an independent variable is correlated with the random error term and what is meant by an inconsistent estimator. Here, we simply call attention to the problem. Specifying a production function in intensive form does not solve any inherent problems of bias and inconsistency because of the simultaneous choice of inputs.

A further difficulty with the intensive form is that it still requires a measure of capital stock to estimate the production function. This may strike you as a rather startling statement. Realistic production functions must clearly include capital as an input. Don't we have to have a measure of capital to estimate a production function? Isn't such a measure absolutely essential? In reality, an accurate measure of capital is often very difficult or impossible to obtain.

When economists include capital and labor in a production function, they understand that these variables represent flows of homogeneous capital and labor services. Labor services are typically measured by employed labor hours.

But how is the flow of capital services measured? Econometricians first try to derive a measure of capital stock net of depreciation. But depreciation in the accounting sense, which is usually the only measure available, is often very different than actual depreciation in the economic sense. Further, only working capital should be included in the production function. Idle capital stock is obviously not relevant, and its inclusion will bias the estimation results. But data on capacity utilization are often either incomplete or impossible to obtain. Finally, a firm's capital stock seldom represents a homogeneous input. It includes different kinds of machines purchased at different times, inventories, and the plant itself. Due to this lack of homogeneity, it is far from clear what is measured by values for capital stock. Given all these measurement problems, an econometrician may either be unable to derive a measure of capital stock or feel very uneasy about using an existing measure.

Because of problems of measurement error and simultaneity, the intensive form of the Cobb–Douglas function is often further constrained by conditions derived from the assumptions of perfect competition and profit maximization. With these additional assumptions, the marginal productivity of an input equals the input's real rate of payment. For the Cobb–Douglas production function, this condition can be shown to imply

$$\beta_2 = \frac{rK}{PQ} \tag{7.15}$$

$$\beta_3 = \frac{wL}{PQ} \tag{7.16}$$

where P is the price of the output, w the wage rate of labor, and r the rental rate of capital. Using the rules of logarithms and a little algebra, Equation 7.16 can be written

$$\log \frac{Q}{L} = \log \frac{W}{P} - \log \beta_3 \tag{7.17}$$

With the addition of a disturbance term, Equation 7.17 can be estimated by ordinary least-squares. The random error term is assumed to capture errors that firms make in choosing their profit-maximizing combination of inputs.

When a production function is estimated using Equation 7.17, it is said to be estimated by the **marginal productivity method**. Notice that the regression intercept term provides the estimate of β_3. Also notice that a regression coefficient for $\log \frac{W}{P}$ is computed, even though this coefficient is 1 in Equation 7.17.

Sometimes this coefficient is assumed to be 1 and a value for $\frac{wL}{PQ}$ is computed for each data case. The geometric mean of these values is used then as the estimate for β_3. This approach is referred to as the **factor shares method**. Neither method requires a measure of capital stock, and the problem of simultaneity is assumed away by the constraints imposed on the production function.

But the involved process of estimating Equation 7.17 raises troubling questions. Because Equation 7.17, like Equation 7.14, assumes constant returns to scale, we obviously cannot test the validity of constant returns to scale. Further, the validity of perfect competition and profit maximization cannot be examined for any estimates derived from Equation 7.17 because the estimates are constrained by the assumptions of perfect competition and profit maximization. All these restrictions are analytically convenient, but are they justified? Is it possible that they introduce distortions that are worse than those causing the original problems? These are not academic questions because the different forms generally produce different estimates. Only good judgment can determine which form of the production function is most suited to the particular estimation problem being considered. The issue of appropriate form becomes more complex when questions are raised concerning the applicability of the Cobb–Douglas production function itself. Specifically, the Cobb–Douglas function can be shown to be a special case of another production function called the constant elasticity of substitution (CES) production function.[1]

This section has shown some of the conceptual problems associated with linear constraints for the Cobb–Douglas production function. It is by no means a full discussion of the problems associated with estimating production functions. For example, some of the measurement issues raised about capital services also can be raised about labor services. Hours of labor may be no more homogeneous over the labor force than are units of capital stock. If you are interested in a more general discussion of estimation issues, see "Suggested Readings."

Specification Search

In working through the modeling problems in this and preceding lessons, you may have speculated on or been troubled by the ease with which econometric software allows you to run a large number of alternative models as you grope toward finding the "right" model. This **specification-search** process is not consistent with classical statistical methods, which assume a model is given. Nevertheless, specification search clearly describes the process used by most econometricians do their work. One monetary theorist, for example, admitted that he ran well over 1000 regressions before deciding on the "right" specification for the demand for money.

Edward Leamer has isolated six varieties of specification search, which are the subject of Lesson Note 7.1.[2] Economists differ in their opinions on how specification search affects classical statistical inference. Professor Leamer notes that there is a spectrum of professional opinion with "believers" at one end and "agnostics" at the other. "Pragmatists" fall somewhere between the two extremes. We close this lesson with Leamer's description of the types of researchers. Are you a believer, agnostic, or pragmatist?

"Believers" use ad hoc techniques to search for specification, throwing out insignificant variables here and there, for example, but they continue to regard the end result of such a methodology to be identical to the end result obtained in the experimental sciences (or at least cynically to act that way). Believers report the summary statistics from the nth equation as if the other n − 1 were not tried, as if the nth equation defined a controlled experiment.

At the other extremes are the agnostics, who gladly admit the irrelevance of classical inference. They argue that a nonexperimental scientist is merely identifying relationships that exist in the historical data. He is describing the salient features of the data accurately but economically. Ideally, the data analysis generates hypotheses that need new data to be tested. Agnostics may thus discount any statistical result until it has been employed in a prediction outside the data period. We might interpret such statements in a statistical context as the absence of information concerning the standard errors. A point estimate without an associated standard error does not imply an hypothesis test, nor can it determine unambiguous inferences.

Somewhere between these two extremes is a group of pragmatists. They feel that the believers' contentment stems only from ignorance but that the agnostics have gone too far. This group argues that estimated standard errors are properly enlarged by a specification search but not to the extent they become infinite.[3]

Lesson Note 7.1

The Six Varieties of Specification Searches

A theory of specification searches can be constructed first by identifying the reason a researcher engages in a search, and second by building formal inferential models that properly carry out his legitimate intentions. By observation of economists analyzing data, I have come to the conclusion that there are six different reasons for specification searches. . . .

For illustrative purposes, imagine a researcher interested in exploring empirically the theory of demand. In its simplest form the theory may be stated as follows: "*Ceteris paribus*, an individual's purchases of some commodity depends on his income and on the price of the commodity." The problem of the empirical worker is to translate this theoretical assertion into a statement about observable phenomena. He must identify the observable counterparts of the theoretical variables, he must select other variables that may significantly affect purchases, he must choose a particular functional relationship between the variables, and he must decide which individuals are actually to be observed. Because he cannot make these decisions with complete confidence, the researcher is willing to change his mind if his original choices seem not to work out as well as he might have liked. He does so by changing the specification of his statistical model. He may include more explanatory variables; he may omit certain variables; he may substitute one variable for another; he may discard observations, or he may include new observations.

Suppose the initial model is $\log D_i = \alpha + \beta \log Y_i + \gamma \log P_i + u_i$, where D_i is the purchases of oranges by household i, Y_i is monetary income, P_i is the price of the commodity, and u_i is a "random disturbance" assumed to be normally distributed, independent of u_j, for $i \neq j$. The variables are observed by asking a random se-- lection of heads of households, "How much did you earn last month, how many oranges did you purchase, and how much did they cost?" Using the replies of 150 households, the following regression equation is estimated:

$$\log D_i = 6.2 + .85 \log Y_i - .67 \log P_i, \qquad R^2 = .15,$$
$$\quad\quad (1.1) \quad\quad (.21) \quad\quad (.13)$$

with standard errors in parentheses. For a variety of reasons, it is likely that other equations would be estimated with the same data set. Without endorsing the procedures, I now describe a typical search program.

Of special interest is the hypothesis that the fraction of income spent on oranges is not a function of price, $\gamma = -1$. To test this hypothesis, the equation is reestimated with the constraint applied:

$$\log D_i + \log P_i = 7.2 + .96 \log Y_i, \qquad R^2 = .14.$$
$$\quad\quad (1.0) \quad\quad (.20)$$

Using a standard F test, this hypothesis is rejected at the .05 level, and it is inferred that the data cast doubt on the hypothesis $\gamma = -1$. This is an example of an hypothesis testing search in which different specifications describe different hypotheses about the phenomenon.

The theory of demand describes the behavior of a single individual, but this sample varies across individuals. The nutritional importance of oranges is greatest in areas with the least sunlight, and it may be inappropriate to treat southerners as if they were identical to northerners in their taste for oranges. Separate regressions are therefore computed for southerners and northerners:

$$\log D_i^N = 7.3 + .89 \log Y_i^N - .60 \log P_i^N \quad R^2 = .18,$$
$$\quad\quad (1.9) \quad (.41) \quad\quad (.25)$$

$$\log D_i^S = 7.0 + .82 \log Y_i^S - 1.10 \log P_i^S \quad R^2 = .19.$$
$$\quad\quad (2.2) \quad (.31) \quad\quad (.26)$$

These regressions suggest that in the North, income is the relatively more important variable and price the relatively less important variable, but the hypothesis that the coefficients are different is not rejected at the .05 level. This is an example of a *data-selection search*. The same theoretical hypothesis underlies all three specifications: the one estimated with all the data and the pair estimated with subsets. The specifications differ in their choice of data sets.

Next it must be observed that the answer to the income question may be a very poor measurement of the household's true income. As it turns out, households were asked to report their expenditures on a fairly inclusive list of other commodities, and it may be that their total expenditures E_i is a better measurement of income than Y_i. The variable E_i is substituted for Y_i, and the estimated equation becomes

$$\log D_i = 5.2 + 1.1 \log E_i - .45 \log P_i, \quad R^2 = .18.$$
$$\qquad\quad (1.0) \quad (.18) \qquad\quad (.16)$$

The R^2 has increased, and the coefficient on the income variable has become more significant, which suggests that E_i is the better measurement of income. This is a *proxy variable search*. Competing specifications in a proxy variable search all derive from the same underlying hypothesis. Different estimated regressions reflect different ways of measuring a common set of hypothetical variables.

The R^2s in all these equations are unhappily low. Perhaps there are other variables that might be added to the specification to improve the fit. After all, the theory makes use of the Latin phrase, *ceteris paribus*, other things constant, yet it is the nature of nonexperimental research that other things are not held constant. Although I prefer oranges, if grapefruit are on sale, I will sometimes buy them instead. Adding the price of grapefruit π_i to the equations yields the result

$$\log D_i = 3.1 + .83 \log E_i + .01 \log P_i - .56 \log \pi_i$$
$$\qquad\quad (1.0) \quad (.20) \qquad\quad (.15) \qquad\quad (.60)$$
$$R^2 = .20.$$

This specification represents the broader theory: "*Ceteris paribus*, an individual's purchases of some commodity depends on his income, on the price of the commodity, and on the price of 'similar' commodities." The process of revising the underlying theory in response to the data evidence is called *post data model construction*, and the resulting hypothesis is called a *data-instigated* hypothesis. Whereas all other specifications are implicit in the original theoretical statement, a data-instigated hypothesis is not.

In the regression last reported, the coefficients on the price variables are insignificant and of the "wrong" sign. Furthermore, the sum of the coefficients (.83 + .01 − .56 = .28) is rather far from zero. The presumption that these coefficients sum to zero derives from the homogeneity postulate that asserts the following. "There is no money illusion: if money income and all prices are multiplied by the same constant, purchases will not change." Applying this homogeneity constraint yields the regression

$$\log D_i = 4.2 + .52 \log E_i - .61 \log P_i + .09 \log \pi_i$$
$$\qquad\quad (.9) \quad (.19) \quad (.14) \qquad\quad (.31)$$
$$R^2 = .19.$$

The R^2 has fallen only slightly, and the coefficients all have the right sign, two of them significantly so. Thus the constraint seems to improve the specification. This is an example of an *interpretive search*. The underlying hypothesis is taken as given. Restrictions are imposed in the hopes that the estimates may be "improved."

The regression equation now includes three variables, one with a very small coefficient and the other two with coefficients approximately the same size in absolute value. A simple equation would result if π were omitted and the other two coefficients set equal to each other (but opposite in sign):

$$\log D_i = 3.7 + .58 \log(E_i / P_i) \qquad R^2 = .18.$$
$$\qquad\quad (.8) \quad (.18).$$

The R^2 is only slightly smaller, and this simple equation is selected. This sixth and final search is a *simplification search*, the function of which is to find a simple but useful model.

The six kinds of specification searches may not yet be clearly different in your mind. In practice, there is little effort made to distinguish one from the other, and it is unsurprising that at first consideration it is difficult to discern the real differences. Moreover, since the searches differ sometimes only in the intent of the researcher and not in his actions, it may be difficult to infer which kind of search actually occurred. By this I do not mean to imply that it is *unimportant* to identify the type of search. Quite the contrary, the effectiveness of a search must be evaluated in terms of its intentions. An apparently successful simplification search may be judged completely unsuccessful as an interpretive search, and so forth.

Source: Leamer, E. E. *Specification Search* (New York: Wiley, 1978), 5–9.

Suggested Reading

A good discussion of the constraints implied by economic theory is found in Chapters 7 and 8 of M. D. Intriligator, *Econometric Models, Techniques, and Applications* (Englewood Cliffs, N.J.: Prentice-Hall, 1978). You may not understand some of the material in these two chapters unless you have had a course in intermediate microeconomics. But you will be able to follow most of the discussion on how economic theory is used to provide the foundation for estimating demand functions and production functions. The two chapters also give many examples of how actual production functions and demand functions have been estimated. Another good discussion is found in Chapter 2 of K. F. Wallis, *Topics in Applied Econometrics*, 2d. ed. (Minneapolis: The University of Minnesota Press, 1979).

Dummy Variables

1. To learn how to estimate a model including a dummy variable using econometric software

2. To learn some of the complexities and problems associated with the seasonal adjustment of data

3. To learn how to use the seasonal adjustment procedure in econometric software

Qualitative or categorical variables are often significant in explaining dependent variables in regression models. For example, consumption spending during wartime is argued to be different than consumption spending during peacetime. During wartime, governments take a variety of actions to restrict consumption to free up resources for the war effort. **Dummy variables** can be used to measure such qualitative or categorical variables. A dummy variable is equal to 1 when a data case possesses the qualitative attribute and equal to 0 when the data case does not possess the qualitative attribute.

A dummy variable can be added to the simple consumption function model to evaluate the argument about wartime consumption spending.

$$C_t = \beta_0 + \beta_1 Q_t + \beta_2 D_t + u_t, \quad \text{where } D_t = 0 \text{ for war years}$$
$$D_t = 1 \text{ for peace years}$$

During war years, the dummy variable equals 0, and the regression model is

$$C_t = \beta_0 + \beta_1 Q_t + u_t$$

During peace years, the dummy variable equals 1 and the regression model is

$$C_t = (\beta_0 + \beta_2) + \beta_1 Q_t + u_t$$

Parameter β_2 measures the shift in the regression line caused by the presence of peace. The effect of the dummy variable is shown graphically in Figure 8.1. Notice that for this example the slope of the regression line does not change with different values of the dummy variable; only the intercept changes value.

Dummy variables are one of the most useful techniques in the econometrician's toolbox. They can be structured to include several qualitative variables in a regression model. They also can be used to examine the possibility that regression slopes are influenced by qualitative variables. Because they are such an important tool, various applications of dummy variables are treated at length in most econometric texts.

This lesson gives you practice using dummy variables by asking you to deseasonalize monthly department store sales. Because seasonally adjusted data are used with such frequency in economic analysis, the lesson also discusses the alternative **decomposition technique** used by government agencies. Data are

Figure 8.1
Effect of a Dummy Variable

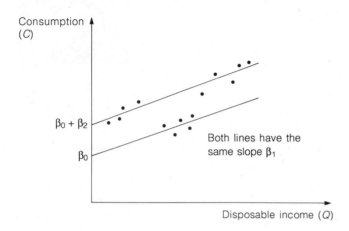

usually deseasonalized with a decomposition technique, not with dummy variables. But anyone doing applied econometrics must understand the issues involved in the seasonal adjustment of economic data. This lesson thus has the dual purpose of giving you practice using dummy variables *and* going over some of the issues posed by seasonally adjusted data. It is unfortunately the case that seasonal adjustment continues to pose significant interpretation problems in economic analysis.

Seasonal Adjustment with Dummy Variables

Figures 8.2 and 8.3 show several years of data for monthly department store sales and unemployment rates. It is clear that sales and unemployment vary systematically over the year. A variable that shows a systematic pattern across the year is said to have a *seasonal trend*. It is very difficult to interpret variables that show a strong seasonal trend. When department store sales rose in December of 1983, for example, did this rise indicate a general strengthening of the economy, or did it reflect the normal rise in seasonal retail activity? The answer to this kind of question is critical to assessing the true state of the economy. To provide meaningful answers, economists *deseasonalize* variables: They take out the variation in the variables caused by seasonal factors. How are data deseasonalized? An examination of Figures 8.2 and 8.3 suggests that the impact of seasonal factors can be accounted for by dummy variables.

EXERCISE 8.1

Use a regression model containing dummy variables to deseasonalize department store sales. Because department store sales show an upward trend over time, you must include time as a variable in your model, as well as dummy variables for the months. The Data Bank contains monthly department store sales from January 1967 to December 1983 under the heading "SEASONALLY UNADJUSTED DATA" (USALES). The Data Bank also contains dummy variables for months under the names JAN to NOV and

Figure 8.2
Monthly Retail Sales for Department Stores, Seasonally Unadjusted,
Selected Years

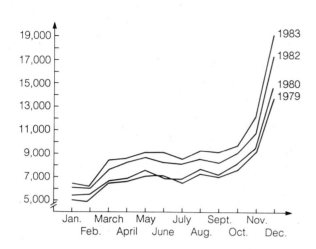

Figure 8.3
Civilian Unemployment Rate, Seasonally Unadjusted, Selected Years

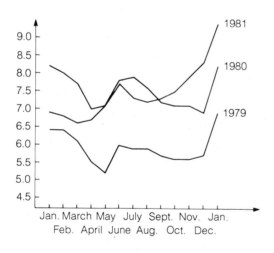

a monthly time index under the name MTIME. Make sure you understand why only eleven monthly dummies are used instead of twelve. Don't look at the dummy variables in the Data Bank until you feel confident that you know *how* these dummies should be included in your model. Write your estimated regression below.

Are all the signs as you expected? Should you test the significance of each parameter estimate or examine the overall goodness of fit?

_____

_____

_____

_____

Examine the relationship between the predicted department store sales computed from your model and the original actual values. Plot the predicted and actual values for 1979–1983 in Figure 8.4. If your econometric software does the plot, attach the plot to the figure. Are you satisfied with your results, or does something seem wrong? (Think about the assumption underlying the time-trend variable in your model. That is, how does the predicted value for January 1983 differ from the predicted value for January 1980? Is this assumption reasonable? The regression model reflects movements in USALES with respect to a time trend and seasonal factors.)

_____

_____

_____

_____

Deseasonalize department store sales for 1983. The dummy variable coefficients give the seasonal shift for each month. Calculate the mean of these coefficients. Next, subtract the mean from each coefficient. The resulting figures give a seasonal series that fluctuates around zero. Finally, subtract this seasonal series from the original unadjusted data to generate the seasonally adjusted values for 1983.

January	July
February	August
March	September
April	October
May	November
June	December

What kinds of judgments can you make about the state of the economy in 1983?

_____

_____

Figure 8.4
Predicted Sales and Actual Sales

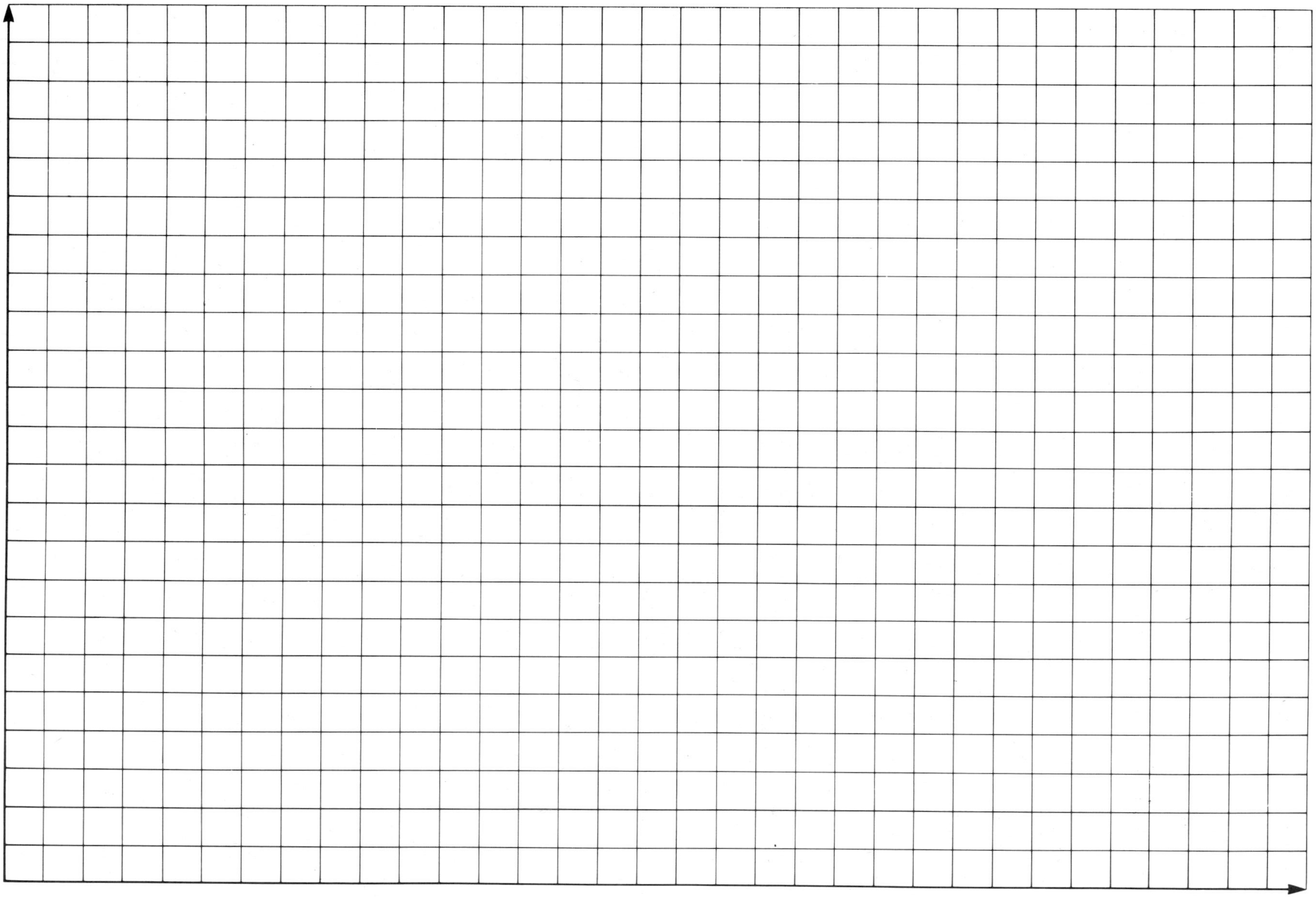

When is it appropriate to deseasonalize data using dummy variables?

_____

_____

_____

_____

_____

Decomposition Method

In formulating your dummy variable regression model for seasonal adjustment, you assumed that department store sales vary with both time and the month of the year. In other words, you assumed that the data contain a *seasonal component* and a *long-term time-trend component*. Economists who deal with data like department store sales, often called time-series data, argue that changes in the data can be explained by four such components. The other two are a *business-cycle component* and an *irregular, or random component*. Movements in a time series are assumed to be caused by these four components.

If a time series could be decomposed, split into its four parts, it would be possible to remove the effects of the seasonal component from the effects of the other components. The resulting series then would be free of seasonal variation. Such decomposition techniques have been developed, and it is these techniques that generate the seasonally adjusted data reported by government agencies. The basic assumptions underlying the decomposition methodology can be shown by examining how a simple decomposition procedure is used to deseasonalize department store sales.

Think about department store sales at time t as being the product of the four components:

$$D_t = L_t S_t C_t R_t \tag{8.1}$$

where L is the long-term time component, S is the seasonal component, C is the business-cycle component, and R is the random component.

EXERCISE 8.2

Notice that there are other ways to write the component model. How, for example, would the component model for sales differ from the multiplicative model shown by Equation 8.1 if the four components are assumed to be *additive*. Which specification do you feel is realistic?

_____

_____

_____

_____

The decomposition method works through four steps to arrive at indices for deseasonalizing a variable. First, it removes the seasonal and random components from the time series. It does this by computing a moving average based on the length of seasonality, in this case twelve months:

$$\bar{D}_t = \frac{1}{12}(D_{t+6} + D_{t+5} + D_{t+4} + D_{t+3} + D_{t+2} + D_{t+1} + D_t + D_{t-1} + D_{t-2} + D_{t-3} + D_{t-4} + D_{t-5})$$

(8.2)

Notice that the moving average is centered around t. It is not based on the previous twelve periods. Statisticians argue that this centering tends to generate a more stable time series. Economists argue that this moving average should be free of seasonal and random components. That is, Equation 8.2 can be written as

$$\bar{D}_t = L_t C_t$$

(8.3)

Second, the combined seasonal and random components are estimated.

Because the values for $\bar{D}_t$ are assumed to have removed these components from the time series, the desired estimate is obtained by dividing the original time series by $\bar{D}_t$:

$$D_t^* = \frac{D_t}{\bar{D}_t} = \frac{L_t S_t C_t R_t}{L_t C_t} = S_t R_t$$

(8.4)

The resulting values for D_t^* are often referred to as seasonality ratios.

Third, the random component is removed from D_t^*, leaving only the seasonal component. How can the random component be removed? The most common method is to average the values of D_t^* for each month. That is, average all the seasonality ratios for January, for February, for March, and so on. The highest and lowest values in each month are usually removed before computing the average. This adds stability to the resulting seasonal indices. Notice that this method assumes that the averaging process smooths out random fluctuations. The resulting twelve averages are the seasonal adjustment indices. It is necessary, however, to make one last adjustment before using these indices to adjust department store sales.

Fourth, the seasonal indices are adjusted to sum to 1. The twelve averages should sum to 1, but may not do so if a long-term trend remains in the data series. The twelve averages are added, and the resulting sum divided into 12. Each of the twelve averages is then multiplied by the resulting ratio. The revised indices now sum to 12.

EXERCISE 8.3

Use the decomposition technique described above (or the decomposition technique provided by the econometric software) to compute seasonal indices for department store sales. Use the twelve seasonal indices to deseasonalize 1983 department store sales. To do this, simply divide each month's sales by its corresponding seasonal index. Record the seasonally adjusted values below. (Your econometric software may generate the seasonally adjusted values for you.)

January	July
February	August
March	September
April	October
May	November
June	December

How do the results differ from those observed with the dummy variables technique?

_____

_____

_____

_____

Why do you get different results?

_____

_____

_____

_____

_____

The actual seasonal indices used by the Commerce Department and other government agencies are computed by a large computer program. This program is based on the decomposition methodology, but its calculations are much more complex than are the simple decomposition calculations you worked through in Exercise 8.3. By analyzing thousands of time series, government economists have been able to both improve decomposition procedures and design a number of tests to examine the accuracy of these procedures.

To give you some idea of how carefully the deseasonalized data are scrutinized, consider a recent problem with seasonal indices for department store sales uncovered by economists at the Commerce Department. Once every seven years Christmas falls on a Sunday, and most department stores stay open only one-half day on the preceding Saturday. This early closing on a trading day in December, which has Christmas on a Sunday, has not been fully accounted for in the seasonal indices. Government economists are cognizant of the problem, but they are not sure that they can deseasonalize the data adequately for these years. Events that happen once every seven years do not provide many degrees of freedom. More generally, economists concerned with deseasonalizing data must be constantly alert to possible changes in seasonal patterns. For example, the rapid rise in energy prices in the early 1970s changed the seasonal pattern for a number of energy-consumption time series. Until historical evidence accumulated on the consumption behavior, it was not possible to generate reliable seasonally adjusted figures.

The decomposition technique itself requires simplifying assumptions. Think about the assumptions that you had to make to apply the decomposition procedure. You can probably think of alternative assumptions that are just as reasonable. These alternative assumptions obviously generate different values for the indices. Despite the attention given to calculating deseasonalized data, a strong ad hoc element remains in the procedures. Even with the complexity of computer programs, we cannot be sure that all seasonality has been removed from a time series. Worse, it is possible that the procedure has removed more than the seasonal trend. It is not surprising then that seasonality issues still occur in interpreting economic data. During certain periods of time, seasonal adjustment controversies may be quite significant. Lesson Note 8.1 discusses some specific instances of controversy.[1]

Finally, it may have occurred to you while working through the decomposition method that this method could be used as a forecasting tool. If seasonal and random components are removed from a time series, the remaining values reflect the long-term trend and business-cycle components. These two components are of great interest to some economists involved in forecasting future economic activity. These economists use decomposition techniques to produce a time series containing only the long-term trend and business-cycle components. This time series is called the trend–cycle curve.

Lesson Note 8.1

Seasonal Variations Seen Causing Big Swings in Economic Statistics

WASHINGTON—Economists are frequently twitted for inaccurately forecasting the future, but in recent months they have even found it difficult to explain the recent past.

The problem is government statistics, which showed the economy slowing in December and booming again in January. Many analysts blame the contradictory signals on the difficulties of adjusting figures for seasonal variations in business patterns. More signals are due this week: The government issues February retail-sales figures today and its February industrial-production report on Thursday.

Initial government reports for December convinced analysts that economic activity had slowed considerably. Retail sales rose a sluggish 0.1%, durable-goods orders declined 1.1%, and industrial production climbed a moderate 0.5%. On top of that, the Commerce Department's preliminary report of the gross national product for the fourth quarter showed the nation's output of goods and services rising at a 4.5% annual rate after inflation, down sharply from the third quarter's 7.6% pace.

Swayed by the sluggish numbers, some analysts announced an end to the economy's boom. Growth had settled down to a more sustained rate, they declared, and the fears of renewed inflation and higher interest rates had been reduced.

Then came a parade of robust figures for January. Retail sales bounced up 2.2%, while industrial production rose 1.1%, and durable-goods orders increased a strong 2.7%. Housing starts startled the statistics watchers by jumping to their highest level in five years. And even some of the December figures, such as durable-goods orders, were revised sharply upward.

Dazzled by the new numbers, analysts scurried back to their computers to revise their forecasts. Maury Harris, chief economist at Paine Webber Inc., pushed his estimate for first-quarter economic growth to 6.9% from 5.1%. James Smith, chief economist at Union Carbide Corp., went to 6% from 2.9%.

The numbers seemed to suggest that the economy was on a seesaw, down one month, up the next. But most of the seesawing was only in the statistics, which for several reasons were subject to large distortions. In truth, says Lawrence Chimerine, chairman of Chase Econometrics in Bala Cynwyd, Pa., the economy was neither as weak in December nor as strong in January as the numbers suggested.

Part of the December slowdown reflected the one-time effects of cold weather, which held down retail sales and industrial production. The January numbers reflected a rebound from those weather-depressed levels.

Beyond that, the swing from December to January illustrates the current vagaries of monthly statistics. "We still have the best data system in the world," says Edward Guay, chief economist for Cigna Corp. in Hartford, Conn. "But it is more difficult right now to take the data and make judgments about the economy than it has been at any time in the last fifteen years." The primary reason for that difficulty, says Mr. Guay, is the seasonal-adjustment process.

Government statisticians adjust their numbers for predictable variations during the course of a year. But such adjustments are imprecise. And because they are based on the experience of recent years, the adjustments become particularly difficult at times like the present, when a year of unusually robust economic activity follows on the heels of five years of sluggish growth.

"It's very hard to seasonally adjust data when you have gone through the sort of turmoil we have in the last few years," says Mr. Guay.

Adjustment problems are particularly troublesome in winter, when the Christmas season causes unusual bulges in retail sales, and when severe weather forces construction to a halt in many areas.

The December retail-sales figures illustrate the point. Everyone who drove past a shopping mall in December knew that people were buying more than they had in the previous month. Before seasonal adjustment, retail sales in December were a full 21% above their November level. But the seasonal adjustment for the normal Christmas-sales boom brought that down to a meager 0.1% increase.

Among the factors distorting that adjustment process, according to a Census Bureau statistician, was the fact that both Christmas Eve and New Year's Eve were on Saturdays. The computer program that makes the adjustments gives a heavier weight to sales on Saturdays, because they are normally heavy shopping days. But shopping at grocery stores and general-merchandise stores was light on the holiday eve, and many stores closed early. As a result, those two Saturdays looked weak relative to those in previous Decembers, pulling down the entire sales estimate.

January housing starts are a similar case, but in the opposite direction. After adjustment, the annual rate of 1.9 million starts was the highest for any one month since December 1978. But January clearly isn't the best month for starting a house: Before adjustment, the housing-start rate was less than 1.3 million. So a full third of the final figure was the result of seasonal adjustment. And since the adjustment was based on a period of history in which housing was severely depressed, a pretty good January trend looked even better by contrast. Thus the adjusted figure may well have been distorted upward.

"I don't think it is possible to do a good job of seasonal adjustment," says Michael Sumichrast, chief economist of the National Association of Home Builders. "It's very, very dangerous to pay too much attention to any one month's figure."

The caprice of monthly statistics can also be seen in the size of the revisions made to the initial figures. That 1.1% decline in durable-goods orders, for instance, was revised to a 1.7% increase a month later. Ruth Runyan of the Commerce Department says the department's survey of orders and durable goods, products intended to last for more than three years, is especially weak in December because many companies are closing out their books and therefore are unable to give accurate, early estimates of their orders. December data are "always difficult to interpret," she says.

With this sort of seesawing, how much attention should be paid to monthly, seasonally adjusted economic statistics? Not much, says Geoffrey Moore, who heads Columbia University's Center for International Business Cycle Research.

"Month-to-month changes in statistics are very unreliable in many, many ways," Mr. Moore says. "They get revised, they are affected by all sorts of ephemeral things, and it's much better to look at a longer interval."

Mr. Moore's organization compares the seasonally adjusted monthly numbers to an average of the previous twelve months. Others prefer to look at three-month averages of the statistics. And some holdouts from an earlier era look only at unadjusted statistics and com pare them with unadjusted statistics for the same month a year earlier, although that method is also subject to distortion and misses key turning points in the economy.

Mr. Guay of Cigna Corp. says he doesn't expect any improvement soon in the seasonal-adjustment problems. It will take four or five years, he says, to "wash out" the distortions caused by the turmoil of the last few years. In the meantime, Mr. Guay says, "it's going to be very hard to read the data."

Changing Statistics
(Rise or fall from previous month)

	November	December (Initial)	December (Revised)	January
Retail Sales	1.2%	0.1%	0.1%	2.2%
Industrial Production	0.3%	0.5%	0.6%	1.1%
Durable Goods Orders	3.4%	−1.1%	1.7%	2.7%
Housing Starts (Annual rate in millions)	1.73	1.67	1.67	1.92

Source: The Commerce Department and the Federal Reserve Board

Source: Murray, Alan. "Seasonal Variations Seen Causing Big Swings in Economic Statistics," *The Wall Street Journal*, 13 March, 1984.

Suggested Reading

If you would like more information on the decomposition method and its use as a forecasting tool, read B. E. Majani, "Decomposition Methods for Medium-Term Planning and Budgeting," in S. Makridakis and S. C. Wheelwright (eds.), *The Handbook of Forecasting* (New York: Wiley, 1982). A good discussion of the assumptions underlying contending seasonal adjustment methods is by J. P. Burman, "Seasonal Adjustment—A Survey," in S. Makridakis and S. C. Wheelwright (eds.), *Forecasting* (New York: North Holland Publishing, 1979).

Heteroscedasticity

1. To learn how regression results are affected by heteroscedasticity
2. To learn how to correct for heteroscedasticity using econometric software

In specifying the general regression model, assumptions are made about the behavior of the random error term. This lesson and the next deal with what happens to ordinary least-squares estimators when two of these assumptions are violated. The two assumptions are

$$E(u_i u_j) = \sigma_u^2 , \qquad \text{for } i = j; \ i,j = 1, \ldots, n$$

The random error term has a constant variance. In other words, the random error term is **homoscedastic**. When this assumption is violated, the random error term is **heteroscedastic**.

$$E(u_i u_j) = 0 , \qquad \text{for } i \neq j; \ i,j = 1, \ldots, n$$

The random error terms are uncorrelated. When this assumption is violated, the random error terms are said to exhibit **autocorrelation** or **serial correlation**.

Examine the estimated regression lines shown in Figure 9.1. The scatter of data cases around the regression line in Figure 9.1a is consistent with the assumptions of homoscedasticity and no autocorrelation. The scatter of data cases in Figure 9.1b suggests that the variance of the random error term increases with the value of the independent variable. The random error term appears to be heteroscedastic. The scatters of data cases in Figures 9.1c and 9.1d suggest that successive values of the random error term are correlated with each other. In Figure 9.1c, positive values of the random error term follow other positive values, and negative values follow other negative values. In Figure 9.1d, positive and negative values consistently alternate with each other. The random error terms in Figures 9.1c and 9.1d thus appear to exhibit autocorrelation.

This lesson discusses heteroscedasticity; Lesson 10 considers autocorrelation. In general, ordinary least-squares estimators no longer have superior sampling properties in the presence of heteroscedasticity or autocorrelation. Ordinary least-squares estimators remain unbiased but no longer have minimum variance among linear unbiased estimators; they are no longer efficient estimators. Econometric texts give very complete explanations of both heteroscedasticity and autocorrelation. While these lessons give some background information, they do not attempt to duplicate the discussions in your text. Instead, they

Figure 9.1
Sample Data Sets with Estimated Regression Lines

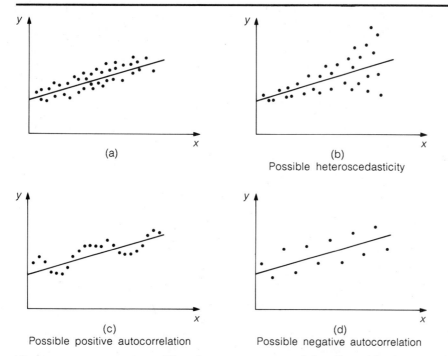

(a)

(b)
Possible heteroscedasticity

(c)
Possible positive autocorrelation

(d)
Possible negative autocorrelation

focus on two questions. First, how are your models affected by heteroscedasticity and autocorrelation? Second, how can you employ efficient estimators to estimate your models. It is important to stress that we are guided by the desirable properties of estimators in correcting for heteroscedasticity or autocorrelation. Our corrected regression *for a specific sample* may not perform as well as our uncorrected regression for that sample. What matters is not a specific estimate but employing estimators with superior properties.

Residuals as an Information Source

Although we used scatters of data cases in Figure 9.1 to discern the presence of heteroscedasticity and autocorrelation, regression residuals usually are used to make this diagnosis. Once a regression contains more than one independent variable, graphic analyses as those shown in Figure 9.1 are not possible. Residual plots must be used. If you feel heteroscedasticity or autocorrelation is a problem, residuals from a regression should be plotted against the estimated values of the dependent variable and the values for each independent variable.

Looking at regression residuals is not new to you. Throughout your econometric course, residuals are used as a source of information about the underlying model. Residuals are used to estimate the standard error of a regression and often point to a misspecified model. For example, if we assume that the growth of some variable is linear when it is actually exponential, an examination of the residuals indicates something is wrong with the linear specification. Figure 9.2 shows an example of such a misspecification and the resulting residual pattern. Notice the residuals are plotted against both the dependent and independent variable. In this case, either plot shows something is seriously amiss.

Finally, residuals are used to find **outliers**, data cases where the regression model fits poorly. If, for example, you did not think about union strike activity when you constructed your auto-demand model, you undoubtedly found a few years with much larger residuals than others. Some research on the automobile industry reveals these residuals as years of strike activity. More gener-

Figure 9.2
A Misspecified Model and Autocorrelation

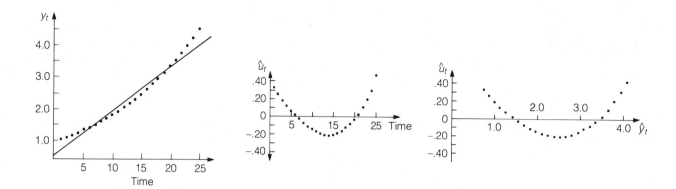

ally, an examination of outliers may suggest a significant variable has been excluded from your regression model.

Residuals are clearly one of the most important diagnostic tools available to an econometrician. It thus seems quite reasonable to look at residuals for evidence of heteroscedasticity and autocorrelation. There is a problem, however, with "eyeballing" residual patterns. Residuals are influenced by the values of the independent variables in the regression as well as the true random error term. To see this, consider the regression model in deviation form:

$$y_i = \beta_1 x_i + u_i \tag{9.1}$$

When Equation 9.1 is estimated using ordinary least-squares, the residual for any data case i is

$$\hat{u}_i = y_i - \hat{\beta}_1 x_i \tag{9.2}$$

Because y_i is assumed to be generated by Equation 9.1, Equation 9.1 can be substituted for y_i in Equation 9.2. This substitution gives

$$\hat{u}_i = u_i + (\beta_1 - \hat{\beta}_1) x_i \tag{9.3}$$

Only through improbable luck will we be fortunate enough to estimate β_1 without error for a *given data set* such that $(\beta_1 - \hat{\beta}_1)$ equals 0. As a consequence, the values of x_i influence the values of the residuals for a given data set. Examine Equation 9.3 carefully. Assume that the values of x_i increase. The residuals may also increase as a consequence of the increasing x values and show a pattern similar to that generated by heteroscedasticity. Next, assume that successive values of the independent variable are highly correlated. In other words, values of the independent variable are themselves autocorrelated. Under this assumption, the residuals may show a pattern similar to that generated by autocorrelation in the random error term. You can clearly be misled about the presence of either heteroscedasticity or autocorrelation by simply looking at residuals. For this reason, it is very important that statistical tests be performed to decide whether the ordinary least-squares assumptions are violated. Correcting for either heteroscedasticity or autocorrelation when they are not present poses no real difficulties if the sample is large and the proper estimation technique is used. But such improper correction may well pose difficulties if the sample is small and the proper estimation technique is not clear. As we will see, one of the difficulties with heteroscedasticity is that the estimation procedure often reflects an ad hoc judgment, which could be incorrect.

Causes and Problems

What Causes Heteroscedasticity?

In cross-sectional data, the variance of the dependent variable often becomes larger or smaller as the value of an independent variable increases. For example, the variance of consumption spending usually increases as disposable income increases in cross-sectional budget studies. The changes in the dependent variable, consumption spending, are of a different order of magnitude over the range of the independent variable, disposable income.

But why should the variance of the dependent variable increase as the independent variable increases? It is argued that large economic units have a wider range of choices than do small economic units. In cross-sectional data, this causes the variance of the random error term to increase for the larger units. A high-income family, for example, has more discretionary income than does a low-income family. A high-income family thus has a much wider range of saving–consumption choices than does a low-income family. This difference in variation seldom occurs in time-series data, where both aggregate variables increase together over time. Thus, an examination of the residuals for the aggregate consumption function does not show obvious heteroscedasticity.

Models influenced by learning behavior may also exhibit heteroscedasticity. For example, students who study more for exams tend to have a smaller variance in their scores than do students who study less. As students study more, they learn more and decrease their chances of making errors.

Why Is Heteroscedasticity a Problem?

Recall from Lesson 1 that the assumption of homoscedasticity is *not* needed to show that the ordinary least-squares slope estimator is unbiased. But the *classical* ordinary least-squares variance formula does require the assumption of homoscedasticity. The variance of the ordinary least-squares slope estimator is

$$E(\beta_1 - \hat{\beta}_1)^2 = \Sigma w_i^2 E(u_i^2) = \Sigma w_i^2 \sigma_i^2 \tag{9.4}$$

where w_i is the ordinary least-squares weight for the ith data case. It is no longer valid to assume that $E(u_i^2) = \sigma_u^2$ when heteroscedasticity is present. The classical ordinary least-squares assumptions, however, state that $E(u_i^2) = \sigma_u^2$.

Thus, the variance of all random error terms is *assumed* to be constant and moved outside the summation sign. This yields the classical ordinary least-squares formula for the variance of the slope estimator:

$$E(\beta_1 - \hat{\beta}_1)^2 = \sigma_u^2 \Sigma w_i^2 = \frac{\sigma_u^2}{\Sigma x_i^2} \tag{9.5}$$

What are the consequences of using Equation 9.5 when heteroscedasticity is present? This is a difficult question. First, let's consider what would happen if we know the σ_i^2 terms and computed the variance of the slope estimator using not Equation 9.5 but Equation 9.4. In minimizing the sum of the squared residuals, ordinary least-squares gives more weight to observations with large error variances than to observations with small error variances. This happens because the residuals associated with the large variance observations are likely to be larger than are the residuals associated with small variance observations. In minimizing the sum of the squared residuals, ordinary least-squares generates a good fit for the large variance observations. But it can be shown that the ordinary least-squares slope estimator is not efficient. An alternative linear unbiased estimator of β_1 exists that has a smaller variance.

To gain some intuitive feeling for why this is the case, look at Figure 9.1b. In *repeated samplings*, the estimated regression line will be very sensitive to the large residuals associated with the large values of the independent variable. A few large positive residuals will cause the line to tilt up; a few large negative residuals will cause the line to tilt down. Because negative and positive residuals are equally likely, the ordinary least-squares estimator remains unbiased. But on average, the fluctuation in the regression line will generate a larger variance than does the fluctuation associated with an estimator that gives less weight to the large residuals.

Another way to think about the inefficiency of ordinary least-squares estimators is as follows: The ordinary least-squares criterion gives *equal weight* to all data cases. Remember that the ordinary least squares criterion is to minimize the sum of the squared residuals

$$\Sigma(y_i - \hat{y}_i)^2$$

Obviously, the ordinary least-squares criterion places a high priority on finding the regression line that reduces large residuals. But notice that the summation over each data case in the formula gives equal weight to each data case. This is reasonable when all error terms come from the same distribution. But when random error terms are generated by different distributions, a random error term from a distribution with a small variance gives more accurate information about the regression line than does a random error term from a distribution with a large variance. To reflect this more accurate information, the efficient estimator gives a greater weight to data cases that have been generated by a distribution with a small variance. Specifically, it can be shown that the efficient estimator assigns a weight to each data case that is inversely proportional to the true variance of the error term for the data case. In effect, this efficient estimator minimizes a "weighted" sum-of-squared residuals. The efficient estimator, called the **generalized least-squares** or **weighted least-squares estimator**, gives less weight to observations expected to have large residuals and more to observations expected to have small residuals.

Ordinary least-squares estimators may not be efficient in the presence of heteroscedasticity, but they are nevertheless unbiased. We thus have unbiased estimators with larger variances than some unbiased alternative estimators. In the world of applied econometrics, this is not a disastrous state of affairs. But when we apply the *classical* ordinary least-squares solution we do not use Equation 9.4; we use Equation 9.5. The variances of the classical ordinary least-squares estimators must be unbiased to meaningfully test hypotheses or construct confidence intervals. Unfortunately, it can be shown that Equation 9.5 yields a biased estimate of the variance of β_1.

It is the possibility of such bias that makes heteroscedasticity such a perplexing empirical problem. The direction of this bias is clearly important for assessing the impact of heteroscedasticity on hypotheses tests and confidence intervals computed with ordinary least-squares information. Specifically, we could be led to make very serious errors in statistical inference if the variances of the ordinary least-squares estimators reflect serious downward bias. It is not possible to state unambiguously what the direction of the bias is. The bias can be positive or negative, depending on how heteroscedasticity is related to the independent variable. In other words, the evaluation of the biased properties of ordinary least-squares variances requires *sample-specific information*. Concern that variance estimates are too small more than offsets the efficiency concerns associated with heteroscedasticity.

Examination of a case occurring frequently in applied econometric work shows why such concern is justified. This is the case where the variance of the random error term varies directly with an independent variable. Let's examine this in detail. Assume that

$$\sigma^2_i = c_i \, \sigma^2 \qquad\qquad (9.6)$$

where σ^2 is some constant, and c_i is some constant for data case i. Notice that the set of c_i terms is a set of constants; the c_i s are not random variables. Substituting Equation 9.6 into Equation 9.4 gives

$$E(\beta_1 - \hat{\beta}_1)^2 = \Sigma w_i^2 c_i \sigma^2 = \sigma^2 \Sigma w_i^2 c_i \qquad\qquad (9.7)$$

Remembering that the $w_i = \dfrac{x_i}{\Sigma x_i^2}$ is the ordinary least-squares weight for the ith data case, Equation 9.7 becomes

$$E(\beta_1 - \hat{\beta}_1)^2 = \left[\frac{\sigma^2}{\Sigma x_i^2} \right] \frac{\Sigma x_i^2 c_i}{\Sigma x_i^2} \qquad\qquad (9.8)$$

The term in brackets in Equation 9.8 can be thought of as representing the variance given by the classical ordinary least-squares solution, the variance associated with the assumption of homoscedasticity (Equation 9.5). Examine Equation 9.8. When the variance of the random error term varies directly with the independent variable, x_i^2 and c_i are positively correlated. If, in addition, $\dfrac{\Sigma x_i^2 c_i}{\Sigma x_i^2}$ is greater than 1, the true variance of $\hat{\beta}_1$ is larger than that shown by the classical ordinary least-squares formula. The classical ordinary least-squares formula thus *underestimates* the variance of $\hat{\beta}_1$. In other words, the computed ordinary least-squares variance is too small. Because the variance of $\hat{\beta}_1$ is underestimated, the associated t value is overstated, and the slope estimator looks better than it actually is. The same results can be shown for the intercept estimator.

EXERCISE 9.1

Develop a model to explain state expenditures on elementary and secondary schools (EXES) based on state characteristics and examine how heteroscedasticity affects the model. You will find the data you need in the Data Bank under the heading "STATES DATA". Do *not* transform any of these variables when you estimate your initial model. Write your estimated model in the following space.

Next examine the data for possible heteroscedasticity. Plot the residuals for your regression against the dependent and independent variables on the graphs provided in Figure 9.3. If your econometric software prints these plots, attach the printout to Figure 9.3. Do the residual plots suggest that heteroscedasticity may be present?

_____

_____

_____

_____

Your econometric text discusses various tests for heteroscedasticity. Select the test you feel is most appropriate for your expenditures model and evaluate your regression results for the presence of heteroscedasticity. Does your model show statistically significant heteroscedasticity? If so, discuss the *likely* impact of heteroscedasticity on the *t* tests of your parameter estimates.

_____

_____

_____

_____

_____

_____

Treatment

What can be done about heteroscedasticity? The problem is that ordinary least-squares criterion assigns the *wrong weights* to the observations. A different set of weights generates unbiased estimators with minimum variances. The solution to heteroscedasticity is to find these weights and recompute the regression. Can we use ordinary least-squares to estimate these weights directly? We can, but this procedure has difficulties, the explanation of which goes beyond a beginning course. The more traditional approach is to *assume* a relationship between the variance of the random error term and one of the independent variables. This relationship reflects the econometrician's ad hoc judgment about what seems reasonable for a given problem. Two commonly assumed relationships are

$$E(u_i^2) = \sigma^2 X_i^2 \tag{9.9}$$

$$E(u_i^2) = \sigma^2 X_i \tag{9.10}$$

Figure 9.3
Residual Plots for Higher Education Expenditures Model

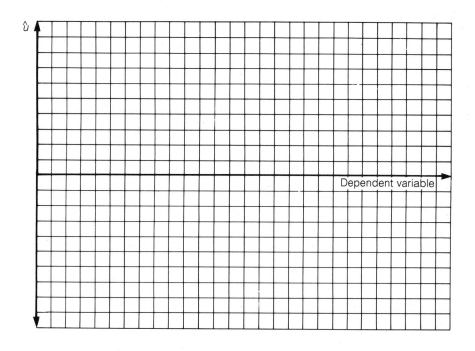

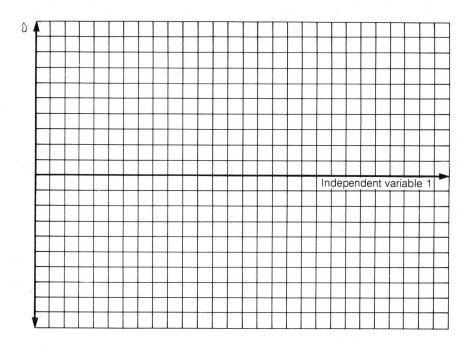

Figure 9.3 (continued)
Residual Plots for Higher Education Expenditures Model

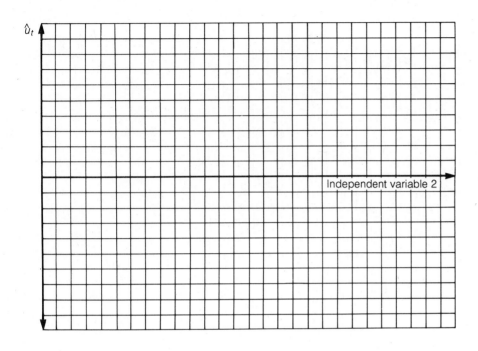

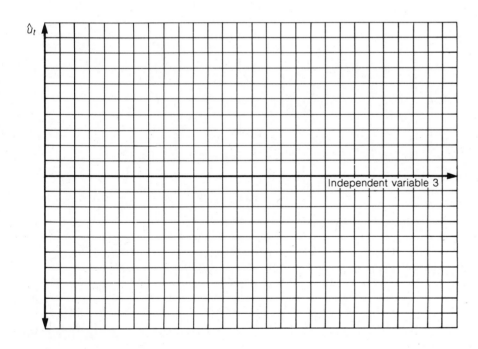

where σ^2 is an unknown constant. Equation 9.9 indicates that the error variance is proportional to the square of the independent variable X, whereas Equation 9.10 indicates that the error variance is proportional to X. Given the linear model

$$Y_i = \beta_0 + \beta_1 X_i + u_i \tag{9.11}$$

your text shows that the weighted sum of squares solution yields the efficient estimator

$$\sum \frac{(Y_i - \hat{\beta}_0 - \hat{\beta}_1 X_i)^2}{\sigma^2_{u_i}} = \sum \frac{\hat{u}_i^2}{\sigma^2_{u_i}} \tag{9.12}$$

Equation 9.12 reflects the properly weighted sum of squares. In other words, minimizing the sum of squares associated with Equation 9.12 yields an efficient estimator.

Take a moment to examine Equation 9.12. The observations in the squared sum are weighted such that they are inversely proportional to the variance of the random error term associated with each observation. Thus, observations with large variances are given less weight than in the ordinary least-squares solution. The new weighting corrects for heteroscedasticity. Notice that the weighted least-squares criterion is equivalent to the ordinary least-squares criterion when the random error term is homoscedastic.

Let's see how to actually estimate a weighted least-squares regression. Assume that Equation 9.9 is the true state of the world. Given this assumption, Equation 9.11 can be transformed to

$$\frac{Y_i}{X_i} = \beta_0 \left[\frac{1}{X_i}\right] + \beta_1 + v_i \tag{9.13}$$

where $v_i = u_i / X_i$. This transformation is accomplished by dividing every term in Equation 9.11 by X_i. Notice that the random error term v in Equation 9.13 is homoscedastic.

$$E(v_i^2) = E\left[\frac{u_i}{X_i}\right]^2 = \frac{1}{X_i^2} E(v_i^2) = \sigma^2$$

If Equation 9.9 is true, estimation of Equation 9.13 by ordinary least-squares yields efficient parameter estimates. In other words, the weighted least-squares solution is obtained by applying ordinary least-squares to the transformed equation, reflecting new observation weights. Notice that the dependent variable is weighted by $1/X_i$ and that the estimate for the slope of Equation 9.11 is obtained from the *intercept term* in Equation 9.13. The intercept for Equation 9.11 is obtained from the slope estimate for the new variable $1/X_i$ in Equation 9.13.

Some econometric texts advise trying to redefine a model to avoid heteroscedasticity by expressing the model in per-capita variables, percentage-change variables, and the like. While these transformations are an implicit correction for heteroscedasticity, they are not formally equivalent to the generalized least-squares solution. It seems that the issue here is whether the redefined model stands on its own in a *behavioral sense*. For example, does it make sense to try to explain per-capita educational expenditures among the states? If the redefined model does make behavioral sense and heteroscedasticity disappears as a problem, most econometricians would feel comfortable advising beginning students to estimate the redefined model, especially if the alternative is to impose an ad hoc judgment about the form of heteroscedasticity.

EXERCISE 9.2

Show how you would transform Equation 9.11 if the true state of the world is Equation 9.10.

_____

_____

_____

_____

Discuss which relationship, Equation 9.9 or Equation 9.10, is most realistic for your expenditures model.

_____

_____

_____

_____

_____

_____

Using weighted least-squares, reestimate your expenditures model and write your re-estimated model below.

How has correcting for heteroscedasticity changed your regression results?

_____

_____

_____

_____

_____

Are the changes in your regression results what you expected?

_____

_____

_____

_____

_____

We close this lesson with some notes of caution, which are especially significant for small data sets. Heteroscedasticity poses ambiguous problems for econometricians. There is no single, generally accepted test for heteroscedasticity. There is also no single, generally accepted procedure for correcting for heteroscedasticity. All existing tests and correction procedures require some explicit assumptions about the pattern of heteroscedasticity or the properties of the resulting estimators. In general, the need to correct for heteroscedasticity depends on the extent to which homoscedasticity is violated. Beginning students are advised to proceed with caution in both assessing the presence of heteroscedasticity and correcting for what appear to be heteroscedastic errors.

Autocorrelation

1. To learn how regression results are affected by autocorrelation
2. To learn how to correct for autocorrelation in models

Lesson 9 discussed how models are affected by heteroscedasticity. This lesson focuses on how models are affected by autocorrelation. You first construct an interest-rate model in the *absence* of autocorrelation concerns. You then evaluate the consequences of autocorrelation and re-estimate the interest-rate model using efficient estimators.

Interest-Rate Model

We begin by reviewing some of the variables that economists feel affect the real interest rate. There is theoretical controversy about many aspects of economic theory, none more so than interest-rate determination. Nevertheless, the following discussion should get you started on building your interest-rate model.

Figure 10.1a shows how many economists view short-run money market equilibrium: The equilibrium interest rate is determined by the interaction of money demand and supply functions. It is essential that the difference between *real* and *nominal* variables be made clear in discussing money market equilibrium. For example, suppose that the nominal demand for money for some consumer is $500. If the price level doubles, the consumer's demand for nominal money rises to $1000. But the consumer's real demand for money, the demand for real balances, stays the same in terms of purchasing power.

The demand for real balances is a function of two arguments. *Liquidity preference theory* argues that quantity demanded decreases as the real interest rate rises. Risk-averse consumers have a "speculative motive" for demanding money. The interest rate represents the cost of holding money instead of an interest-earning bond. The higher the interest rate, the more costly it is to hold money. The demand for money also depends on the level of real income (Q). As real income increases, consumers increase their demand for real balances to finance purchases. Consumers have a "transaction motive" for demanding money. This causes interest rates to rise, as shown in Figure 10.1b.

The supply of money is generally determined by the Federal Reserve System, which determines the nominal supply of money. The real money supply is equal to the nominal money supply divided by the price level. We have also given the money supply curve in Figure 10.1 some sensitivity to the interest rate. Many economists feel this is more realistic than a perfectly vertical supply curve, because the banking system seems to expand nominal balances as the interest rate rises. Figures 10.1c and 10.1d show the change in the interest rate

Figure 10.1
Determination of the Real Interest Rate

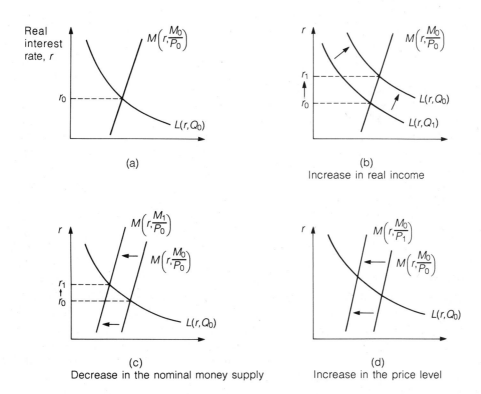

(a)

(b)
Increase in real income

(c)
Decrease in the nominal money supply

(d)
Increase in the price level

due to a decrease in the nominal money supply and an increase in the price level.

To develop an interest-rate model, you must have a measure of the money supply. As is frequently the case in econometric investigation, there is controversy on the appropriate measure. Before you develop your interest-rate model, read Lesson Note 10.1.[1] This reading goes over some of the issues involved with different measures of the money supply. The reading is taken from D. E. W. Laidler's book on estimating the demand function for money. The difficulties posed by the need to match an empirical measure to a theoretical concept in estimating the demand for money are discussed. Structural change in financial institutions is also shown to pose measurement issues in assessing time-series data.

Another measurement difficulty concerns how to assess price level changes. The real interest rate is equal to the nominal interest rate minus the *expected* rate of inflation. Actual price-level changes may provide a poor measure of expected price-level changes. Finally, as in the case of the consumption function, you are asked to assume a single-equation model when a multiple-equation model is more appropriate. The interest rate is clearly determined by the *simultaneous* interaction of demand and supply. Estimation issues concerning simultaneity are discussed in Lesson 14.

Measuring the Money Supply

Consider first the problem of finding an empirical measure of money. There is no sharp distinction in the real world between money and other assets, but rather a spectrum of assets, some more like one's rough idea of money than others. Theories based on the transactions motive emphasize the proposition that a demand for money exists because, unlike other assets, money is a means of exchange. They are theories of the demand for assets which are readily acceptable and transferable in everyday transactions, and the money concept to which they apply was, until the early 1970s, rather easily defined at least in the context of the U.S. economy; there were but two assets that clearly had such a characteristic. These were currency and demand deposits at commercial banks. The sum of these assets available to the public at that time was widely agreed to constitute the relevant measure of the money stock as far as theories of the transactions demand for money were concerned. Matters have become a little more complicated in the last decade. In the early 1970s, beginning in New England, there were introduced "NOW" accounts, transferable by check like demand deposits but unlike them bearing explicit interest, albeit at a regulated rate. In 1981 such accounts became available on a nationwide basis and are believed by many to belong in a definition of money used to test transactions demand theories against recent data. However, such accounts are more expensive to transfer than demand deposits, and it is possible to argue plausibly that they do not really constitute "transaction balances" in the same sense as do demand deposits.

Each economy raises its own problems in measuring "means of exchange." For example, in the British economy currency and current accounts at commercial banks might be regarded as generally acceptable and readily available means of exchange. But the availability of economic overdrafts to bank customers has led some to argue that unused overdraft limits also constitute "money" in a meaningful sense. Or

again, in Canada certain classes of deposits at trust companies (institutions somewhat similar to savings and loan associations) and certain classes of time deposits at chartered banks have long been transferable by check. In these cases the charges levied for making transfers by check are sometimes sufficiently high as to deter people from using such assets as if they were the equivalent of ordinary checking accounts, and so it is far from obvious a priori whether or not it is appropriate to treat all such assets as equally efficient means of exchange. Moreover, as with the United States, the situation in Canada began to change in the 1970s and has continued to do so as the commercial banks introduced new types of interest-bearing low-cost checkable deposits, notably, in 1981, accounts paying interest on a daily basis; these new assets probably do belong in a definition of money that is relevant to testing theories about transactions demand.

All in all there is little, if anything, that one can say about the issues involved in measuring the money stock relevant to transactions demand theories that is generally true of all times and places. In some economies it is clear which assets are means of exchange and which are not, but not in all, as the above examples show; nor do the dividing lines between means of exchange and other assets stay put over time in any particular economy. The boundary shifts as the financial system evolves, and the most that one can say in general is that the economist seeking to test transaction demand theories needs to be sensitive to the institutional framework of the economy generating his data.*

Not all theories of the demand for money are based on the transactions motive. As a result, even if the borderline between means of exchange and other assets was clearcut, it would be hard to settle on an appropriate and generally acceptable definition of money on a priori grounds. Theories of the speculative demand for money downplay its characteristic as

---

*The problem of the continuity of the meaning of a money supply series is one that is particularly amenable to solution by the construction of an index number series to measure money. . . .

a means of exchange and emphasize instead the fact that it is an asset whose capital value does not vary with the rate of interest. In the United States currency and demand deposits, and these days NOW accounts, have this characteristic to be sure, but they are not the only assets that possess it. Time deposits at commercial banks, deposits at mutual savings banks, and savings and loan association shares are, in this sense, just as much "money" in the United States as are their equivalents in other economies. Moreover such assets yield an interest income to their holders at a rate higher than that borne by checkable deposits and currency. The extent to which checkable deposits bear interest varies from time to time and place to place, but it would be hard to find a case of their bearing interest at a rate equal to, let alone higher than, that available on noncheckable deposits.

Currency—except very occasionally in the past in the case of notes issued by privately owned banks—is an asset that bears no interest at all. Despite this, individuals hold currency, not to mention low- or zero-interest checkable deposits, in significant amounts, and the speculative motive for holding money can be of little relevance as far as the demand for such "narrow money" is concerned. It is more likely to play a role in determining the demand for assets such as noncheckable time deposits and perhaps savings and loan association shares. Hence its importance can best be tested in the context of the demand for money defined over a broader spectrum of assets than currency and checkable deposits.

Theories based on the precautionary motive are no better at yielding a clearcut guide as how best to define money for empirical purposes. There is no doubt that currency and demand deposits may be held for precautionary reasons. However, in the context of the United States it can be argued that the costs of transferring funds from, say, a money market mutual fund or a time deposit to a demand deposit when they are needed to cover an unexpected cash outflow are small relative to those involved in converting, say, certificates of de-

posit or savings and loan association shares into a demand deposit. If this argument is correct, it will follow that money market mutual funds and time deposits can reasonably be included in a definition of money to which the theory of the precautionary demand for money is relevant but that the other above-mentioned assets should be excluded. At the very least, the existence of such an argument prevents such a possibility from being ruled out a priori.

Theories of the demand for money which rest simply on the proposition that money yields a flow of unspecified services to its owners raise similar problems. Every asset yields services to its owner, and in defining one set of assets as being money and another as not being money, one is really arguing that the services yielded by the various assets in the first category are sufficiently similar to one another as to make it possible to treat them as if they were all one asset, and sufficiently different from those yielded by other assets to disqualify the latter from being put in the same category. It is the asset holder's decision, rather than that of the economist studying his behavior, that determines which assets are close substitutes for one another and which are not. The only way to find out what asset holders think is to study their behavior; in the context of this more general approach to the problem of the demand for money, the correct definition of money becomes an empirical matter, at least within rather broad boundaries laid down by one's "rough idea" of what money is.*

In the light of the foregoing arguments, it is hardly surprising that several definitions of money have been employed in the course of testing theories of the demand for money. As far as the United States economy is concerned, the bulk of the work carried out down to the mid-1970s confined the definition of money to currency plus demand deposits at commercial banks, "old M_1," as it is now called or currency plus demand deposits plus time deposits at commercial banks, "old M_2." There was a good reason for so limiting the definition of money, for in addition to clarifying the theory of the

---

*The notion that the question of the correct way to measure money for purposes of carrying out empirical work on the demand for money and related problems is itself an empirical issue is set out and defended in Laidler (1969) and Friedman and Schwartz (1970, Part 1). For a criticism of this approach to the problem, see Mason (1976), who argues with considerable justice that this approach carries with it a grave danger of leading one into circular arguments—the definition of money that enables a theory to work well is chosen as appropriate and then evidence generated using it is cited as supporting the theory in terms of which the data were selected in the first place. This danger undoubtedly exists in principal, but . . . there seems to be enough results concerning the demand-for-money function that do not depend on the precise variable chosen to measure money that Mason's objection may not be a fatal one.

demand for money per se, these empirical tests were supposed to throw light on the scope of economic policy, particularly monetary policy. One wished, then, to know about the role played in the economy by assets whose volume could be controlled by the monetary authorities, and these assets were currency in circulation and the liabilities of commercial banks. It was thus not unreasonable to concentrate on these assets to the exclusion of others. As we have already noted, however, from the 1970s onward, developments in the banking system began to undermine the relevance of these simple notions of what constituted narrow and broad money. In particular, NOW accounts have come to be included in the narrow-money concept ("new M_1") while the broader concept ("new M_2") has had to be extended to include such assets as, for example, shares in money market mutual funds and money market certificates issued by commercial banks. The process of financial innovation which has required these adjustments is an ongoing one, and ideas about the "appropriate" definition of money in the U.S. economy will undoubtedly continue to change in the future as they have in the recent past.

One novel approach to the problem of measuring money currently under investigation involves the construction of index numbers to measure the quantity of money. Instead of simply adding up what are, after all, heterogenous assets on a dollar-for-dollar basis, it is argued that those assets that are more readily and cheaply transferred should be given more weight in measuring the aggregate money stock than those that are less liquid. One type of index number that has been used . . . to generate aggregate money supply indices is the so-called Divisia Index whereby each type of asset to be included in the total money supply is weighted by the difference between the rate of return it earns and some representative market rate of interest. The argument underlying this procedure is that the greater is this difference, the greater must be the "liquidity services" the asset in question yields to its holder, and hence the more is it "money."

The difficulty here is that the difference between rates of return in question measures, at best, liquidity on the margin rather than the average liquidity of a particular asset. If one were to picture a perfectly competitive banking system in which all types of bank liabilities bore interest at the market rate, the Divisia Index would yield the peculiar result that the money stock was equal to zero.* This is a theoretically extreme example, not likely to be encountered in practice, and it may well be that in current circumstances the Divisia Index is a reasonably good one to employ. However, this example does, at least, warn us that the use of this index is not theoretically satisfactory in all circumstances and that experiments with other types of index are worthwhile. A promising line of enquiry here uses turnover rates on different classes of assets as weights, the idea being that the more frequently an asset is transferred, the more useful do agents find it as "money." . . .

Far more work has been done on the demand for money in the U.S. economy than in any other, but many other countries have been studied with less thoroughness. To discuss the details of definitions of money used in studies of these other countries would require us to deal with their individual financial systems to an extent that would be quite inappropriate in a book such as this. Suffice it to say that, as far as possible, people working on countries other than the United States have tried to utilize definitions of money roughly corresponding to those used in studying U.S. data. It should also be noted that because financial innovation over the last decade or so has not been confined to the United States, people working in other countries too have found it necessary to adjust their notions of how to measure money in order to accommodate such changes. In a number of cases . . . experiments with Divisia Index numbers have also been carried out.

One final point concerning the measurement of money should be made. As we have stressed again and again in the first two parts of this book, the demand for money is a demand for *real* balances. The concepts of the money

---

*The problems involved here stem from certain fundamental issues in monetary theory that are beyond the scope of this [article] . . . . The basic point is that in an economy that uses token as opposed to commodity money, the marginal cost of producing real balances is essentially zero. Under competitive conditions real balances become a free good to the economy, and all the very difficult questions that arise in general about accounting for the services provided by free goods in measuring income, wealth, and economic welfare are relevant to the case of money. The reader who wants to follow up this issue is referred to Friedman (1969) and Johnson (1969), two of the fundamental papers on the matter. Fried and Huwitt (1983) discuss closely related issues.

stock we have been discussing here are measured in nominal terms. To get to a measure of real money from nominal money, it is necessary to divide by an appropriate price index. The selection of the latter variable is relatively uncontroversial. It is generally accepted that a broadly based index such as, in the case of the United States, a gross or net national product deflator is an appropriate choice, but sometimes a consumer price index is used, particularly for those countries where national product deflators are either unreliable or unavailable. By and large, one measure of a broad spectrum of prices moves in harmony with another, and little seems to hinge on such a choice in most cases. Sometimes, though, price indices are distorted by being heavily weighted with officially set prices, particularly in countries where governments seek to control inflation by direct price controls, and this can raise problems in particular instances.

As we shall see in due course, many important empirical results concerning the demand for money are rather insensitive to the precise way in which money is measured and how that measurement evolves over time. However, "many" is not "all," and we shall have to return to some of the issues raised above, particularly those having to do with financial innovation, when we discuss the outcome of empirical work. For the moment it will suffice for the reader to be aware that the problem of measuring money in the real world, in a way that corresponds to the concepts underlying theroretical work on the demand for money, raises real problems for those intent on empirically testing rival hypotheses about the nature of the function.

Source: Laidler, D. E. W. *The Demand for Money: Theories, Evidence, and Problems,* 3rd ed. (New York: Harper & Row, 1985), 81–86.

EXERCISE 10.1

Develop a model to explain quarterly short-term interest rates. Use the interest rate on three-month Treasury bills as your measure of the short-term interest rate. (You will find this variable in the Data Bank under the name QTBILL.) Specify your model below.

Discuss your reasons for including each independent variable and the sign you expect for each parameter estimate.

_____

_____

_____

_____

_____

_____

_____

_____

_____

Estimate your model. Write the estimated model below.

Discuss the estimation results. Do your parameter estimates have the expected signs? What is the overall goodness of fit of your model?

_____

_____

_____

_____

_____

_____

_____

_____

_____

Compute the predicted or fitted values for the short-term interest rate. Plot the fitted values with the actual values in Figure 10.2. If the econometric software does the plot, attach the printout to Figure 10.1. Do the fitted values seem to be consistently above then below the actual values? What do you think would happen if you tried to use the model to forecast future interest rates?

_____

_____

_____

_____

Figure 10.2
Actual and Fitted Values for the Short-Term Interest Rate

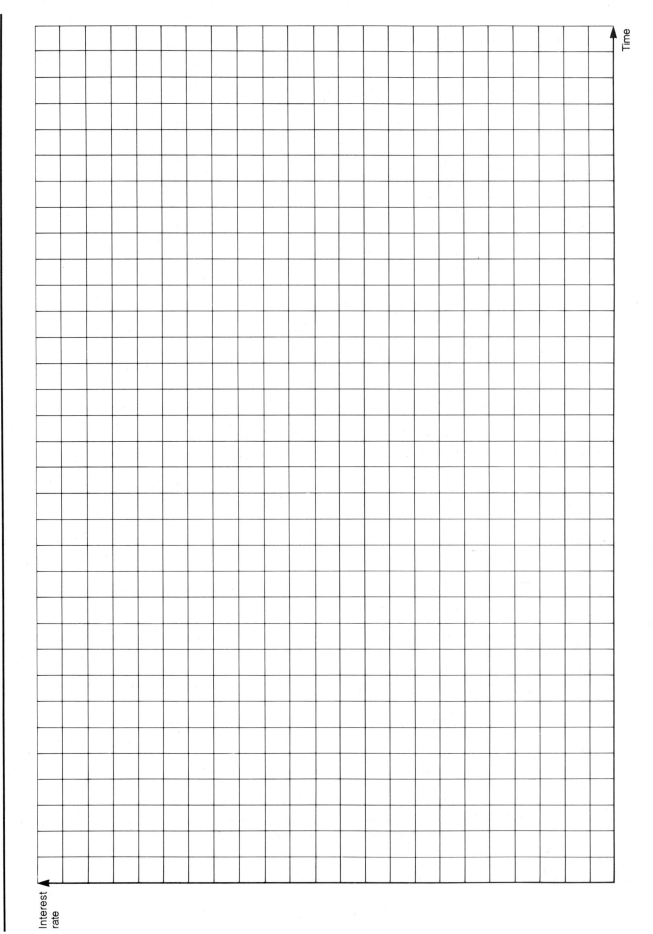

Interest rate

Time

Causes and Problems

When fitted values are consistently above, then below, the actual values, the random error term in one period influences the random error term in the following period. The residual pattern for your interest-rate model looks much like the residual pattern for the regression shown in Figure 9.1c. Positive autocorrelation is present. Figure 10.1d shows negative autocorrelation, which is so uncommon in economic analysis that it is usually ignored in the beginning course.

Why should autocorrelation concern the econometrician? Recall from Lesson 1 that the assumption that the independent random error terms are uncorrelated is *not* needed to show that the ordinary least-squares slope estimator is unbiased. As in the case of heteroscedasticity, however, ordinary least-squares estimators are not efficient. But this inefficiency concern is more than offset by the underestimation of estimator variances associated with the ordinary least-squares solution in the presence of autocorrelation.

To see why underestimation occurs, let's examine the solution for the variance of the ordinary least-squares slope estimator:

$$E(\hat{\beta}_1 - \beta_1)^2 = \frac{\sigma_u^2}{\Sigma x_i^2} + 2w_1 w_2 E(u_1 u_2) + \ldots + 2w_{n-1} w_n E(u_{n-1} u_n) \qquad (10.1)$$

It is no longer valid to assume $E(u_i u_j) = 0$ when autocorrelation is present. Nevertheless, the *classical* ordinary least-squares variance estimator continues to assume $E(u_i u_j) = 0$. Thus, the classical ordinary least-squares variance estimator is

$$E(\hat{\beta}_1 - \beta_1)^2 = \frac{\sigma_u^2}{\Sigma x_i^2} \qquad (10.2)$$

Equation 10.2 tends to *underestimate* the variance associated with Equation 10.1 in the presence of positive autocorrelation because the expected values of the $u_i u_j$ terms are positive. To make matters worse, the variance σ_u^2 in Equation 10.2 is not known but estimated from regression residuals. In the presence of positive autocorrelation, this sample estimate can be shown to *underestimate* σ_u^2.

The variance of $\hat{\beta}_1$ thus is unambiguously underestimated in the presence of positive autocorrelation. The regression looks better than it actually is. The same results can be shown to hold for the ordinary least-squares intercept estimator.

What causes autocorrelation? In Lesson 1, you learned that the random error term can be thought of as capturing the net effects of independent variables that are *excluded* from the model. When these independent variables move together, they may cause autocorrelation in the random error term. Some years ago, Ames and Reiter examined yearly data for 100 economic variables. They found that the average correlation coefficient between observations in successive years was .84, with 56 variables having correlation coefficients greater than .90.[2] Because most economic variables move in phase together over time, it is not surprising that autocorrelation is often a problem when time-series data are used.

Another cause of autocorrelation is specification error. You saw an example of specification error in Figure 9.2. When there are several variables in a model, misspecification is not as easily detected. In these cases, economists fit different functional forms to the data and make judgments on whether autocorrelation is being caused by specification error. The solution to this type of autocorrelation is to find the correct functional form.

To develop a general solution for autocorrelation, it is necessary to model the autocorrelation process itself. How exactly do past errors affect the current error? The standard model used in beginning econometric texts assumes that the current error is linearly related to the previous error. The regression model becomes

$$Y_t = \beta_0 + \beta_1 X_{1t} + \beta_2 X_{2t} + \ldots + \beta_m X_{mt} + u_t \tag{10.3}$$

$$u_t = \rho u_{t-1} + v_t \tag{10.4}$$

where v is a normally distributed random variable with a 0 mean and constant variance. Although it is no longer valid to assume $E(u_t u_{t-1}) = 0$, all other assumptions used to specify the general regression model remain intact. Values for random variable v at different time periods are assumed to be independent of each other and of values for random variable u.

The standard test for examining the null hypothesis of no autocorrelation ($\rho = 0$) is the Durbin–Watson test, as discussed in your text.

EXERCISE 10.2

Using the Durbin-Watson statistic for your interest-rate model, test the null hypothesis of no autocorrelation.

What does the error process described by Equation 10.4 imply about the influence of past errors on the current error? To answer this question, we need to know the covariances between the errors at different times. For example, the covariance between u_t and u_{t-1} is

$$
\begin{aligned}
\sigma_{u_t u_{t-1}} = E(u_t u_{t-1}) &= E\left[(\rho u_{t-1} + v_t) u_{t-1}\right] \\
&= E\left[\rho u_{t-1}^2 + v_t u_{t-1}\right] \\
&= E\left[\rho u_{t-1}^2\right] + E\left[v_t u_{t-1}\right] \\
&= \rho \sigma_u^2
\end{aligned}
$$

Similarly, the covariance between u_t and u_{t-2} is

$$
\begin{aligned}
\sigma_{u_t u_{t-2}} = E(u_t u_{t-2}) &= E\left[(\rho u_{t-1} + v_t) v_{t-2}\right] \\
&= E\left[(\rho(\rho u_{t-2} + v_{t-1}) + v_t) u_{t-2}\right]
\end{aligned}
$$

Figure 10.3
Example Correlograms

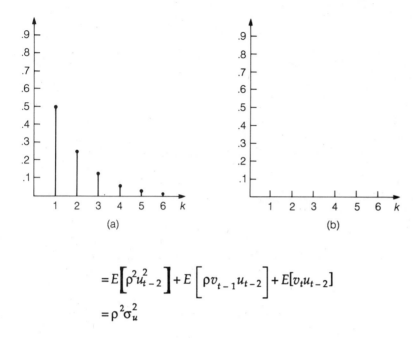

(a)   (b)

$$= E\left[\rho^2 u_{t-2}^2\right] + E\left[\rho v_{t-1} u_{t-2}\right] + E[v_t u_{t-2}]$$

$$= \rho^2 \sigma_u^2$$

Examining these derived covariances shows that the current error is determined by all past errors, with the importance of the past errors diminishing geometrically over time. We can show this relationship formally with the **autocorrelation function**. The autocorrelation function for lag period k is defined as

$$R_k = \frac{E(u_t u_{t-k})}{\sqrt{E(u_t^2)E(u_{t-k}^2)}} = \frac{\sigma_{u_t}\sigma_{u_{t-k}}}{\sigma_u^2} \tag{10.5}$$

For example, given the error process indicated in Equation 10.4,

$$R_1 = \frac{\sigma_{u_t}\sigma_{u_{t-1}}}{\sigma_u^2}$$

The autocorrelation function is nothing more than the correlation coefficient between errors at different time periods. Thus, another way to think about R_k is that it is the correlation coefficient between error terms in time period t and error terms in time period $t-k$. Notice that the autocorrelation coefficient of lag 1 for the error process described by Equation 10.4 is ρ.

When the autocorrelation function is plotted against time, the resulting figure is called a **correlogram**. Figure 10.3a shows the correlogram for the autocorrelation process $u_t = .5u_{t-1} + v_t$.

EXERCISE 10.3

Plot the autocorrelation function for $u_t = .9u_{t-1} + v_t$ in Figure 10.3b. Which autocorrelation function has a better "memory" of the distant past?

Other formulations of the error process are possible. In fact, the error process indicated by Equation 10.4 is really a special case of the general **autoregressive process**

$$u_t = \phi_1 u_{t-1} + \phi_2 u_{t-2} + \cdots + \phi_s u_{t-s} + v_t \qquad (10.6)$$

Equation 10.6 defines an autoregressive process of order s. Thus, the error process assumed in your text is a first-order autoregressive process, often indicated by the notation $AR(1)$, with ρ being equal to ϕ_1. The behavior of higher-order error processes is addressed under the topic of **time-series analysis** in advanced econometrics.[3] The autocorrelation function for varying lag periods is estimated using the residuals from a regression and used to develop an appropriate error process for the model. The error process indicated by Equation 10.4 is a reasonable process for the econometric applications dealt with in your course. If your econometric software computes the autocorrelation function, you may want to examine the autocorrelation function for your interest-rate model to see if the residuals generate the expected pattern for a first-order autoregressive process.

Treatment

Because Equation 10.3 must be true for all time periods, we can write

$$Y_{t-1} = \beta_0 + \beta_1 X_{1,t-1} + \beta_2 X_{2,t-1} + \cdots + \beta_m X_{m,t-1} + u_{t-1} \qquad (10.7)$$

Multiplying both sides of Equation 10.7 by ρ and subtracting the resulting equation from Equation 10.3 gives

$$(Y_t - \rho Y_{t-1}) = \beta_0(1-\rho) + \beta_1(X_{1,t} - \rho X_{1,t-1}) + \cdots + \beta_m(X_{m,t} - \rho X_{m,t-1}) + (u_t - \rho u_{t-1}) \qquad (10.8)$$

This procedure is called **generalized differencing**. If ρ is known, values for the variables in their differenced form can be computed, and Equation 10.8 can be estimated with ordinary least-squares. The reason for following the generalized differencing procedure is clear when the random error term associated with Equation 10.8 is examined. The random error term is simply v_t in Equation 10.4, the kind of well-behaved random error term assumed by the ordinary least-squares model. Thus, efficient parameter estimates are obtained when Equation 10.8 is estimated using ordinary least-squares.

EXERCISE 10.4

Write your interest-rate model in generalized difference form.

The generalized difference form of your interest-rate model yields efficient parameter estimates. But to estimate the new equation you must know ρ, which is obviously not known. In reality, ρ is estimated from sample information. Several estimation procedures are discussed in the econometric literature. A common procedure, included in most econometric software, is the **Cochrane–Orcutt procedure.**[4] Exercise 10.5 shows how this procedure works using your interest-rate model.

EXERCISE 10.5

Using the residuals from your Exercise 10.1 model, estimate the error process shown in Equation 10.4 as you would any linear regression with the constant term suppressed. (Remember, the error process does not have an intercept term.) The regression slope is used to estimate ρ; write your estimated ρ below:

Now take the value obtained for $\hat{\rho}$ and estimate your model in its generalized difference form. Write your estimated model below.

This regression yields new parameter estimates for the interest-rate model. Next, substitute these new parameter estimates into your *original* interest-rate model, the model prior to generalized differencing. A new set of residuals is associated with the new parameter estimates. Compute the sum of the squared residuals. How does this value differ from the value of the sum of the squared residuals in the original model?

You have just generated the first iteration of the Cochrane–Orcutt procedure. You could keep going, using the new residuals to estimate a new $\hat{\rho}$, generating new parameters for the generalized difference form, substituting the new parameters back into the original model, generating new residuals, and so on. Luckily, econometric software does the work for you. Software programs typically stop iterating when the new $\hat{\rho}$ differs from the old $\hat{\rho}$ by less than some specified value, usually .01 or .005. Some software programs let you specify this value. A few simply run through a set number of iterations. Each iteration produces new parameter estimates that are better in the sense that they generate a smaller sum of the squared residuals than do the previous parameter estimates.

The problem with the Cochrane–Orcutt procedure is that there may be some set of parameter estimates that generates a smaller sum of the squared residuals. The Cochrane–Orcutt procedure finds a *local* optimal $\hat{\rho}$, a $\hat{\rho}$ that generates the smallest sum of the squared residuals in the neighborhood of the iterations. It does not check to see if values outside this neighborhood may be better. Another problem associated with the treatment of the first observation is discussed in advanced econometric texts.

Econometricians concerned about the local nature of the Cochrane–Orcutt solution often use an alternative procedure called the **Hildreth–Lu procedure** to generate a global solution.[5] A set of grid values for $\hat{\rho}$ is specified. A good initial set of grid values for most problems is .0, .1, .2, .3, .4, .5, .6, .7, .9, .8, and 1.0. Equation 10.8 is then computed for each grid value. The equation with the smallest sum of the squared residuals is selected as the best equation for the grid. The procedure continues, with new grid values set around the best $\hat{\rho}$ for the previous grid, until the econometrician is satisfied with the results. Careful use of the Hildreth–Lu procedure ensures that a global solution is found.

If your econometric text has a section on forecasting with autocorrelated error terms, you may want to try your hand at forecasting interest rates for the next four quarters, using your interest-rate model.

EXERCISE 10.6

Reestimate your interest-rate model using the Cochrane–Orcutt procedure. How do the estimation results differ? Is this what you would expect?

_____

_____

_____

_____

Plot the fitted values for the reestimated model in Figure 10.4. How does the relationship between the fitted and actual values compare with what you observed for your initial interest-rate model?

_____

_____

_____

Figure 10.4
Actual and Fitted Values for the Short-Term Interest Rate,
Corrected for Autocorrelation

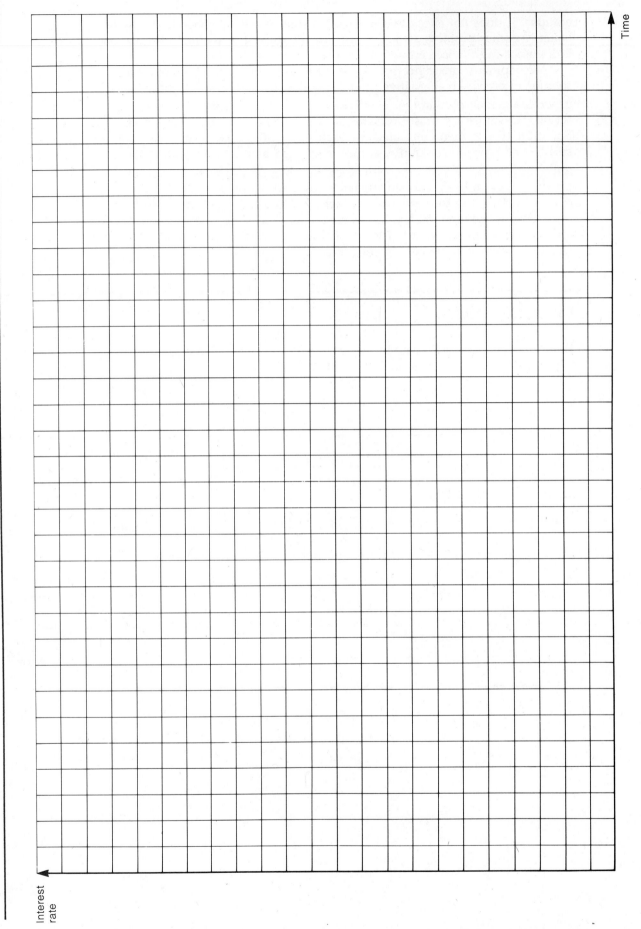

Geometric Lags I

1. To learn how to specify models that assume partial adjustment behavior or adaptive expectations behavior

2. To learn how to estimate a partial adjustment model using econometric software

3. To review the general distributed lag and geometric lag models

A dependent variable may take several time periods to completely adjust to a change in an independent variable. The total change in the variable is distributed over several time periods. The dependent variable is said to respond with a lag. This lesson focuses on lagged relationships that can be explained by a *geometric function*. Two types of behavior—**partial adjustment behavior** and **adaptive expectations behavior**—are shown to fit geometric lag patterns. Examples of each type of behavior are given, and you are asked to restructure some of your models to reflect these behaviors. The two following lessons develop additional distributed lag topics.

General Distributed Lag Model

Most students initially try to account for delayed adjustment by including lagged values of independent variables in their models. For example, you may have included last period's disposable income, along with the current period's disposable income, as an independent variable in your auto demand model. You may also have discovered that some of your models simply fit better when one or more of the independent variables is lagged, without thinking too much about why this should be the case.

It may seem reasonable to lag independent variables, but this lagging is pretty ad hoc. How do you decide how many periods to lag a variable? Do you try to *average* the values of some variable over several time periods and use this average as a single variable? Do you have any notion which lag period exerts the strongest effect on the current value of the dependent variable?

One way to answer these questions is to let the data select the model's lag structure. Is there anything wrong with this procedure? To answer this question, let's examine the general form of the **distributed lag model**:

$$Y_t = \gamma + \beta_0 X_t + \beta_1 X_{t-1} + \beta_2 X_{t-2} + \ldots + u_t \tag{11.1}$$

The current value Y is explained by the current value X and all past values of X. The random error term is assumed to be well behaved. Other independent variables can be included in Equation 11.1.

The β_ks are called **lag parameters**. Our task is to estimate the β_ks, to determine the model's lag structure. Because none of the ordinary least-squares assumptions are violated by Equation 11.1, the lag parameters can be estimated directly if the lag periods are restricted to a finite number. Letting the data determine a model's lag structure is thus a valid procedure in principle.

But, by this time in the course, you should be skeptical of this kind of data analysis. We sometimes appear to let the data select the model, but this procedure is always heavily influenced by cognitive judgments. In the case of Equation 11.1, we have already assumed a great deal about the structure of the economic world *before* turning to ordinary least-squares to estimate the lag parameters.

In addition to theoretical ambiguity, there are some practical problems with estimating Equation 11.1 directly. First, the lag parameters may be quite sensitive to the time period over which the model is estimated. You have undoubtedly observed that some of your models fit the estimating period well but perform poorly when forecasting beyond the estimating period. Second, if the lag structure involves many time periods, small data sets may not provide enough degrees of freedom for useful inference. Finally, the values of independent variables in successive time periods are likely to be highly correlated. Multicollinearity thus looms as a serious problem. The coefficients in Equation 11.1 still can be estimated, but they have intolerably large standard errors and wide confidence intervals.

EXERCISE 11.1

A student decides to estimate the lag structure for the simple consumption function directly from the data. To see the problems raised by multicollinearity in direct estimation of lag structures, consider the student's regression results shown in Table 11.1. The student starts running regressions, with each new regression including one more lag period. When a nonsignificant lag parameter is generated on the last period, the student concludes that the lag structure does not extend to this period. The next to the last regression is then used to estimate the consumption function's lag structure. How successful is the student in determining the lag structure directly? Do you see any evidence of multicollinearity? (Each regression is corrected for serial correlation using the Cochrane–Orcutt procedure. Disposable personal income is noted as NPI and personal consumption expenditures are noted as NCE.)

_____

_____

_____

_____

_____

_____

For both practical and theoretical reasons, econometricians usually restrict the lagging process. Specifically, they assume the lag parameters follow some functional form. This "solves" most of the practical problems posed by the direct estimation of distributive lag models, although new problems of proper estimation techniques emerge. Of course, models that are analytically convenient are not necessarily correct from the standpoint of economic theory or useful for predictive purposes. Try to gain a clear conception of the *structure* of the economic world assumed by the various lag functions as you work through this and the next two lessons. The most important question to address in constructing a distributed lag model is whether the lag function is a realistic approximation to economic reality.

Table 11.1
Direct Estimation of the Simple Consumption Function Lag Structure

SMPL 1961.2–1985.2
97 Observations
LS // Dependent Variable is NCE

Variable	Coefficient	Std. Error	T Stat.	Two-Tail Sig.
C	3.7125804	11.670878	0.318063	0.751
NPI	0.9012078	0.0175240	51.427032	0.000

R squared	0.998162	Mean of dependent var	579.8094
Adjusted R squared	0.998123	S.D. of dependent var	111.5397
S.E. of regression	4.832342	Sum of squared resid	2195.044
Durbin–Watson stat	2.265130	F statistic	25526.19
Log likelihood	−288.9205		

SMPL 1961.3–1985.2
96 Observations
LS // Dependent Variable is NCE
Convergence achieved after 2 iterations

Variable	Coefficient	Std. Error	T Stat.	Two-Tail Sig.
C	−1.0682326	14.074351	−0.0758992	0.940
NPI	0.6368266	0.0547265	11.636534	0.000
NPI (−1)	0.2736697	0.0546760	5.0052960	0.000

R squared	0.998499	Mean of dependent var	581.9649
Adjusted R squared	0.998450	S.D. of dependent var	110.0757
S.E. of regression	4.333152	Sum of squared resid	1727.411
Durbin–Watson stat	2.004847	F statistic	20404.47
Log likelihood	−274.9396		

SMPL 1961.4–1985.2
95 Observations
LS // Dependent Variable is NCE

Variable	Coefficient	Std. Error	T Stat.	Two-Tail Sig.
C	−0.0992385	15.442072	−0.0064265	0.995
NPI	0.6050710	0.0619098	9.7734259	0.000
NPI (−1)	0.2395881	0.0628527	3.8119012	0.000
NPI (−2)	0.0652360	0.0620429	1.0514666	0.296

R squared	0.998464	Mean of dependent var	584.1558
Adjusted R squared	0.998395	S.D. of dependent var	108.5351
S.E. of regression	4.347685	Sum of squared resid	1701.213
Durbin–Watson stat	2.000091	F statistic	14622.59
Log likelihood	–271.8471		

SMPL 1962.1–1985.2
94 Observations
LS // Dependent Variable is NCE

Variable	Coefficient	Std. Error	T Stat.	Two-Tail Sig.
C	–1.6823992	16.450620	–0.1022696	0.919
NPI	0.5804746	0.0678518	8.5550402	0.000
NPI (–1)	0.2254458	0.0653888	3.4477722	0.001
NPI (–2)	0.0441779	0.0658585	0.6708012	0.504
NPI (–3)	0.0628905	0.0680606	0.9240364	0.358

R squared	0.998423	Mean of dependent var	586.3148
Adjusted R squared	0.998333	S.D. of dependent var	107.0463
S.E. of regression	4.370187	Sum of squared resid	1680.671
Durbin–Watson stat	1.988980	F statistic	11142.19
Log likelihood	–268.9120		

Variable Correlation Matrix

	NCE	NPI	NPI (–1)	NPI (–2)	NPI (–3)
NCE	1.000000	.9976363	.9960119	.9936463	.9910610
NPI	.9976363	1.000000	.9982490	.9961640	.9937811
NPI (–1)	.9960119	.9982490	1.000000	.9982940	.9961987
NPI (–2)	.9936463	.9961640	.9982940	1.000000	.9983227
NPI (–3)	.9910610	.9937811	.9961987	.9983227	1.000000

Geometric Function

The **geometric lag model** assumes that the current value of the dependent variable is related to the current value of the independent variable and weighted values of the lagged independent variable. The weights are positive and decline geometrically. Assuming a geometric lag structure, the ith lag parameter is

$$\beta_i = \beta_0 w^i, \qquad \text{where } 0 < w < 1 \text{ for } i = 0, 1, \ldots \tag{11.2}$$

When Equation 11.2 is substituted into Equation 11.1, the distributed lag model becomes

$$Y_t = \gamma + \beta_0(X_t + wX_{t-1} + w^2 X_{t-2} + \ldots) + u_t \tag{11.3}$$

which may be rewritten as

$$Y_t = \gamma + \beta_0 \sum_{i=0}^{\infty} w^i X_{t-i} + u_t$$

It may seem as if we have made little progress in estimating the lag structure. There are still an infinite number of time periods associated with Equation 11.3, and the practical problems discussed in the last section are still present. But a simple transformation, the **Koyck transformation**, generates a dramatic simplification in the estimating problem.[1] The Koyck transformation is described in your text, but let's review the steps as they apply to Equation 11.3.

EXERCISE 11.2

Step 1: Rewrite Equation 11.3 to explain the value of Y at $t-1$ instead of t. This is perfectly valid because the equation must be true for all time periods.

(11.4)

Step 2: Multiply both sides of Equation 11.4 by w. This also is valid because multiplying both sides of an equality by a constant leaves the equality unchanged.

(11.5)

Step 3: Subtract Equation 11.5 from Equation 11.3.

(11.3) $y_t = \gamma + \beta_0 X_t + w\beta_0 X_{t-1} + w^2\beta_0 X_{t-2} + \ldots u_t$

(11.5) ___ = _____

(11.6) =

Notice that all the lagged values of X drop from resulting Equation 11.6, which is usually written for estimating purposes as

$$Y_t = (1-w)\gamma + \beta_0 X_t + wY_{t-1} + v_t, \qquad \text{where } v_t = u_t - wu_{t-1} \tag{11.7}$$

Equation 11.7 can be estimated by ordinary least-squares.

But there is a problem with estimating Equation 11.7. Unfortunately, the error term v cannot be assumed to be well behaved. The Koyck transformation generates a serially correlated error term. This is much more damaging than it may first appear because the lagged dependent variable Y_{t-1} is now used as an independent variable. Consequently, v_t and Y_{t-1} are correlated, with v_t and $Y_{t\,1}$ being affected by u_t. This correlation does not disappear as the sample gets large. In such cases, ordinary least-squares estimators are biased and inconsistent. Serial correlation alone *without* a lagged dependent variable used as an independent variable yields unbiased estimators. A lagged dependent variable used as an independent variable with a well-behaved random error term yields biased but consistent estimators. But when the two estimation issues occur together, ordinary least-squares estimators become inconsistent.[2] How this estimation problem is dealt with depends on the assumptions made about the error process. Your econometric text and instructor will discuss which procedures are appropriate under different sets of assumptions.

The geometric lag function clearly solves some of the practical problems of estimating a distributed lag model, but is it consistent with the behavior suggested by economic theory? It turns out that two commonly assumed economic behaviors—partial adjustment behavior and adaptive expectations behavior—generate geometric lag patterns. Because the models reflecting these behaviors are so commonly used in applied econometric work, we will discuss each in detail. We will also see how partial adjustment and adaptive expectations assumptions can be used to improve some of the models you formulated in previous lessons.

Partial Adjustment Behavior

Because of institutional and structural rigidities in the economy, the desired level of some dependent variables cannot be realized in a single time period. Let's look at two examples. Assume that an increase in sales causes firms to increase their desired level of capital stock. The firms perceive that the increase in sales is permanent, and they decide to add to their plant and equipment to meet the new demand. But capacity limits in the capital-goods industry cannot satisfy the orders for new equipment and plant in one time period. Thus, the new capital stock is produced over several time periods. As the second example, consider the adjustment of consumers to the rise in gasoline prices in the 1970s. In the short run, consumers could not switch to more fuel-efficient autos, move closer to work, or expand mass transit. As a result, short-run consumer behavior did not reflect the full adjustment to the higher gasoline prices. Consumers appeared to be less responsive to rising energy prices than was indeed the case in the long run.

In formulating a partial adjustment model, it is necessary to distinguish between the *desired level* of the dependent variable and the *actual value* of the dependent variable. Let Y_t^D indicate the desired value of Y at time t. Then Y_t^D is determined as follows:

$$Y_t^D = \alpha + \beta X_t + u_t \tag{11.8}$$

A change in X causes a change in the desired level of Y. Equation 11.8 may look like an ordinary regression equation at first glance, but it cannot be estimated directly because we do not have a measure of Y_t^D. We only have the observed values of Y, which are obviously different than the desired levels. We need an equation that describes the adjustment process in moving from an actual value of Y to the desired value of Y. This adjustment process is usually written

$$Y_t - Y_{t-1} = \phi(Y_t^D - Y_{t-1}), \quad \text{where } 0 < \phi < 1 \tag{11.9}$$

Coefficient ϕ, often called the **adjustment coefficient**, determines how quickly the desired value is realized.

EXERCISE 11.3

What does an adjustment coefficient of .5 imply about the adjustment process? How close will the observed value of Y be to the desired value of Y four periods after a change in X?

The partial adjustment coefficient is a constant. Do you feel that this is a realistic way to model the adjustment processes for capital stock and gasoline prices? If not, what alternative processes would be more realistic?

_____

_____

_____

_____

_____

In 1986 oil prices declined dramatically. Assume that you had previously estimated consumer response to oil prices in the 1970s using a partial adjustment model. Would you feel comfortable using this model to explain consumer response to the oil-price decline?

_____

_____

_____

_____

_____

EXERCISE 11.4

Assume that Y_t^D is a linear function of three variables such that

$$Y_t^D = \alpha + \beta_1 X_{1t} + \beta_2 X_{2t} + \beta_3 X_{3t}$$

Does it matter which variable changes in terms of the partial adjustment process, or does the model assume that the adjustment process is the same for *all* independent variables?

_____

_____

_____

_____

_____

To see how partial adjustment behavior can be estimated as a geometric lag model, substitute Y_t^D in Equation 11.8 into Equation 11.9 and solve for Y_t.

$$Y_t = \alpha\phi + \phi\beta X_t + (1 - \phi)Y_{t-1} + \phi u_t \qquad (11.10)$$

Notice that Equation 11.10 is not quite equivalent to Equation 11.7. The error process in the two formulations is not the same. If u_t is assumed to be a well-behaved random error term, then ϕu_t is also well behaved. While Y_{t-1} is affected by u_{t-1} and all error terms previous to u_{t-1}, it is not affected by u_t. As a result, it can be shown that ordinary least-squares generates consistent estimators. If the error term is not well behaved and exhibits serial correlation, we have a more difficult estimation problem. Once again, the appropriate estimation techniques depend on the assumed error process.

EXERCISE 11.5

Because consumer demand is often distorted in the short run by structural rigidities, demand functions are frequently estimated assuming partial adjustment behavior. Restructure the beef-demand model estimated in Lesson 6 (Exercise 6.7) to allow for partial adjustment with respect to the price of beef. You may have difficulty working a partial adjustment process into your log-linear model. Econometricians write the adjustment process to be consistent with the model for estimation purposes. Thus, if the demand function is

$$Y_t^D = AX_t^\beta \qquad (11.11)$$

the adjustment process consistent with this specification is

$$\left[\frac{Y_t}{Y_{t-1}}\right] = \left[\frac{Y_t^D}{Y_{t-1}}\right]^\phi e^{ut} \qquad (11.12)$$

Write your beef-demand model assuming partial adjustment by showing the equivalent equations for Equations 11.11 and 11.12. (HINT: Substitute your equivalent of Equation 11.11 into your equivalent Equation 11.12.)

Estimate the new model. Write the new estimated model below.

How does the short-run price elasticity differ from the long-run price elasticity?

_____

_____

_____

EXERCISE 11.6

Despite its "bread-and-butter" use by econometricians, many have questioned the applicability of the partial adjustment process to durable goods. What time path for adjustment is assumed by the partial adjustment model? Why might this time path be unreasonable for a durable good?

_____

_____

_____

_____

_____

Others have suggested the partial adjustment process is not valid when more than one independent variable is included in the model. Discuss the relevance of this issue for your beef-demand model. (HINT: What is the adjustment parameter for each independent variable in your partial adjustment beef model? Is this realistic for the beef market?)

_____

_____

_____

_____

_____

Adaptive Expectations Behavior

Economists often argue that a change in some dependent variable is related to the expected level of an independent variable. Formally,

$$Y_t = \alpha + \beta X_t^* + u_t \tag{11.13}$$

where X_t^* is the expected level as opposed to the actual value of X_t. A firm might decide how much labor to hire based on the expected wage rate rather than on the actual wage rate. Because there are costs to hiring and laying off workers, it is more reasonable for a firm to use the expected wage over a period of time rather than the current wage in its profit-maximizing decisions. For similar reasons, a consumer may decide to buy a house on the basis of expected income rather than on current income. It also has been suggested that firms make investment decisions on the basis of expected rather than actual sales.

But how is the expected level of a variable determined? One possibility is to assume that people are basically backward-looking. They determine the current expected level of a variable by looking at past values of the variable. This expectation is revised as new observations occur. If the current value differs from their expected level, people adjust their expected level for the current period. Specifically, the expected level for the current period is assumed to be a weighted average of the current value of the variable and the expected level of the variable in the previous time period.

$$X_t^* = \phi X_t + (1 - \phi)X_{t-1}^*, \qquad \text{where } 0 < \phi < 1 \qquad\qquad (11.14)$$

Equation 11.14 indicates that people adapt their expectations every time period. Coefficient ϕ determines how quickly new evidence is reflected in expectations.

EXERCISE 11.7

How quickly do people adapt their expectations if $\phi = .9$? If $\phi = .1$?

_____

_____

_____

What sort of factors determine the size of ϕ? What magnitude would you associate with slow and fast learners? What magnitudes would you associate with very cautious consumers?

_____

_____

_____

The adaptive expectations model assumes that ϕ is a constant. Are you comfortable with this assumption, or do you feel there are times the assumption may not be correct? Under what conditions would you feel uneasy about assuming ϕ is a constant?

_____

_____

_____

To see how the adaptive expectations model fits the geometric lag specification, rewrite Equation 11.14 for the time period $t - 1$. Remember, if an equation is true at t, it must also be true at $t - 1$:

$$X_{t-1}^* = \phi X_{t-1} + (1 - \phi)X_{t-2}^*$$ (11.15)

Next, substitute Equation 11.15 into Equation 11.14:

$$X_t^* = \phi X_t + (1 - \phi)(\phi X_{t-1} + (1 - \phi)X_{t-2}^*)$$

$$X_t^* = \phi X_t + \phi(1 - \phi)X_{t-1} + (1 - \phi)^2 X_{t-2}^*$$

If this process is continued, substituting for X_{t-2}^*, X_{t-3}^*, and so on, the following function is generated:

$$X_t^* = \phi X_t + \phi(1 - \phi)X_{t-1} + \phi(1 - \phi)^2 X_{t-2} + \phi(1 - \phi)^3 X_{t-3} + \phi(1 - \phi)^4 X_{t-4} + \cdots$$

$$= \phi \sum_{S=0}^{\infty} (1 - \phi)^s X_{t-s}^s$$

Thus, the adaptive expectations model described by Equation 11.13 becomes

$$Y_t = \alpha + \beta\phi \sum_{S=0}^{\infty} (1 - \phi)^s X_{t-s} + u_t$$ (11.16)

EXERCISE 11.8

Apply the Koyck transformation to Equation 11.16.

_____

_____

_____

Notice that the adaptive expectations model and the Koyck geometric model share the same error term.

The adaptive expectations model plays a large role in macroeconomic theory. It is not, however, accepted by all macroeconomists. A significant number of economists feel that the adaptive expectations model is simply wrong. Lesson Note 11.1, taken from a book by Otto Eckstein, discusses some of the econometric evidence and controversy concerning lagging price expectations.[3] Eckstein defines "core inflation" as the trend rate of increase in the cost of the factors of production. His references to equations are to the 800–equation Data Resources, Inc. (DRI) model and a much smaller but related core-inflation model. Notice that price expectations are introduced by constructed variables. The lag pattern for these variables is predetermined, not estimated from the regression discussed in the lesson note. We turn our attention in more detail to issues of price-expectation formulation in Lesson 15, when we examine the empirical issues raised by the Phillips curve. The regression results for the fourth variable look different from the results you are used to seeing. The fourth variable reflects the use of a different kind of lag structure, a polynomial distributed lag structure, which is the topic of Lesson 13.

Lesson Note 11.1

Price Expectations and Core Inflation

The persistence of core inflation is principally due to the extended process by which the price expectations underlying wage and capital cost trends are formed. The delay in the transmission of demand and supply-shock impulses to actual inflation is defined by the lags in the equations which translate these impulses into actual inflation experience (equations 22–27). These lags average two quarters for the various supply shocks and about three quarters for the demand effect. These are short intervals, short enough to be approximated by models of instantaneous adjustment. But the average lag for price expectations in the wage equation is ten quarters and in the interest rate equation it is six quarters, thereby creating very slow adjustment processes.

Before accepting the generally pessimistic conclusions of the core inflation analysis, it is necessary to examine more closely the dynamic processes by which expectations are formed. In this chapter, the empirical underpinnings of this critical element in the core inflation theory are examined through a series of statistical tests of the specifications of the critical wage and interest rate equations.

1. The Rational Expectations Viewpoint

The theory of rational expectations invented by Muth[*] and developed by Lucas[†] is consistent with the core inflation theory in some versions and quite contradictory to it in others. The rational expectations hypothesis maintains that economic agents properly consider the available information in making decisions, and that these decisions will, on the average, be free of systematic forecasting bias. In the case of prices, where the theory has been most commonly applied, this hypothesis asserts that price expectations will be formed on the basis of a mental model which correctly derives the long-term inflation outlook from historical observations and assumptions about monetary policy. Of course, inflation contains an unpredictable element, but under rational expectations the expected value of a probability distribution of future prices would be correct.

The empirical implementation of the Core Inflation Model is consistent with this "weak" version of the rational expectations theory. As the equation displayed in [Table 11.2] shows, the coefficients on the price expectations terms in the DRI model's wage equation sum to 0.84, sufficiently close to unity not to be significantly different. Price expectations in the long-term interest rate equation . . ., the other important testing ground of the rational expectations assumption, also show a value close to unity. Thus, at this level of specificity, the core inflation theory is consistent with the rational expectations viewpoint.

The widely heralded and debated policy conclusions of the rational expectations theory depend upon a stronger set of assumptions, however. If individuals anticipate the inflationary results of policy correctly, they would sharply reduce, and in a limiting case fully defeat, the intended results of policy. Easier money would immediately produce higher inflation and no change in output or unemployment. This reasoning requires instant learning, i.e., that expectations are not only free of bias, but that they are formed and acted on immediately upon receipt of new information. This is

---

[*]John F. Muth, "Rational Expectations and the Theory of Price Movements," *Econometrrca*, July 1961, pp. 315–335.
[†]R. E. Lucas, Jr., "Econometric Policy Evaluation, A Critique," in Karl Brunner and Allan H. Meltzer, eds., *The Phillips Curve and Labor Markets* (Amsterdam: North-Holland Publishing Co., 1976), pp. 19–46; and R. J. Gordon, "Can Econometric Policy Evaluation Be Salvaged? A Comment," *ibid.*, pp. 47–61.

the "strong" rational expectations hypothesis.

Under this "strong" rational expectations viewpoint, the core inflation theory could not be correct. The gradual determination of the core inflation rate depends upon the existence of slow learning processes by which price expectations are formed. Thus, the smoothness and persistence of the inflation expectations build-up is created by the slow learning processes by which individuals extract additional information from actual economic data, letting several years of experience accumulate before changing their fundamental judgment on the inflation outlook.

The same disagreement applies to ex ante calculations about the future of core inflation. If "strong" rational expectations apply, the announcement of a changed economic policy regime, such as the adoption of monetarist rules with modest targets, would be processed through the mental models in the minds of economic agents and would result in an immediate lowering of inflation expectations. Long-term interest rates would therefore fall and wage claims would decline drastically, reducing core inflation upon receipt of the announcement. Even if policy announcements lack credibility with a public insisting on actual experience, a quick learning process might still produce a close approximation to the "strong" rational expectations result. Tight money would lower aggregate demand and reduce sensitive commodity prices to produce reductions in the short-term inflation record. Demand effects might still take two or three quarters to affect the price indexes, but this observed information would then be quickly processed into lower inflation expectations.

The key factual and theoretical issue, therefore, dividing the "strong" rational expectations viewpoint from the core inflation approach is the assumption about the speed of learning of households and businesses from actual experience or from policy announcements. If learning processes are rapid, the rewards for anti-inflationary demand policies would be great, and the costs in terms of lost output and unemployment would be small. On the other hand, if the kinds of equations built into the DRI model, embodying gradual learning processes, describe the empirical reality, then core inflation is stubborn indeed, and the progress

that could be achieved by politically plausible demand policies, including the monetarist recipe of an orderly reduction of money growth, would be disappointingly small.

2. Price Expectations in the Wage Equation: Has Learning Speeded Up?

Traditional wage equations rely on extended distributed lags to define the price expectations which define wage claims. An earlier paper using data through 1976 tested alternative equations with different expectation mechanisms. Gradual learning from actual experience rather than quick learning from recent data about prices or money proved to be the better explanation of the data.*

One might conjecture that the period of extreme inflation has accelerated the learning processes by which price expectations are formed. If learning has quickened, then the equations based on the statistical record of a much longer postwar interval would not be representative of conditions in the future and would portray too pessimistic a prospect. If price expectations adapt more quickly now than they did in the past, the rate of wage increase would retreat more rapidly in response to the better price performance that could be created by weak demand and favorable shock experience, and the labor cost element of core inflation would show bigger improvement.

What has happened to price expectations of workers and employees during the last six years of rapid inflation? To begin to answer this question, a series of statistical tests have been performed using wage equations which follow the standard formulation of the literature. The results are quite surprising, both for the assessment of the core inflation analysis and for the strong version of the rational expectations theory.

The wage equation in the DRI model, shown in [Table 11.2], relies on the inverse of a demography-corrected national unemployment rate, proxy variables for the period of intense guidepost policy in the mid-1960s and the wage-price controls of 1971–74, as well as a dummy variable for the first quarter of 1964 when there appears to have been a major measurement error in the official data. The price expectations factor in the wage equation is

---

*Otto Eckstein, "Economic Theory and Econometric Models," Paper presented to Ann Arbor Conference on Econometric Models, August 1978 (to be published in the Conference volume).

modeled through two variables: expectations based on the short-term price experience of the preceding four quarters with a coefficient of .21, and expectations based on a longer experience using a decay factor of .15, with a coefficient of .63. The sum of the price coefficients, .84, is sufficiently close to unity to be consistent with rational expectations.

While this is an equation with good statistical properties, it has a systematic bias beginning in 1974. The equation overpredicts wage changes, indicating that, as a first approximation, the reaction of wages to prices has become weaker, not stronger, since the OPEC burst of energy inflation.

Table 11.2
Wage Equation in the DRI Model

Ordinary Least-Squares

Quarterly (1956:1 to 1979:1)—93 Observations
Dependent Variable: 400*log(JAHEADJEA/JAHEADJEA(–1))

		Coefficient	Standard Error	t-Stat	Independent Variable
1)	....	0.206108	0.06456	3.192	100*log(PC(–1)/PC/(–5))
2)	....	0.629963	0.07306	8.623	PCEXP85
3)		11.1579	0.6999	15.94	1/(RU-RUADJ)
4)	....				PDL(%MINWAGE400,1,4,FAR)
/0	....	0.0102843	0.003743		
/1	....	0.00771322	0.002808		
/2	....	0.00514215	0.001872		
/3	....	0.00257107	0.0009359		
Sum	....	0.0257107	0.009359	2.747	
Average	....	1.00000	0.0	NC	
5)	....	0.605270	0.2026	2.988	DGPOST
6)	....	2.13063	0.5253	4.056	ALTP1
7)	....	–2.25031	0.7629	–2.950	DMY641

R-Bar squared: 0.8573
F-statistic (7,86): 764.5
Durbin–Watson statistic: 1.4632
Sum of squared residuals: 47.34
Standard error of the regression: 0.7419   Normalized: 0.1393

JAHEADJEA is the index of hourly earnings of private nonfarm production workers,
PC is the implicit price deflator for personal consumption expenditures,
PCEXP85 is the expected rate of inflation for personal expenditures deflator (numerals indicate persistence factor),
RU is the unemployment rate for all civilian workers,
RUADJ is the adjustment to the full-employment unemployment rate,
%MINWAGE400 is the logarithmic first difference of MINWAGE,
DGPOST is the guidepost dummy,
ALTP1 is a dummy variable for Phase 1 of the Nixon Controls Program,
DMY641 is the dummy for the break in the JAHEADJEA series, apparent data error.

Source: Eckstein, O. *Core Inflation* (Englewood Cliffs, N.J.: Prentice-Hall, 1981), 72–76.

Geometric Lags II

1. To learn how the permanent-income hypothesis can be empirically defined using a geometric lag model

2. To learn how to restructure the Lesson 3 consumption function model to reflect the permanent-income hypothesis

3. To learn how to estimate demand models for consumer durables using the permanent-income hypothesis

Consumption Function

It is time to return to the story of the consumption function, which we left dangling rather unceremoniously in Lesson 3. You will remember that the most troubling aspects of Duesenberry's formulation centered on the assumptions of proportionate response and irreversible behavior. A function reflecting a partial adjustment of consumers to income changes seemed to many to be more in accord with consumer behavior. Duesenberry himself discussed the possibility of a gradual adjustment based on consumer psychology. But it was T. M. Brown who first estimated a consumption function based on what he termed the "persistence of habit in consumer behavior."[1]

Brown argued that the effect of past habits on current consumption behavior declines continuously over time rather than discontinuously as in Duesenberry's relative income formulation. During a recession, for example, consumers cling to their old habitual level of consumption. Given this argument, it is not surprising that Brown structured his consumption function in terms of a partial adjustment process.

The partial adjustment consumption function is

$$C_t^D = \beta_0 + \beta_1 Q_t + u_t \tag{12.1}$$

where C_t^D is the desired level of consumption. The partial adjustment process is given by

$$C_t - C_{t-1} = \phi(C_t^D - C_{t-1}) \tag{12.2}$$

Substituting Equation 12.1 into Equation 12.2 gives

$$C_t = \phi\beta_0 + \phi\beta_1 Q_t + (1 - \phi)C_{t-1} + u_t \tag{12.3}$$

While some economists were thinking about fitting a lag structure to the consumption function to improve Duesenberry's specification, others were thinking about the theory underlying the consumption function itself. It was argued that current disposable income is *not* the correct income variable. This argument emerged from two different but compatible hypotheses of the consumption function: the **permanent-income hypothesis** and the **life-cycle hypothesis**. Today, economists use a consumption function that combines elements of both hypotheses. To see how an empirical specification is developed from this modern consumption function theory, we will discuss the permanent-income hypothesis developed by Milton Friedman in some detail.[2] The life-cycle hypothesis adds to the resulting specification by strengthening the case for including wealth in the consumption function.

Friedman argues that the consumer does not determine his or her consumption spending in terms of current disposable income. Instead, the consumer uses his or her permanent income. What is permanent income? Friedman formally defines permanent income as the amount the consumer could consume while maintaining his or her wealth intact. Permanent income is thus a much longer-run income concept than is current disposable income.

Friedman further argues that the consumer determines permanent consumption as a direct proportion of permanent income. Letting k be a constant, the consumption function is

$$C_t^P = kQ_t^P \tag{12.4}$$

Permanent income and permanent consumption in general will not be the same as observed disposable income and observed consumption. Friedman defines the difference between permanent income and current income as a transitory component, which can be positive or negative. The same is true of the difference between permanent consumption and observed consumption. Letting Q_t^T and C_t^T be the transitory components, current income and consumption at time t are

$$C_t = C_t^P + C_t^T \tag{12.5}$$

$$Q_t = Q_t^P + Q_t^T \tag{12.6}$$

Friedman next assumes that the mean values of the transitory components are zero and that the transitory and permanent components are independent. He also assumes that transitory components of income and consumption are independent.

This last assumption remains controversial. It implies that a windfall gain in income must be saved and not spent on consumption goods. Some economists have argued that a small positive correlation is consistent with the permanent-income hypothesis if consumers are assumed to have a less-than-infinite time horizon. The most significant thing to understand about this controversy is that Friedman, like many other economists, assumes that consumption does not include consumer durables; consumer durables are treated as saving. Thus, transitory income that is spent on items such as cars and refrigerators is treated as saving.

How does Friedman solve the empirical puzzles associated with the simple consumption function? Because permanent consumption is proportional to permanent income and transitory fluctuations in consumption and income average out to zero, the long-run ratio of consumption to income is constant. Thus, the permanent-income hypothesis explains the constant average propensity to consume found in long-run historical data.

The other empirical puzzles are explained by extending the argument that observed income is a poor measure of permanent income. Consider an increase in observed income during an economic expansion. This increase will not immediately change consumers' perceptions of their permanent incomes by an equal amount. Consumption spending continues to be based on permanent income. Figure 12.1 shows what happens as aggregate income increases from Q_0 to Q_1. Consumption shifts from point N_0 on the long-run consumption function to N_1 on a short-run consumption function. Only after consumers recognize Q_1 as the new level of permanent income will they move to N_2 on the long-run function. The short-run consumption function drifts upward as Q_1 becomes accepted as the new level of permanent income. The discrepancy between observed and permanent income thus resolves the puzzle between the long-run consumption function with no intercept term and the short-run consumption function with an intercept term.

At the level of the individual consumer, the discrepancy also explains the consumption results associated with family-budget studies. Relatively high-income families are likely to be experiencing large, positive transitory components in their income. These families base their consumption spending on their lower level of permanent income. Similarly, low-income families are likely to be experiencing large, negative transitory components in their income. These consumers base their consumption spending on their higher level of permanent income. When contrasted with middle-income families, high-income families appear to save proportionately more and low-income families proportionately less.

Friedman's permanent-income hypothesis reconciles the empirical puzzles that could not be solved by the simple consumption function. It also is an extremely rich hypothesis in terms of its empirical predictions. For example, self-employed individuals have proportionately greater transitory components in their income than do salaried workers. It follows that self-employed individuals as a group should have a lower average propensity to consume. This prediction is confirmed by empirical studies.

We may have a consumption function grounded in theoretical elegance, but how does the econometrician deal with unobservable variables like permanent income and permanent consumption? From the econometrician's perspective, this appears to be a problem in measurement error. Given the assumptions made by Friedman, the "error" in consumption, the dependent variable, can be assumed to be captured by the random error term. The measurement error in income, however, represents measurement error in an independent variable. Unlike the measurement error in the dependent variable, this type of error can be shown to cause biased and inconsistent ordinary least-squares estimators.

How can an empirically meaningful measure of permanent income be constructed for purposes of estimating the aggregate consumption function? Friedman resolves the measurement problem by arguing that permanent income can be measured by applying adaptive expectations to current and past levels of disposable income. In other words, consumers can be thought of as viewing their permanent income as a geometrically weighted sum of current and past income. Thus, permanent income at time t is

$$Q_t^P = \beta \sum_{i=0}^{\infty} \gamma^i Q_{t-1} + u_t \qquad (12.7)$$

Figure 12.1
The Consumption Function for Permanent Income

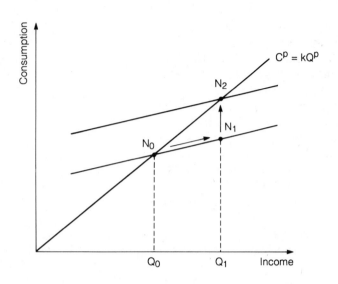

EXERCISE 12.1

Using the Koyck transformation, show how Friedman's consumption function can be estimated with ordinary least-squares.

_____

_____

_____

_____

EXERCISE 12.2

Do you see any difference between the Koyck-transformed consumption function and Equation 12.3? Be careful; make sure you look at the error process described by each formulation.

_____

_____

_____

_____

_____

If you added a second variable, such as wealth, to the consumption function, how would the two formulations differ?

_____

_____

_____

_____

Answering the two items in this exercise should convince you that equations that look similar may have different implications when we consider *all* the assumptions that go into their formulation. Econometricians must be very careful when constructing models.

We have come a long way from Keynes's intuitive passage in Lesson 3. Initial research on the simple consumption function generated new questions, which led to new arguments and ultimately to formal theories of the consumption function. The story is not over. Recent research once again has raised some puzzling questions. These questions center on the reaction of consumers to transitory-income changes and on the motives for saving. The reaction to transitory-income changes and saving appears to be too large.

EXERCISE 12.3

Reestimate the consumption function you estimated in Lesson 3. First, restructure your Lesson 3 consumption function to reflect the permanent-income hypothesis. Write your new model below.

Estimate both the old and new model for the time period 1961.1–1980.4. Write your estimated equations below.

Forecast consumption spending for 1981.1 to 1986.4 using both models. Plot the forecast values for each model along with the actual values in Figure 12.2. (If your software does the plot, attach the plot to the figure.) Which consumption function do you prefer?

_____

_____

_____

_____

_____

Compare the lag structure in your permanent-income model with that found by the student in Table 11.1. Which estimation technique determines the "right" lag structure?

_____

_____

_____

_____

_____

_____

Permanent Income and Consumer Durables

In Lesson 5, you constructed a model of the demand for new automobiles. It was noted then that autos are a durable good, with consumers purchasing autos for the flow of services they provide. It is the consumption of automobile services, not the autos themselves, that constitutes the correct dependent variable in your model. The Data Bank does not give you a service measure because such a measure is not regularly calculated. Even if it were, measurement difficulties are such that the variable would reflect a substantial amount of error. The permanent-income hypothesis can help resolve this measurement dilemma.

The permanent-income hypothesis implies that the consumption of services from durable goods should be proportional to permanent income, just as the consumption of nondurables and services is proportional to permanent income. Let S be the flow of consumption services from autos. It follows from the permanent-income hypothesis that

$$S_t = kQ_t^P = k \sum_{i=0}^{\infty} w^i Q_{t-i} + u_t$$

(12.8)

Next, assume that the flow of services is proportional to the stock of autos. Let A be the stock of autos. It follows that A_t is equal to

$$A_t = k' \sum_{i=0}^{\infty} w^i Q_{t-i} + u_t \tag{12.9}$$

where k' is the new constant. Applying the Koyck transformation to Equation 12.9 gives

$$A_t = \beta' Q_t + w A_{t-1} + v_t \tag{12.10}$$

Equation 12.10 is not, however, structured to answer questions directly about the demand for *new* autos. This is easily remedied once it is remembered that new autos add to the stock of autos. Thus, the purchase of new autos at time t is added to the stock of autos at time $t - 1$ to give the existing level of automobile stock. Let D be consumer purchases of new autos. Then,

$$D_t = A_t - A_{t-1} \tag{12.11}$$

Solving Equation 12.11 for A_t and substituting for A_t in Equation 12.10 gives

$$D_t = \beta' Q_t + w A_{t-1} - A_{t-1} + v_t \tag{12.12}$$

We are not quite finished. Unlike nondurable goods, durable goods *depreciate*. Thus, a certain amount of new automobile purchases is not an addition to the stock of autos but a replacement of old autos. Recall from your economic principles course that depreciation measures in the economist's sense of depreciation are almost impossible to obtain. Accounting depreciation numbers are only loosely associated with true depreciation. Have we reached an impasse in our attempt to estimate automobile demand? Econometricians are very inventive people about such things. Let's see what happens if we assume that depreciation is proportional to the stock of autos. Let B be depreciation. Then, B_t is

$$B_t = \phi A_{t-1} \tag{12.13}$$

Subtracting B_t from the left-hand side of Equation 12.12 and rearranging the equation so that D_t is the only left-handed variable gives

$$D_t = \beta' Q_t - (1 - w - \phi) A_{t-1} + v_t \tag{12.14}$$

This equation can be estimated with ordinary least-squares.

EXERCISE 12.4

Would you estimate Equation 12.14 any differently than Equation 12.12?

_____

_____

_____

In what way would your interpretation of the estimated coefficient for A_{t-1} differ between the two regressions?

_____

_____

_____

_____

_____

_____

EXERCISE 12.5

Restructure your Lesson 5 auto-demand model to reflect the permanent-income hypothesis. Write your new model below.

Estimate the new model. Write the estimated new model below.

Is this new model better than your earlier model?

_____

_____

_____

_____

_____

_____

_____

Polynomial Lags

1. To review the polynomial distributed lag model

2. To learn how to estimate a model with a polynomial lag distribution using econometric software

In the last two lessons, you learned how to include geometric lags in your models. The lag parameters in the general distributed lag model were assumed to be generated by a geometrically declining function. Partial adjustment behavior and adaptive expectations behavior were shown to generate geometric lags. These behaviors have many applications in econometrics, but there are times that other lag structures are suggested by economic theory. Lesson Note 13.1 gives an example of a relationship requiring a complex lag structure; the relationship between the value of a country's currency and its trade balance.

Lesson 5 also introduced a problem requiring a complex lag structure. Think for a moment about the relationship between output and investment spending for new plant and equipment explored in Lesson 5. Does the adaptive expectations model give a realistic description of how firms view the effects of past output on their current investment spending? Specifically, is the previous quarter's output the most significant output influencing the decision? Firms must first decide if a rising or falling output is likely to continue in the future. They must then appropriate funds. This decision process takes time; investment spending itself takes time. All this suggests that a geometric lag pattern for output may not be realistic. Output some quarters previous to the present, not last quarter's output, may be the most significant influence on the current level of investment spending. Figure 13.1 shows a variety of possible lag patterns for such a relationship.

Does one of these patterns seem appropriate for the investment function? If so, how can the lag parameters be estimated? Notice that the last question is really a question about specifying a functional form to describe the lag parameters. Although economists have used various functional forms to examine investment spending, this lesson restricts its attention to the **polynomial function**. The polynomial function is quite flexible and can generate a variety of lag patterns, depending on the degree of the polynomial assumed. Figure 13.2 shows a few of the numerous lag patterns associated with varying degrees of the polynomial function. Not all of the lag structures shown in Figure 13.1 can be estimated with a polynomial lag, but close approximations are possible in each case. This lesson works through a simple example of how polynomial lags are estimated. Once you finish the lesson, you will be able to include polynomial lags in your models.

Estimating models with polynomial lags from scratch is very tedious business, involving considerable algebraic manipulation and variable transformation. For this reason, econometric software includes programs to perform all needed calculations; you need only supply a few pieces of information. The software does the work for you. It is nevertheless important that you understand how the software works. The instructions you give the software impose parameter restrictions, and you must understand these restrictions to interpret your results correctly.

Lesson Note 13.1

The *J*-Curve

In your economic principles course, you learned that there is an inverse relationship between a country's trade balance and the value of its currency. Specifically, if a country's currency depreciates, its imports should decrease while its exports increase. But the suggested inverse relationship takes time to emerge, and it is one of the more significant lag relationships confronting policymakers concerned with improving a country's trade balance.

Following a depreciation, the prices a country pays for its imports rise relative to the prices paid for domestic goods. The physical volume of imports does not change initially. The value of imports in terms of domestic currency must therefore rise. In other words, the country now buys the same volume of imports for a higher price. This *price effect* suggests that a depreciation should be followed by a worsening trade balance. Over time, however, the depreciation causes an adjustment in the volume of imports. It takes time for consumers and business firms to adjust their habits, renegotiate contracts, and find domestic sources of supply. But consumers and business firms do substitute gradually toward domestic goods, which are now cheaper in relative terms. Further, foreigners find that the country's exports are now relatively less expensive than their own goods. Foreigners thus increase their purchases of the country's exports. Unlike the price effect, this *volume effect* improves the country's trade balance.

The long-run result of a depreciation depends on the relative strengths of the price and volume effects. Econometricians have conclusively established that the volume effects are sufficiently large to cause an industrialized country's trade balance to improve in the long run. They also have determined that the trade balance will indeed worsen in the short run. A country's trade balance thus traces out a time path resembling the letter *J*. This is why the relationship between a depreciation and the resulting trade balance is frequently referred to as the *J* **curve effect**.

How long does all this take for the United States? It has been estimated that it takes at least three quarters to achieve 75 percent of the full benefit for imports. In contrast, it takes at least six quarters to achieve 75 percent of the full benefit for exports. This asymmetry with respect to exports and imports is not surprising because a large percentage of United States exports are capital goods. It takes much longer to negotiate capital-goods contracts and deliver capital goods than it does consumption goods. The econometric evidence further suggests that following a major depreciation the United States can expect its trade balance to worsen for approximately one year before it begins to improve.

Figure 13.1
Examples of Lag Structures

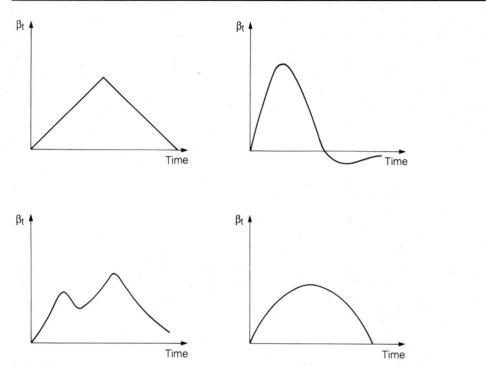

Figure 13.2
Polynomial Lag Examples

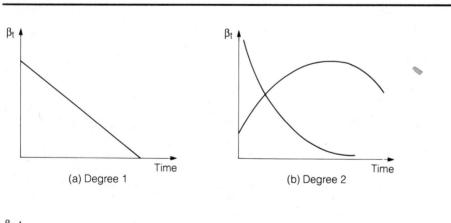

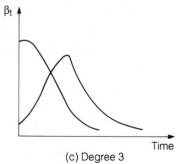

Estimating a Polynomial Lag Structure

How Lag Parameters Are Generated

Before seeing how to estimate a model assuming a polynomial lag, let's go over how a polynomial function generates the lag parameters. You should recall the general distributed lag model from Lesson 11.

$$Y_t = \gamma + \beta_0 X_t + \beta_1 X_{t-1} + \beta_2 X_{t-2} + \dots + u_t \qquad (13.1)$$

Lag parameters are now assumed to be generated by a polynomial function. If we assume a second-degree polynomial function, the lag parameters are described by

$$\beta_i = \alpha_0 + \alpha_1 i + \alpha_2 i^2 \qquad (13.2)$$

where i is the lag period and α_0, α_1, and α_2 are constants. Notice that Equation 13.2 is a polynomial function. The independent variable is the lag period. The dependent variable is the lag parameter. The lag parameters for the first three periods are

$$\begin{aligned}
\beta_0 &= \alpha_0 \\
\beta_1 &= \alpha_0 + \alpha_1 + \alpha_2 \\
\beta_2 &= \alpha_0 + 2\alpha_1 + 4\alpha_2 \\
\beta_3 &= \alpha_0 + 3\alpha_1 + 9\alpha_2
\end{aligned} \qquad (13.3)$$

The current period effect of the independent variable is shown by β_0.

EXERCISE 13.1

What are the lag parameters for the fourth and fifth periods?

$\beta_4 =$

$\beta_5 =$

To generate the lag parameters, the degree of the polynomial must be assumed. But how do econometricians determine the degree of the polynomial? If they don't have any idea about how the lag parameters should look, they simply guess. But in general, the degree of the polynomial should be one more than the number of turning points thought to exist in the lag structure.

Once the degree of the polynomial is selected, the econometrician's task to derive estimates of the α_js. It is these values that determine the β_ks, the lag parameters. Figure 13.3a shows the lag parameters for one set of α_js estimated for Equation 13.2.

Figure 13.3
Calculation of Lag Parameters

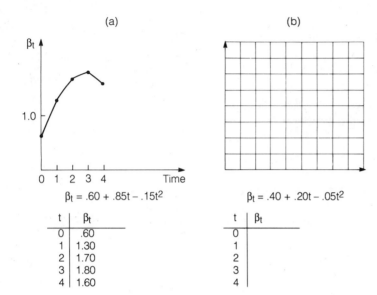

(a)

$\beta_t = .60 + .85t - .15t^2$

t	β_t
0	.60
1	1.30
2	1.70
3	1.80
4	1.60

(b)

$\beta_t = .40 + .20t - .05t^2$

t	β_t
0	
1	
2	
3	
4	

EXERCISE 13.2

Solve for the lag parameters associated with $\hat{\alpha}_0 = .40$, $\hat{\alpha}_1 = .20$, and $\hat{\alpha}_2 = .05$ in Figure 13.3b. Assume a four-period lag. Record your values in the area provided.

Estimation Procedure

Besides the degree of the polynomial, the number of lag periods must be assumed before any estimation attempt is made. Unless there is some economic argument for determining the lag period, which there almost never is, the econometrician selects a "reasonable" value. This value must be larger than the degree of the polynomial. To keep the algebra simple, assume the lag period is four. The procedure for estimating the αs is then straightforward.

Begin by substituting for the βs in Equation 13.1 using Equation 13.2.

$$Y_t = \gamma + \alpha_0 X_t + (\alpha_0 + \alpha_1 + \alpha_2)X_{t-1} + (\alpha_0 + 2\alpha_1 + 4\alpha_2)X_{t-2} + (\alpha_0 + 3\alpha_1 + 9\alpha_2)X_{t-3} +$$
$$(\alpha_0 + 4\alpha_1 + 16\alpha_2)X_{t-4} + u_t \tag{13.4}$$

To estimate the α_js, the terms in Equation 13.4 must be regrouped:

$$Y_t = \gamma + \alpha_0(X_t + X_{t-1} + X_{t-2} + X_{t-3} + X_{t-4}) + \alpha_1(X_{t-1} + 2X_{t-2} + 3X_{t-3} + 4X_{t-4}) +$$
$$\alpha_2(X_{t-1} + 4X_{t-2} + 9X_{t-3} + 16X_{t-4}) + u_t \tag{13.5}$$

Notice that new variables must be constructed from the original X values. Once this is done, Equation 13.5 can be estimated with ordinary least-squares.

Unlike the Koyck procedure, the polynomial lag procedure does not change the random error term, which is assumed to be well behaved. We don't have to worry about complications introduced by using a lagged dependent variable as an independent variable on the right-hand side of the regression equation. Also, other independent variables can clearly be included in Equation 13.5. We did not indicate additional variables to keep the algebra relatively simple. Although polynomial lags can be assumed for any or all of other independent variables in a model, it is highly unusual to assume polynomial lags for more than a few variables. Consequently, most econometric software limits the number of polynomial weighted variables.

Restrictions

The discussion to this point indicates that you must tell your econometric software the *degree of the polynomial* and the *number of lag periods* assumed for your lag structure. The software may also ask you for "head" and "tail" restrictions or "near" and "far" restrictions. This allows you to force the lag parameters for the near and far end of the distribution to 0.

Let's see what happens when we restrict the near end of our second-degree polynomial. Examine the lag parameters shown in Equation 13.3. If the near-end lag parameter is 0, β_0 must be 0; however, this implies that α_0 is 0. The resulting lag parameters are

$$\beta_0 = 0$$
$$\beta_1 = \alpha_1 + \alpha_2$$
$$\beta_2 = 2\alpha_1 + 4\alpha_2$$
$$\beta_3 = 3\alpha_1 + 9\alpha_2$$

In other words, the new polynomial lag structure is

$$\beta_i = \alpha_1 i + \alpha_2 i^2 \tag{13.6}$$

Once we have the new "restricted" lag structure, we proceed as before. Equation 13.6 is substituted into Equation 13.1 to yield the new regression model.

It should be emphasized here that econometricians realize that all the restrictions they impose on polynomial lag parameters are probably incorrect. As a result, the parameter estimators are biased; but these biased estimators have smaller variances than the unrestricted estimators associated with the model.

EXERCISE 13.3

Derive the regression model associated with Equation 13.6, assuming a four-period lag structure.

_____

_____

_____

_____

_____

A student estimates an investment function for plant and equipment spending (BFI72) assuming a second-degree polynomial with a ten-quarter lag for the independent variable GNP. The student also restricts the near end of the polynomial. The regression results, adjusted for serial correlation using the Cochrane–Orcutt procedure, are shown in Table 13.1. Fill in the blank areas of the lag coefficients table. (HINT: PDL1 and PDL2 are *dependent* random variables.)

Table 13.1
Polynomial Regression

SMPL 1961.3–1985.2
96 Observations
LS // Dependent Variable is BFI72

Variable	Coefficient	Std. Error	T Stat.	Two-Tail Sig.
C	–39.811345	11.501751	–3.4613292	0.001
PDL1($\hat{\alpha}_1$)	0.0075954	0.0015095	5.0316722	0.000
PDL2($\hat{\alpha}_2$)	–0.0007463	0.0002131	–3.5030566	0.001

R squared	0.992792	Mean of dependent var	113.5662
Adjusted R squared	0.992557	S.D. of dependent var	32.97406
S.E. of regression	2.844745	Sum of squared resid	744.5167
Durbin–Watson stat	0.969998	F statistic	4223.950
Log likelihood	–234.5407		

Estimator Variance–Covariance Matrix

	C	PDL1	PDL2
C	132.290267	–.00345238	.00022786
PDL1	–.00345238	2.2786 D-06	–3.1969 D-07
PDL2	.00022786	–3.1969 D-07	4.5391 D-08

Lag Coefficients

Lag Distribution of GNP72	Lag		Coef.	S.E.
*	0	0.00000	0.00000	
: *	1	0.00685	0.00130	
: * *	2		_____	_____
: * *	3	0.01607	0.00263	
: * *	4	0.01844	0.00268	
: * *	5	0.01932	0.00233	
: * *	6	0.01870	0.00166	
: * *	7	0.01660	0.00115	
: * *	8	0.01300	0.00209	
: *	9	0.00791	0.00403	
: *	10	0.00132	0.00651	

Investment Functions in Differenced Form

Because this lesson focuses on estimating investment good models, we need to discuss a general estimation difficulty associated with these models. Specifically, a capital-stock variable is often not available. Even if a capital-stock variable is available, the numerous difficulties associated with measuring capital stock frequently cause econometricians to have little confidence in the measure. It is sometimes not clear which is the lesser of two problems: having or not having a capital-stock measure. The issue cannot be ignored because economic theory suggests that the demand for an investment good is inversely related to the stock of the good.

When a capital-stock variable is not available, or not to be trusted, the econometrician may be able to take advantage of an identity. Investment spending must, by definition, be equal to the change in the stock of capital plus depreciation. In other words, gross investment is equal to net investment plus replacement investment:

$$I_t = (K_t - K_{t-1}) + D_t \tag{13.7}$$

where I_t is investment spending during time period t, K_t is the level of capital stock during time period t, and D_t is depreciation during time period t.

Let's see how this identity can be used to get around the problem of not having a capital-stock measure. Assume an econometrician has developed the following linear model of business spending on plant and equipment:

$$I_t = \beta_0 + \beta_1 Q_t + \beta_2 R_t + \beta_3 K_t + u_t \tag{13.8}$$

This model assumes a great deal. Specifically, capital stock is assumed to operate separately from income (Q) and the interest rate (R) in determining investment spending. If you are skeptical of this assumption, your skepticism is justified. But we are still dealing with single-equation models. The relationship between the interest rate, output level, and investment spending is the stuff of simultaneous models and advanced econometrics.

Suspending his or her disbelief to estimate Equation 13.8, the econometrician first writes the model for time period $t - 1$:

$$I_{t-1} = \beta_0 + \beta_1 Q_{t-1} + \beta_2 R_{t-1} + \beta_3 K_{t-1} + u_{t-1} \tag{13.9}$$

When Equation 13.9 is subtracted from Equation 13.8, the resulting equation is referred to as the model in **differenced form**:

$$(I_t - I_{t-1}) = \beta_1(Y_t - Y_{t-1}) + \beta_2(R_t - R_{t-1}) + \beta_3(K_t - K_{t-1}) + (u_t - u_{t-1}) \tag{13.10}$$

Identity 13.7 can now be substituted for $(K_t - K_{t-1})$ in the differenced form model:

$$(I_t - I_{t-1}) = \beta_1(Y_t - Y_{t-1}) + \beta_2(R_t - R_{t-1}) + \beta_3(I_t - D_t) + (u_t - u_{t-1}) \tag{13.11}$$

which is usually written as

$$(I_t - I_{t-1}) = \beta_1(Y_t - Y_{t-1}) + \beta_2(R_t - R_{t-1}) + \beta_3 I_t - \beta_3 D_t + (u_t - u_{t-1}) \tag{13.12}$$

Equation 13.12 meets all the conditions necessary to apply ordinary least-squares. The effect of capital stock is estimated by the regression coefficient for β_3. Depreciation is sometimes assumed to be a constant. Under this assumption, the term $\beta_3 D_t$ is a constant. The effect of depreciation is then measured by the model's intercept term.

EXERCISE 13.5

How is Equation 13.12 altered if depreciation is assumed to be *proportional* to the existing capital stock?

$$D_t = kK_{t-1}$$

_____

_____

_____

_____

EXERCISE 13.6

Restructure your Investment model to include at least one independent variable with a polynomial lag. Also make sure that your model includes a capital-stock variable. Specify your new model below:

Explain why you selected the polynomial degree, number of lag periods, and restrictions.

_____

_____

_____

_____

_____

Estimate your model. Write the estimated model below.

Contrast your new model with your earlier model. Which model do you prefer?

_____

_____

_____

_____

_____

_____

_____

_____

Suggested Reading

You might suspect correctly that estimating investment is more complex than discussed in this lesson. Modern investment functions are derived from complex restriction equations based on economic theory. A basic discussion of the issues can be found in Chapter 3 of Wallis's *Topics in Applied Econometrics*, cited in Lesson 7. If you are interested in knowing more about capital-measurement issues, consult D. Usher, ed., "Studies in Income and Wealth," vol. 45, *The Measurement of Capital* (Chicago: The National Bureau of Economic Research, 1980).

Simultaneous Equations

1. To understand the problem of simultaneous equation bias
2. To review the statistical criterion of consistency
3. To learn how to use econometric software to solve a simple simultaneous model

To this point, we have been concerned with single-equation models. Yet the two basic models used by economists, income-determination models and market models, are constructed of more than one equation. Two simple examples are

Income-Determination Model	Market Model
$C_i = \beta_0 + \beta_1 Q_i + u_i$	$q_i^d = \beta_0 + \beta_1 P_i + v_i$
$I_i = \bar{I}$	$q_i^s = \alpha_0 + \alpha_1 P_i$
$Q_i = C_i + I_i$	$q_i^d = q_i^s$
where u is a well-behaved random error term	where v is a well-behaved random error term

Both models contain behavioral equations and equilibrium conditions. Both models generate solutions *simultaneously*. This means that solution values cannot be determined by looking at one equation. The *set* of equations must be used to determine the solution values.

Simultaneous equation models pose two serious problems for econometricians. The first problem is **identification**. The structure of a model may be such that estimates for all the model's parameters are not possible. Identification is not a statistical problem with a statistical solution; it is a problem caused by the *structure* of the model. As such, it has no solution if we believe that the structure of the model is correct.

The second problem is **simultaneous equation bias**. If we estimate one equation in a model using ordinary least-squares, the parameters may be biased. This bias can be assessed and dealt with through alternative estimation techniques. In evaluating these alternative techniques, however, econometricians use probability limits instead of expected values. Because finding a probability limit is a different operation than finding an expected value, a new statistical criterion must be used to assess an estimator. This criterion is **consistency**. Consistency is based on finding the probability limit of an estimator as the sample size goes to infinity. When simultaneous equation bias is present, ordinary least-squares gives biased and inconsistent estimators. Other techniques usually give biased but consistent estimators. Thus, consistency becomes a major criterion for assessing estimators when dealing with simultaneous models.

Your econometric text gives very complete discussions of both identification issues and simultaneous equation bias. This lesson makes no attempt to duplicate these discussions. Instead, the lesson focuses on two basic questions. First, how is simultaneous equation bias generated? Until you understand how simultaneous equation bias comes about, it is hard to come to terms with the complexities of the alternative estimation techniques discussed in your text. Second, why must consistency be used to evaluate estimators? Again, it is very difficult to read your text without understanding why consistency is needed. By working through this lesson, you will gain a better understanding of these two questions. The lesson is organized around estimating the consumption function for the simple income-determination model.

Solving a Simultaneous Model

Graphical Analysis

How are observations generated by a simultaneous model? Examine Figure 14.1, which shows the graphical representation of the simple income-determination model *without* the disturbance term. The two behavioral equations are summed to show total planned expenditures for varying levels of income. The equilibrium condition is shown by the 45° line. Any point on the 45° line is a possible equilibrium point, a point where planned expenditures $(C + I)$ equal the level of income (Q). Equilibrium income is found by observing where the planned expenditures line crosses the 45° line. Equilibrium income is then substituted into the consumption function to find equilibrium consumption spending. The planned expenditures line crosses the 45° line at point w_0 in Figure 14.1. The solution values are Q_0 and C_0.

We can pick any arbitrary level of income and plug it into the consumption function. The resulting consumption spending is what will be observed *if* the arbitrary level of income is the equilibrium level. For example, arbitrarily choose Q_1 as the level of income in Figure 14.1. If Q_1 is the equilibrium level of income, C_1 will be the equilibrium level of consumption spending. But Q_1 is not the equilibrium level of income. We will never observe C_1 and Q_1 as solution values if the model is correct. We can only observe Q_0 and C_0, the solution values for the set of simultaneous equations.

The conclusion that all observations must satisfy a model's equilibrium condition sometimes confuses students. The equilibrium condition is in essence treated as an *identity*, an equation that is true by definition. In fact, some texts write equilibrium conditions with identity signs ($\equiv$) instead of equality signs ($=$). An equilibrium condition is, of course, not an identity. To see the difference, again consider income level Q_1 in Figure 14.1. Assume for a moment that firms mistakenly produce an output level of Q_1, a scenario that is not allowed if the simple income-determination model is correct. The firms find they have overproduced. The planned expenditures line must cross the 45° at point w_1 for Q_1 to be equilibrium income; this is not the case.

But notice that actual income (or output) is still equal to actual consumption spending plus actual investment spending. This is because output not sold is defined by economists as investment spending by firms. It may be unwanted or unplanned investment spending, but it is investment spending nevertheless. Unplanned investment spending is indicated by I_u in Figure 14.1. The sum of actual investment spending $(I + I_u)$ and actual consumption spending (C_1) must be equal to the actual level of output and income (Q_1). The identity must hold re-

Figure 14.1
Simple Income-Determination Model

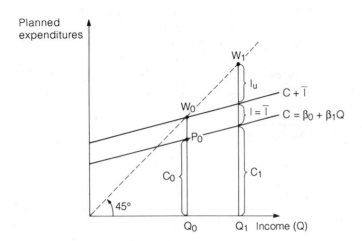

gardless of whether the model is in equilibrium. It is a statement that is true by definition and hence must be true for *any* level of income. In contrast, the equilibrium condition is only satisfied at one income level.

Just remember that when an equilibrium condition is treated as an identity, we are actually assuming that all observations must be consistent with the equilibrium condition. This is a very strong assumption. The assumption may do little damage when models adjust quickly to changes in variables. When models do not adjust quickly, however, disquieting issues are raised. Some of the most controversial, longest running arguments in economics concern how quickly models reach equilibrium. Suffice it to say that when models are allowed to generate disequilibrium values, like Q_1 and C_1, econometricians must structure assumptions about disequilibrium adjustment into their models.

You have already dealt with two such disequilibrium models, adaptive expectations models and partial adjustment models. Similar behaviors can be structured into simultaneous models. The consumption function, for example, is usually structured in an adaptive expectations form in simultaneous equations intended to model real-world economies—usually, but not always. There is currently as much controversy about how to structure disequilibrium adjustments as there is about how quickly markets adjust. The two questions are very much related. New disequilibrium models have been developed that challenge the traditional adaptive expectations mechanism. A discussion of these issues is postponed until the next lesson. Because this lesson is concerned with the more basic issue of simultaneous equation bias, we do not want to complicate the discussion any more than is necessary.

Because we are concerned with estimating the consumption function for the simple income-determination model, let's rewrite the equilibrium condition to show all possible levels of observed equilibrium consumption:

$$C = Q - \bar{I} \tag{14.1}$$

Any solution value for equilibrium consumption spending must lie along this line. Graphically, the 45° line in Figure 14.1 shifts down by the amount $\bar{I}$ and passes through point p_0.

Now assume once again that the model has a disturbance term. To keep our graphical analysis simple, assume that the disturbance term can take on any positive or negative value within some finite range. Because the model solves for equilibrium consumption, we know that we must observe consumption solutions along the equilibrium line. The equilibrium line is shown by $Q - \bar{I}$ in Figure 14.2a. Because the disturbance term varies from period to period, the economy traces out a series of equilibrium values for consumption spending and income between p_1 and p_2.

EXERCISE 14.1

Assume an econometrician estimates a simple consumption model $C = \beta_0 + \beta_1 Q$ using the data shown in Figure 14.2a. What must be the estimate of β_1? If the number of observations increased, would this value change?

_____

_____

_____

_____

What kind of data points would be observed for the market model shown at the beginning of the lesson? What would happen if the econometrician tried to estimate a demand function using this data?

_____

_____

_____

_____

_____

EXERCISE 14.2

Are the econometrician's results in Exercise 14.1 examples of the identification problem discussed in your text?

_____

_____

_____

_____

Figure 14.2
Equilibrium Values for the Income-Determination Model

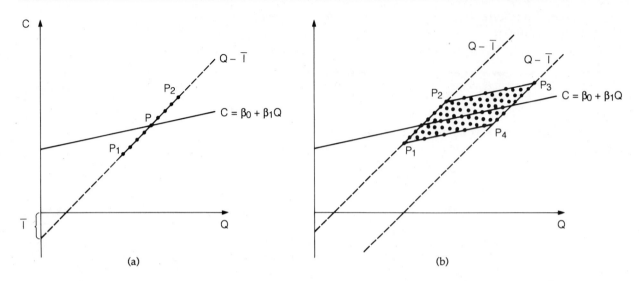

(a) (b)

Now assume that the level of investment spending for the economy varies over several time periods, ranging between I and I'. Observations on equilibrium consumption spending and income must lie within the area $p_1p_2p_3p_4$ shown in Figure 14.2b. The method of ordinary least-squares minimizes the sum of the squared deviations in a *vertical* direction. It follows that the ordinary least-squares regression line computed for the data in Figure 14.2b will tend to pass through p_1 and p_3.[1] If you have trouble seeing this, draw a line through p_1 and p_3 and contrast the deviations around this line with those around the true model $\beta_0 + \beta_1 Q$.

In Lesson 1, you generated consumption spending for a data set of countries using a single-equation model. You were given information about the true model structure and random error term, information an econometrician never has in the real world. We are once again going to assume that you have such information. Only this time, the following simultaneous model is assumed to be true for a set of countries:

$$C_i = 1000 + .6Q_i + u_i, \quad \text{for } i = 1, \dots, n$$

$$Z_i = \bar{Z}_i \tag{14.2}$$

$$Q_i = C_i + Z_i$$

Because we will write the model in deviation form later in the lesson, investment spending is indicated by Z to avoid confusion with the subscript i. The random error term is uniformly distributed between –\$2000 and +\$2000. It is the same random error term assumed in Lesson 2.

EXERCISE 14.3

Plot the true consumption function for the country data set in Figure 14.3. Graphically solve for the values of $p_1p_2p_3$ and p_4 for the country data set assuming investment spending varies between \$200 and \$1100. On the basis of this graphical analysis, evaluate the bias in using ordinary least-squares to estimate the consumption function. (HINT: Contrast the slope of the line through p_1 and p_3 with the slope of the true consumption function.)

_____

_____

_____

_____

_____

_____

Algebraic Solution

While graphical analysis can help us see why simultaneous equation bias comes about, it is obviously limited for dealing with the formal issues of assessing this bias. How are actual numerical solutions for income and consumption spending generated by the simple income-determination model? To answer this question, we must work through three steps.

The first step is to substitute the behavioral equations into the equilibrium condition. This substitution gives

$$Q_i = (1000 + .6Q_i + u_i) + \bar{Z}_i \tag{14.3}$$

This substitution also shows why simultaneous equation bias occurs. The consumption function shows that consumption spending is determined by the random error term and the level of income

But the equilibrium condition also makes consumption a *component* of income. A change in the random error term changes equilibrium consumption spending directly through the consumption function and equilibrium income indirectly through the equilibrium (identity) condition.

This two-way causation is the reason for simultaneous equation bias. In your earlier graphical analysis, the two-way causation was revealed by the introduction of the 45° line. Now we see that the two-way causation is revealed by income occurring on both the right and left of an equal sign in the equation set describing the model's structure.

It should be noted that just because a variable occurs on the right and left sides of equations in a model does not necessarily mean two-way causation is a problem. Consider the following model:

Figure 14.3
True Consumption Function

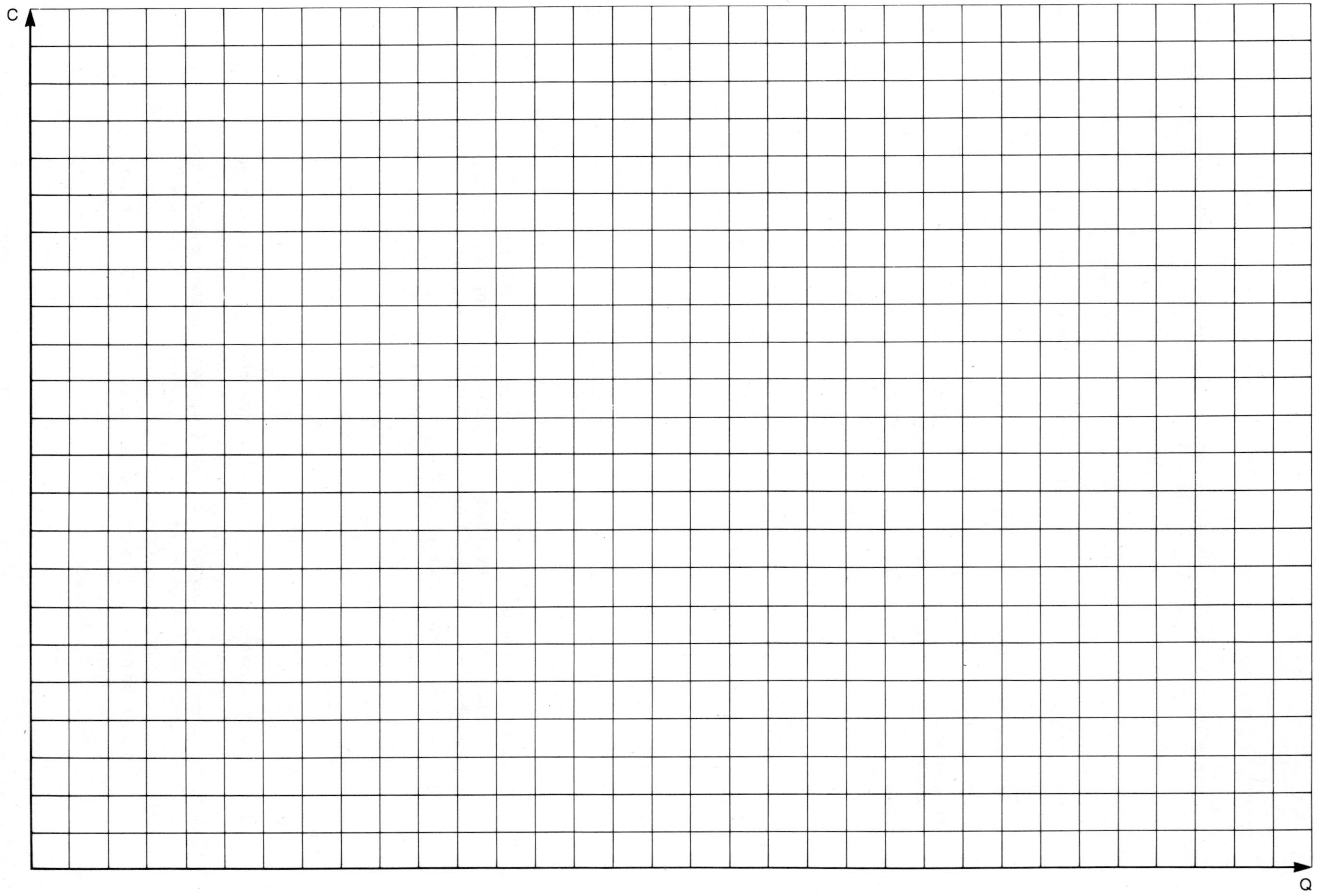

C

Q

$$Y_i = \beta_0 + \beta_1 X_i + u_i$$

$$Z_i = \alpha_0 + \alpha_1 X_i + \alpha_2 Y_i + v_i$$

$$W_i = \gamma_0 + \gamma_1 X_i + \gamma_2 Y_i + \gamma_3 Z_i + t_i$$

where u, v, and t are uncorrelated. The causality implied by this model is

There is no two-way causation in this model and hence no issue of simultaneous equation bias. Put differently, this model does not have to be solved for simultaneously. We first solve for Y in the first equation. We then use this value in the second equation to solve for Z. Finally, we solve for W in the last equation. Such a model is called **recursive**. Each equation in a recursive model can be estimated by ordinary least-squares. Many models used by economists and other social scientists are recursive.

Returning to our problem of how the simultaneous model generates actual data, the second step is to solve Equation 14.3 for equilibrium income. A little algebra gives

$$Q_i = \frac{1000}{(1 - .6)} + \frac{1}{(1 - .6)}\bar{Z}_i + \frac{1}{(1 - .6)}u_i \qquad (14.4)$$

The third step takes the equilibrium level of income and solves for equilibrium consumption spending. Because Equation 14.4 gives the equilibrium level of income, equilibrium consumption spending is found by substituting Equation 14.4 for equilibrium income in the consumption function. This substitution gives

$$C_i = 1000 + .6\left[\frac{1000}{(1 - .6)} + \frac{1}{(1 - .6)}\bar{Z}_i + \frac{1}{(1 - .6)}u_i\right] + u_i \qquad (14.5)$$

which is usually written as

$$C_i = \frac{1000}{(1 - .6)} + \frac{.6}{(1 - .6)}\bar{Z}_i + \frac{1}{(1 - .6)}u_i \qquad (14.6)$$

Equations 14.4 and 14.6 are very important equations to an econometrician; they represent the **reduced form** of the model. The solution values for equilibrium consumption and income are determined within the model. Consumption and income thus are endogenous variables. The level of investment spending is not solved for by the model; its value is determined outside the model and is an exogenous variable. The reduced-form equations show each endogenous variable as a function of the exogenous variables in the model. Your text discusses reduced-form equations in detail. They contain a large amount of information that can be used in estimating structural parameters and forecasting.

What exactly is meant by "determined outside the model"? Exogenous variables are formally assumed to be determined by variables that are independent of both the endogenous variables in the model and the random error term. This is a very strict assumption. The assumption is satisfied if the values for the exogenous variable are a set of fixed constants or the exogenous variable is a random variable distributed independently of the random error term. Given the formal definition of an exogenous variable, it may seem to you that investment spending is not truly an exogenous variable. The level of investment spending in an economy will certainly have endogenous components. You are, of course, right. However, this lesson is intended to clarify foundation concepts, not provide realistic estimates. To keep our minds on the basic issues, we assume that the simple income-determination model is correct. Nevertheless, real-world econometricians are interested in providing realistic estimates. The issues of specifying which variables are exogenous are complex and often controversial. For example, much of the debate on the effect of the money supply on real income centers on the extent to which the money supply includes an endogenous component.

EXERCISE 14.4

To solve for equilibrium consumption (and income) for the country data set, you must know the level of investment spending for each country. These values, shown below, are assumed to be fixed constants. As in Lesson 1, you also need values for the random error term. Use the same values you selected in Lesson 1. Copy these values in Column u. Solve for equilibrium consumption and income using Equations 14.4 and 14.5.

Z	u	Y	C	$\hat{u}$
200	_____	_____	_____	_____
300	_____	_____	_____	_____
300	_____	_____	_____	_____
400	_____	_____	_____	_____
500	_____	_____	_____	_____
800	_____	_____	_____	_____
800	_____	_____	_____	_____
900	_____	_____	_____	_____
1000	_____	_____	_____	_____
1100	_____	_____	_____	_____

As in Lesson 1, an econometrician knows only the values in Columns Z, Y, and C. What happens if an econometrician makes a mistake and assumes that the Lesson 1 model is correct? Estimate the consumption function using the values shown in Columns Y and C. What value do you obtain for $\hat{\beta}_1$?

Calculate the regression residuals and record these in Column $\hat{u}$. Next take all the values for $\hat{\beta}_1$ calculated by your class and draw a frequency distribution for the estimates in Figure 14.4. Is this frequency distribution what you would expect on the basis of your graphical analysis in Figure 14.3?

Calculate the following sums. (HINT: Do you need to calculate sum a, or do you already know the answer?)

a. $\Sigma Y_i \hat{u}_i = $ _____

b. $\Sigma Y_i u_i = $ _____

New Estimator Criterion

To really understand the bias associated with the ordinary least-squares slope estimates in Exercise 14.4, you must be able to derive this bias in a formal manner. Without this formal understanding, you cannot understand how alternative estimators are developed. To simplify the calculations, the model will be discussed in deviation form. The structural model in deviation form is

$$c_i = .6q_i + u_i$$
$$z_i = \bar{z}_i \qquad\qquad (14.7)$$
$$q_i = c_i + z_i$$

The reduced form equations are

$$c_i = \frac{.6}{(1 - .6)}\bar{z}_i + \frac{1}{(1 - .6)}u_i \qquad\qquad (14.8)$$

$$q_i = \frac{1}{(1 - .6)}\bar{z}_i + \frac{1}{(1 - .6)}u_i \qquad\qquad (14.9)$$

The ordinary least-squares slope estimator is

$$\hat{\beta}_1 = \frac{\Sigma c_i q_i}{\Sigma q_i^2} \qquad\qquad (14.10)$$

If the simple income-determination model is the true state of the world, values for equilibrium consumption spending must be generated by the consumption function. Substituting the consumption function for c_i in Equation 14.10 gives

$$\hat{\beta}_1 = \frac{\Sigma(.6q_i + u_i)q_i}{\Sigma q_i^2} = .6 + \frac{\Sigma q_i u_i}{\Sigma q_i^2} \qquad\qquad (14.11)$$

To assess the bias associated with ordinary least-squares, find the expected value of $\hat{\beta}_1$.

$$E(\hat{\beta}_1) = E(.6) + E\left[\frac{\Sigma q_i u_i}{\Sigma q_i^2}\right] \qquad\qquad (14.12)$$

If the Lesson 1 model is the true state of the world, the q_is are fixed constants, and Σq_i^2 is a constant. It follows that

$$E(\hat{\beta}_1) = (.6) + \frac{1}{\Sigma q_i^2}\Sigma q_i E(u_i) \qquad\qquad (14.13)$$

$$E(\hat{\beta}_1) = .6 \quad \text{(because } E(u_i) = 0)$$

The expected value of $\hat{\beta}_1$ is equal to the population parameter. The ordinary least-squares slope estimator is unbiased.

But the Lesson 1 model is not correct. The consumption function is actually part of a larger model, and the q_is are no longer fixed constants. Hence, the argument shown in Equation 14.13 is no longer valid. Variable q_i is now a random variable. If you have trouble seeing this, look around your classroom. Everyone in your class calculated different values for Q in Exercise 14.4. Back in Lesson 1, you all had the same values for Q.

Even though q_i is a random variable, the ordinary least-squares slope estimator is still unbiased *if q_i and u_i are independent*. Let's see why. First, rewrite $E\left[\dfrac{\sum q_i u_i}{\sum q_i^2}\right]$ in terms of its elements:

$$E\left[\frac{\sum q_i u_i}{\sum q_i^2}\right] = E\left[\frac{q_1 u_1}{\sum q_i^2}\right] + E\left[\frac{q_2 u_2}{\sum q_i^2}\right] + \ldots + E\left[\frac{q_{10} u_{10}}{\sum q_i^2}\right] \qquad (14.14)$$

Notice that each term on the right of the equal sign is the product of two random variables:

$$E\left[\frac{\sum q_i u_i}{\sum q_i^2}\right] = E\left[\frac{q_1}{\sum q_i^2} u_1\right] + E\left[\frac{q_2}{\sum q_i^2} u_2\right] + \ldots + E\left[\frac{q_{10}}{\sum q_i^2} u_{10}\right] \qquad (14.15)$$

If q_i and u_i are independent random variables this expression becomes

$$E\left[\frac{\sum q_i u_i}{\sum q_i^2}\right] = E\left[\frac{q_1}{\sum q_i^2}\right] E(u_1) + E\left[\frac{q_2}{\sum q_i^2}\right] E(u_2) + \ldots + E\left[\frac{q_{10}}{\sum q_i^2}\right] E(u_{10}) = 0 \quad \text{(because } E(u_i) = 0 \text{ for all } i) \text{ (14.16)}$$

Thus, $\hat{\beta}_1$ is unbiased when q_i and u_i are independent.

EXERCISE 14.5

On an exam, a student is asked to show that $\hat{\beta}_1$ is unbiased when q and u are independent. The student writes the argument as follows:

$$E\left[\frac{\sum q_i u_i}{\sum q_i^2}\right] = E\left[\frac{q_1 u_1}{\sum q_i^2}\right] + E\left[\frac{q_2 u_2}{\sum q_i^2}\right] + \ldots + E\left[\frac{q_{10} u_{10}}{\sum q_i^2}\right]$$

$$= \frac{E[q_1 u_1]}{E\left[\sum q_i^2\right]} + \frac{E[q_2 u_2]}{E\left[\sum q_i^2\right]} + \ldots + \frac{E[q_{10} u_{10}]}{E\left[\sum q_i^2\right]}$$

$$= 0 \qquad \text{(because } E(q_i u_i) = 0 \text{ for all } i)$$

What is wrong with the student's answer?

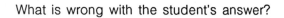

_____

_____

_____

_____

All this means that the econometrician is not in trouble estimating the consumption function with ordinary least-squares if q_i and u_i are independent random variables. After your graphical and algebraic analyses, it should be clear that q_i and u_i are dependent. If you still have trouble seeing this, go back and examine your calculations in Exercise 14.4. Look at Equation 14.5, the equation you used to solve for equilibrium consumption. The value for equilibrium income is shown in brackets. This value is obtained from reduced-form Equation 14.4. Because u_i is a component of equilibrium income, equilibrium income is correlated with u_i. Notice that there is no way you could see this correlation from the regression results. One of the properties of the ordinary least-squares formulas is that $\Sigma q_i \hat{u}_i = 0$. Regression residuals are helpful in diagnosing problems of heteroscedasticity and autocorrelation, but they are not useful in discovering simultaneous equation bias in the first course in econometrics. Advanced econometrics includes some procedures for evaluating simultaneity using residuals.

The ordinary least-squares slope estimator is biased. But what if $\hat{\beta}_1$ *asymptotically* approaches β_1 as the sample size gets very large (goes to infinity). The econometrician still has a biased estimator, but for large samples this bias can be treated as being insignificant. Figure 14.5 shows what the econometrician hopes happens to the distribution for $\hat{\beta}_1$ as the sample size gets large. An estimator that behaves in this fashion is a **consistent estimator**. Because consistency is such an important concept, we are going to go over this concept in some detail.

To see how consistency is defined, examine a very simple case, the sample mean.[2] You should remember from your basic statistics course that the sample mean is an unbiased estimator of the population mean with a variance equal to $\frac{\sigma^2}{n}$, where σ^2 is the variance of the random variable in the population and n is the sample size. Because we are concerned with what happens to the sample mean and its variance as the sample size increases, we add the subscript n to indicate sample size:

$$E(\bar{x}_n) = \mu \qquad \text{var}(\bar{x}) = \frac{\sigma^2}{n}$$

The sample mean is an unbiased estimator of the population mean for any sample size. Sample size is not relevant in establishing that an estimator is unbiased. To malign Gertrude Stein one more time, an unbiased estimator is an unbiased estimator is an unbiased estimator. In contrast, an examination of the variance formula shows that the variance of $\bar{x}_n$ varies with the sample size. As n increases, the variance of $\bar{x}_n$ decreases. The distribution of $\bar{x}_n$ becomes more and more concentrated around μ, as shown in Figure 14.6.

We can describe this increasing concentration around μ with the concept of a *neighborhood*. Let the neighborhood around μ be $\mu \pm \varepsilon$, where ε is some arbitrarily small value. The probability that $\bar{x}_n$ lies in the neighborhood is

$$\Pr(\mu - \varepsilon < \bar{x}_n < \mu + \varepsilon) = \Pr(|\bar{x}_n - \mu| < \varepsilon) \tag{14.17}$$

Figure 14.5
A Consistent Estimator

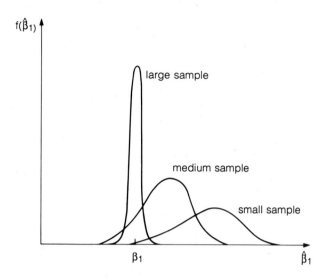

Figure 14.6
An Unbiased Estimator

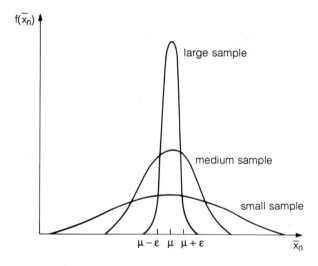

Now, because the variance of $\bar{x}_n$ declines as n increases, there must exist some sample size n^* and ζ ($|\zeta| < 1$) such that

$$\Pr(|\bar{x}_n - \mu| < \varepsilon) > 1 - \zeta \tag{14.18}$$

for all $n > n^*$.

As n increases, the probability of $\bar{x}_n$ lying in the neighborhood becomes larger and larger. Because this probability becomes larger and larger, ζ must become smaller and smaller. In the limit

$$\lim_{n \to \infty} \Pr(|\bar{x}_n - \mu| < \varepsilon) = 1 \tag{14.19}$$

Put differently, we can make the probability of $\bar{x}_n$ lying in the neighborhood as close to one as we wish by making n sufficiently large. The neighborhood, of course, can be made as arbitrarily small as we wish. It is in this sense that a consistent estimator is said to collapse to the true parameter value as the sample size goes to infinity. Equation 14.19 is usually written as

$$\text{plim } \bar{x}_n = \mu \tag{14.20}$$

where plim is the abbreviation for the probability limit.

Notice that plim is an operator. It tells you to find the probability limit of the term to its right. The probability limit operator is easily applied to expressions involving random variables. In fact, it is less restrictive than the expectation operator. Consider the following results for probability limits, where X and Y are random variables and a and b are constants:

$$\text{plim}(a) = a$$

$$\text{plim}(aX + bY) = a \text{ plim}(X) + b \text{ plim}(Y)$$

$$\text{plim}(XY) = \text{plim}(X) \cdot \text{plim}(Y)$$

$$\text{plim}(X^a) = [\text{plim}(X)]^a$$

$$\text{plim}\left[\frac{X}{Y}\right] = \frac{\text{plim}(X)}{\text{plim}(Y)}$$

These results do not depend on X and Y being independent random variables. The results hold when X and Y are dependent.

Returning to our econometrician, can the econometrician at least establish that the ordinary least-squares slope estimator for the consumption function is consistent? To answer this question we must find the probability limit of $\hat{\beta}_1$. To do this, we rewrite the estimator formula (Equation 14.11) to be directly interpretable in terms of variances and covariances. This means that both the numerator and denominator in the last term on the right of the equal sign are divided by $1/n$:

$$\hat{\beta}_1 = .6 + \frac{\frac{1}{n}\Sigma q_i u_i}{\frac{1}{n}\Sigma q_i^2} \tag{14.21}$$

The probability limit of Equation 14.21 is

$$\text{plim } \hat{\beta}_1 = \text{plim}\left[.6 + \frac{\frac{1}{n}\Sigma q_i u_i}{\frac{1}{n}\Sigma q_i^2}\right]$$

$$\text{plim } \hat{\beta}_1 = \text{plim}(.6) + \text{plim}\left[\frac{\frac{1}{n}\Sigma q_i u_i}{\frac{1}{n}\Sigma q_i^2}\right]$$

$$\text{plim } \hat{\beta}_1 = .6 + \frac{\text{plim}\left[\frac{1}{n}\Sigma q_i u_i\right]}{\text{plim}\left[\frac{1}{n}\Sigma q_i^2\right]} \tag{14.22}$$

If $\text{plim } \frac{1}{n}\Sigma q_i u_i = 0$, the ordinary least-squares slope estimator is consistent. How can we evaluate this probability limit? Go back to the reduced-form solution for q:

$$q_i = \frac{1}{(1-.6)}\bar{z}_i + \frac{1}{(1-.6)}u_i$$

Multiply each term by u_i:

$$q_iu_i = \frac{1}{(1-.6)}\bar{z}_iu_i + \frac{1}{(1-.6)}u_i^2$$

Sum this expression over all data cases in the sample:

$$\Sigma\, q_iu_i = \frac{1}{(1-.6)}\Sigma \bar{z}_iu_i + \frac{1}{(1-.6)}\Sigma u_i^2$$

Finally, divide each term by n:

$$\frac{1}{n}\Sigma\, q_iu_i = \frac{1}{(1-.6)}\left[\frac{1}{n}\Sigma \bar{z}_iu_i\right] + \frac{1}{(1-.6)}\left[\frac{1}{n}\Sigma u_i^2\right] \qquad (14.23)$$

We can now solve for the $\text{plim}\left[\frac{1}{n}\Sigma q_iu_i\right]$ by evaluating the probability limit of Equation 14.23.

$$\text{plim}\left[\frac{1}{n}\Sigma\, q_iu_i\right] = \frac{1}{(1-.6)}\,\text{plim}\left[\frac{1}{n}\Sigma \bar{z}_iu_i\right] + \frac{1}{(1-.6)}\,\text{plim}\left[\frac{1}{n}\Sigma u_i^2\right] \qquad (14.24)$$

Because investment is exogenous, it must be independent of u. It follows that the probability limit of $\left[\frac{1}{n}\Sigma \bar{z}_iu_i\right]$ must be 0. But the probability limit of $\left[\frac{1}{n}\Sigma u_i^2\right]$ does not go to 0. It is equal to the variance of the random disturbance term. It follows that the probability limit of $\left[\frac{1}{n}\Sigma q_iu_i\right]$ is

$$\text{plim}\left[\frac{1}{n}\Sigma\, q_iu_i\right] = \frac{\sigma_u^2}{(1-.6)} \qquad (14.25)$$

As n goes to infinity, the sample variance of q, $\frac{1}{n}\Sigma q_i^2$, approaches the population variance σ_q^2. Substituting for the probability limits in Equation 14.22 gives

$$\text{plim}\hat{\beta}_1 = .6 + \left[\frac{\sigma_u^2/(1-.6)}{\sigma_q^2}\right] \qquad (14.26)$$

The variance of q is positive. As long as β_1, assumed here to be .6, is less than 1 but greater than 0, the term in brackets is positive. The ordinary least-squares slope estimator is too large, and this error does not go away as the sample size increases. This error is usually referred to as *asymptotic* bias. It is not the same bias defined by the expectation operator. In other words, econometricians assess bias for an infinitely large sample by using probability limits when evaluating simultaneous equation problems. Because $E(\hat{\beta}_1) \neq \beta_1$, bias also exists for small sample sizes. Thus, the ordinary least-squares slope estimator is *both* biased and inconsistent. The bias does not disappear as the sample size becomes large.

What can the econometrician do? As your text discusses, the econometrician turns to alternative estimation techniques. The two most common alternative techniques discussed in beginning texts are **indirect least-squares** and **two-stage least-squares**. Let's see what happens if the econometrician uses indirect least-squares.

Go back and look at the reduced-form equations. A moment's reflection should convince you that all the required assumptions for ordinary least-squares estimation are satisfied by the reduced-form equations. Assume that the econometrician estimates each reduced-form equation with ordinary least-squares. It follows that $\dfrac{\Sigma\, c_i z_i}{\Sigma\, z_i^2}$ is the best linear unbiased estimator of $\left[\dfrac{.6}{1-.6}\right]$,

and $\dfrac{\Sigma\, q_i z_i}{\Sigma\, z_i^2}$ is the best linear unbiased estimator of $\left[\dfrac{1}{1-.6}\right]$.

The econometrician can form a new estimator for β_1, β_1^*, by forming the ratio of the two reduced-form estimators:

$$\beta_1^* = \frac{\dfrac{\Sigma\, c_i z_i}{\Sigma\, z_i^2}}{\dfrac{\Sigma\, q_i z_i}{\Sigma\, z_i^2}} = \frac{\Sigma\, c_i z_i}{\Sigma\, q_i z_i} = (\hat{.6}) \tag{14.27}$$

Is this indirect least-squares estimator consistent?

$$\text{plim}\,\beta_1^* = \text{plim}\left[\frac{\frac{1}{n}\Sigma\, c_i z_i}{\frac{1}{n}\Sigma\, q_i z_i}\right] = \frac{\text{plim}\left[\frac{1}{n}\Sigma\, c_i z_i\right]}{\text{plim}\left[\frac{1}{n}\Sigma\, q_i z_i\right]} \tag{14.28}$$

To answer this question, we must evaluate the probability limits of $\frac{1}{n}\Sigma c_i z_i$ and $\frac{1}{n}\Sigma\, q_i z_i$. We can do this by once again manipulating the reduced-form equations. Go back to the reduced-form equation for c_i:

$$c_i = \frac{.6}{(1-.6)}z_i + \frac{1}{(1-.6)}u_i$$

Multiply each term by $\bar{z}$:

$$c_i z_i = \frac{.6}{(1-.6)}z_i^2 + \frac{1}{(1-.6)}u_i z_i$$

Sum this expression over all data cases in the sample:

$$\Sigma\, c_i z_i = \frac{.6}{(1-.6)}\Sigma\, z_i^2 + \frac{1}{(1-.6)}\Sigma\, u_i z_i$$

Finally, divide each term by

$$\frac{1}{n}\Sigma\, c_i z_i = \frac{.6}{(1-.6)}\left[\frac{1}{n}\Sigma\, z_i^2\right] + \frac{1}{(1-.6)}\left[\frac{1}{n}\Sigma\, u_i z_i\right] \tag{14.29}$$

Take the probability limit of Equation 14.29:

$$\text{plim}\frac{1}{n}\Sigma\, c_i z_i = \frac{.6}{(1-.6)}\text{plim}\left[\frac{1}{n}\Sigma\, z_i^2\right] + \frac{1}{(1-.6)}\text{plim}\left[\frac{1}{n}\Sigma\, u_i z_i\right] \tag{14.30}$$

The values for investment are a set of fixed constants. Thus, $\frac{1}{n}\Sigma\, z_i^2$ can be treated as a constant being equal to the variance of $\bar{z}$. Because u_i is a well-behaved random error term and z is exogenous, $E(u_i\bar{z}_i) = 0$. It follows that the probability limit of $\frac{1}{n}\Sigma u_i\bar{z}_i$ is 0. Thus, the probability limit of $\frac{1}{n}\Sigma c_i\bar{z}_i$ is $\frac{.6}{(1-.6)}\sigma_{\bar{z}}^2$

EXERCISE 14.6

Solve for plim $\frac{1}{n}\Sigma q_i\bar{z}_i$.

We can now evaluate the consistency of β_1^*.

$$\text{plim } \beta_1^* = \frac{\text{plim}\left[\frac{1}{n}\Sigma c_i\,\bar{z}_i\right]}{\text{plim}\left[\frac{1}{n}\Sigma q_i\,\bar{z}_i\right]} = \frac{\frac{.6}{(1-.6)}\sigma_{\bar{z}}^2}{\frac{1}{(1-.6)}\sigma_{\bar{z}}^2} = .6 \qquad\qquad (14.31)$$

The indirect least-squares estimator is consistent.

The estimator, however, is *biased*. It is true that $E(u_i\bar{z}_i) = 0$, but this is not sufficient to make β_1^* unbiased. Why? The expectation operator cannot be distributed separately over the numerator and denominator, as the plim operator was in Equation 14.28. Remember, $E\left[\frac{X}{Y}\right]$ is not in general equal to $\frac{E(X)}{E(Y)}$. An examination of Equation 14.27 should convince you that it is necessary to have problem-specific information to evaluate the small sample bias associated with the indirect least-squares estimator.

Assessing the small sample bias associated with a least-squares estimator for a specific problem is very time consuming. This is why econometricians usually use probability limits to assess large sample bias, as we did earlier in looking at the ordinary least-squares slope estimator for the consumption function. Consistency replaces the small sample properties of unbiasedness and efficiency as a criterion for evaluating estimators. *But*, knowing that the indirect least-squares estimator is consistent is not very helpful to our econometrician trying to estimate β_1 for the small ten-country data set. An advanced econometric text would also not be helpful. Most of our knowledge about the adequacy of competing estimators comes from stochastic studies. While consistent estimators are superior for large samples, the results of the stochastic studies for small samples are not conclusive.

EXERCISE 14.7

Using the data you generated in Exercise 14.1 and your econometric software, solve for β_1^* using indirect least-squares. What value do you obtain for β_1^*?

Take all the values for β_1^* obtained by your class and draw a frequency distribution for the estimates in Figure 14.7. Compare Figures 14.4 and 14.7. Which estimator would you advise the econometrician to use?

EXERCISE 14.8

Biased and inconsistent estimators can result from applying ordinary least-squares to single-equation models as well as simultaneous models. In Lesson 1, you estimated a consumption function. In selecting the variables to use in your model, you used real-dollar values rather than current-dollar values. If by chance you used current-dollar values, your instructor told you that this was wrong. Economists are concerned about explaining real activity, not nominal activity. But what exactly is wrong with using nominal data to estimate real functions?

Assume that we are interested in estimating the following function:

$$Y_t = \beta_0 + \beta_1 X_t + u_t$$

where Y_t and X_t are real economic variables at time t. Let P_t be the price level in year t. The real function can be expressed in nominal terms by multiplying through by P_t.

$$Y_t P_t = \beta_0 P_t + \beta_1 (X_t P_t) + u_t P_t$$

A real function estimated with nominal variables $Y_t P_t$ and $X_t P_t$ can be shown to yield biased and inconsistent estimates of β_0 and β_1. Show that this is the case for β_1. HINT: The estimated equation is

$$(Y_t P_t) = \alpha_0 + \alpha_1 (X_t P_t) + v_t$$

where $\alpha_0 = \beta_0 P_t$, $\alpha_1 = \beta_1$, and $v_t = u_t P_t$.

Figure 14.7
Frequency Distribution for β_1^*

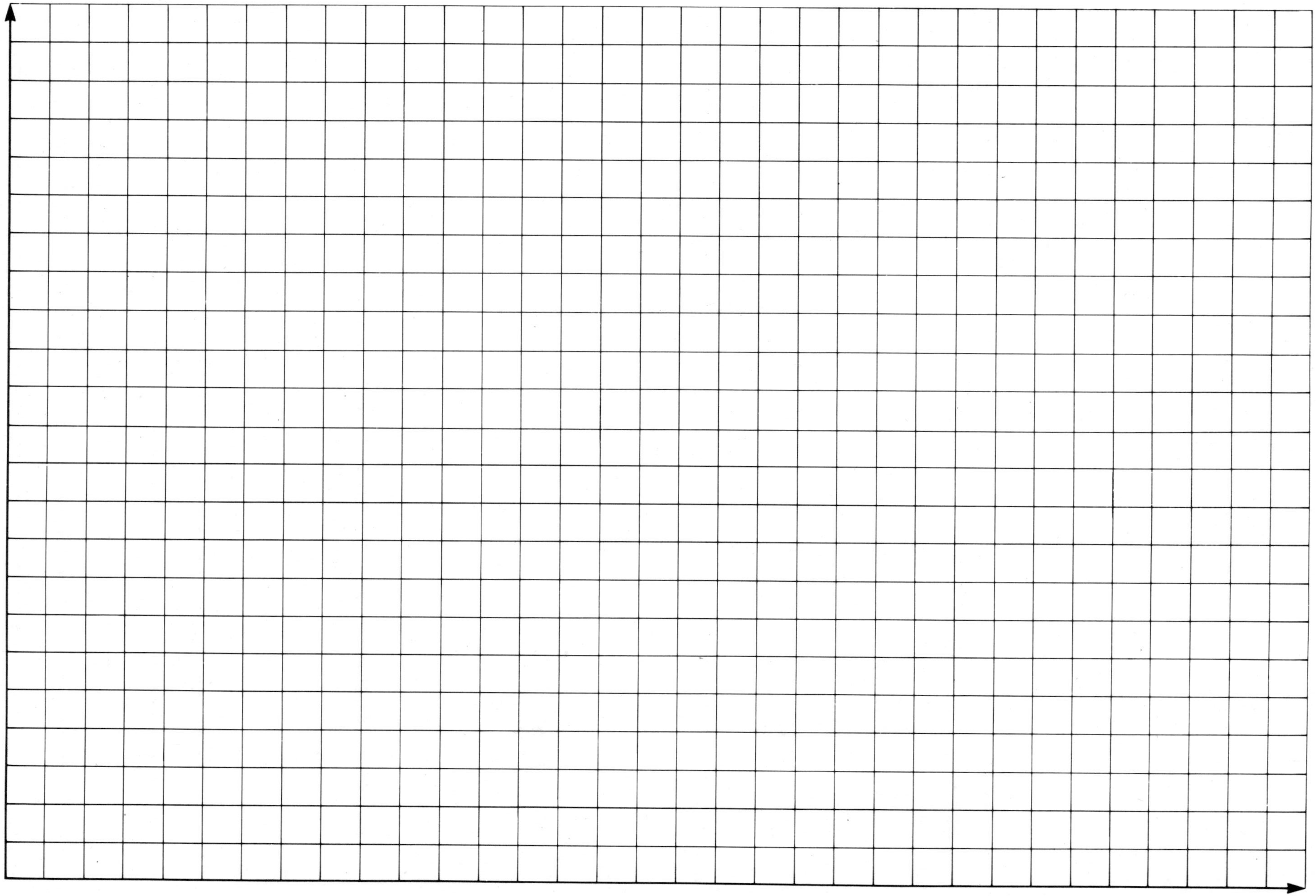

_____

_____

_____

_____

_____

_____

EXERCISE 14.9

Earlier in these lessons you estimated single-equation models for beef demand and auto demand. Reformulate these demand relationships as part of larger simultaneous models. Pay special attention to the timing adjustment of demand and supply reactions in your model. Is it, for example, reasonable to assume that the supply of beef at time t is determined by the price of beef at time $t - 1$? If so, you can reduce the complexity of your estimation problem by specifying a recursive model.

Beef-Demand Model:

Auto-Demand Model:

Evaluate the difficulties, if any, in using ordinary least-squares to estimate the structural parameters for the demand relationships in both models.

_____

_____

_____

_____

_____

_____

_____

_____

_____

_____

_____

_____

_____

_____

_____

_____

_____

EXERCISE 14.10

Using econometric software, estimate the consumption function for the data you qenerated in Exercise 14.4 using two-stage least-squares. You should find that the parameter estimate for $\hat{\beta}_1$ the same as calculated using indirect least-squares. Explain why this is the case.

_____

_____

_____

_____

_____

Do the two alternative estimation techniques always yield the same results?

_____

_____

_____

_____

Suggested Reading

The problems posed by estimating simultaneous equations are difficult to deal with in the beginning econometric course. Their solution usually requires mathematical skills not typically required as a prerequisite to the course. While you may grasp the basic idea of consistency, it is hard to manipulate the probability limit operator unless you have had calculus. Mastering identification issues beyond very simple models requires some matrix algebra.

Most beginning texts try to convey an intuitive sense of the issues. If you want to master this material, you will have to put in the academic roadwork to deal with the discussions in more advanced econometric texts. While this answer often frustrates students, it is nevertheless true. You might be interested in reading how economists first came to deal with simultaneous issues. In fact, it took the profession quite awhile to recognize the formal issues and develop solutions. A good discussion of the early years of quantitative development in economics is C. F. Christ, "Early Progress in Estimating Quantitative Relationships in America," *American Economics Review* 75, no. 6 (Dec. 1985): 39–52.

Econometric Case Study: The Phillips Curve

1. To see how econometricians pursue a research topic by examining a case study
2. To learn to use the *Journal of Economic Literature*

The importance of an underlying economic model to empirical investigation has been stressed throughout these lessons. It has been argued that meaningful inference must rest on a set of assumptions that explain how observations are generated and how variables are related. This seems to suggest that economists first formulate a model, then deduce observable consequences from the model, and finally estimate parameters and test hypotheses. We have seen that model formulation and specification search, while not entirely consistent with this "ideal" process, are evaluated in terms of such an idealization.

Some years ago, Abraham Kaplan drew a distinction between logic in use and reconstructed logic.[1] The cognitive-style economists bring to solving problems is logic in use. The explicit formulation of this logic is reconstructed logic. Kaplan argued that the two types of logic need not coincide. Further, logic in use can be preferred to its reconstructions. Because there are many cognitive styles in any profession, there are many logics in use. The way we actually think about problems in the problem-solving process is thus much more complex than suggested by the reconstruction of this process.

The suggestion that economists start with a model and proceed to empirical estimation is reconstructed logic. As such, it coincides imperfectly with actual logic in use. As you have worked through these lessons, you have seen that there are very different cognitive styles in conducting empirical analysis. There is even a group of economists who seldom look at empirical data, arguing that the strength of economics comes from analytical analysis.

These different cognitive styles become quite important in evaluating economic controversies. Economists often estimate relationships among variables with an incomplete understanding of how the variables are actually related. The evidence gained from such explorations helps economists better understand the relationships and may force them to specify assumptions in a more concise manner. The underlying economic model may become clear only after years of research. How empirical evidence is evaluated in the process of inquiry varies with the logic-in-use practiced by various researchers. The weight assigned to theoretical arguments relative to empirical arguments is an important logic-in-use distinction in the economics profession. You have already seen two examples of this *empirical-theoretical tension*, the consumption function and the investment function. The modern consumption function and investment

Figure 15.1
The Phillips Curve

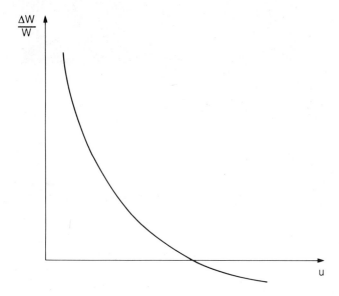

function reflect the combined labors of analytical theory and empirical research conducted over decades.

This lesson focuses on a relationship that has been included in economic principles books for the last thirty years, the **Phillips curve**.[2] The Phillips curve described in today's books, however, shows little resemblance to the original Phillips curve. How the Phillips curve was reformulated is an excellent case study of how the theoretical-empirical tension resolves into new economic models. It also shows how economists can be lulled into theoretical complacency by the current state of the economic environment and how important empirical information can be dismissed in the early stages of investigation. Finally, the case study shows that logic in use may be reconstructed quite differently by economists disagreeing about theoretical issues.

Natural-Rate Hypothesis

The Beginnings

Economists speculated about the relationship between the level of output and the rate of change in money (nominal) wages as early as the 1920s. But serious empirical study of the relationship did not begin until 1958, when British economist A. W. Phillips found an inverse relationship between the rate of increase in money wages and the rate of unemployment.[3] This relationship, shown in Figure 15.1, became known as the Phillips curve.

The Phillips curve rests on the argument that the rate of change in money wages is a direct function of demand conditions in the labor market:

$$\frac{\Delta w_t}{w_t} = f\left[\frac{d_t - s_t}{s_t}\right]$$

(15.1)

where d_t and s_t are the demand for and supply of labor at time t and w_t is the money wage at time t. Phillips used the unemployment rate (u) as the measure of demand conditions in the labor market:

$$\frac{\Delta w_t}{w_t} = f(u_t)$$ (15.2)

Questions were raised about the *theoretical foundations* of the Phillips curve from the moment the initial article appeared in print, but these issues did not draw a great deal of attention. Instead, most economists addressed problems of proper variable measurement and correct functional form. Something like the Phillips curve was integrated into most macroeconomic forecasting models, and the apparent stability of the empirical relationship came to dominate policy discussions on unemployment and inflation. The Phillips curve and the trade-off between inflation and unemployment confronting policymakers became a standard part of every beginning economic text. The noted economist Robert M. Solow summarized the feelings of most economists during this period.[4]

> It did not occur to me that the Phillips curve ... needed any subtle theo-retical justification. It seemed reasonable in a commonsense way that the changes in the money wage, like the change in any other price, should respond to the demand–supply balance in the labor market.
> ... I considered it a defensible hypothesis that excess demand for labor should drive its price up; though of course that leaves entirely open the ques-tion of the mechanism that determines the equilibrium unemployment rate, if there is one.

It was, however, recognized by most economists including Solow that Equation 15.2 is in some sense a misspecification, even though it seemed to fit the data well. Equation 15.2 is written in terms of *money wages*. Very few economists believe that employers and employees bargain over money wages. Most believe that employers and employees bargain over *real wages*. Thus, Equation 15.2 must be expanded to include the rate of change in the price level:

$$\frac{\Delta w_t}{w_t} = f(u_t) + \frac{\Delta p_t}{p_t}$$ (15.3)

If price changes are not perceived or anticipated, money wages are determined by demand conditions in the labor market. If price changes are perceived or an-ticipated, the price changes should be reflected in money-wage changes.

EXERCISE 15.1

Specify a regression model based on Equation 15.3. Notice that you have a lot of choices to make. First, you must specify a functional form that can be estimated using ordinary least-squares. The discussion above is more than a little vague on the specific relationship among the variables. You may also feel that other variables should be included in the model. Specify your model below:

Estimate your model for the years 1950–1966. Use the variables in the Data Bank to measure the variables in your model. Write your estimated function below:

How well does your model explain the rate of change in money wages? How important is the rate of change in the price level in your model?

_____

_____

_____

_____

_____

Use your model to predict the rate of change in money wages from 1967 to the present. Plot the predicted values and the actual values in Figure 15.2. What do you conclude about the predictive ability of your model?

_____

_____

_____

The results of your analysis should convince you, as it did economists, that something was seriously wrong with the Phillips curve after the 1960s. As the economy moved into the 1970s, it became more and more difficult to argue that the Phillips curve was a stable empirical relationship. Milton Friedman and Edmund Phelps suggested that the difficulties lay in an imprecise use of the term unemployment and the wrong price variable.[5] They argued that Equation 15.3 must be rewritten to indicate the *expected* rate of inflation:

$$\frac{\Delta w_t}{w_t} = f(u_t) + \left[\frac{\Delta p_t}{p_t}\right]^*$$

(15.4)

They further argued that there is a **natural rate of unemployment**. The natural rate of unemployment is defined as the rate of unemployment that will exist if the economy is in general equilibrium. Thinking back on your economic principles courses, the natural rate of unemployment is the rate of unemployment that exists when all markets are in equilibrium, when there is no excess demand or supply in individual markets.

Assuming that there is such a natural rate, what happens to the Phillips curve? Consider the case of no inflation and equilibrium in all markets, including the labor market. In other words, assume that the economy is currently at its natural rate of unemployment. With no excess demand or supply in the labor

market and no inflation, there will be no change in the money wages. The economy must be at point A in Figure 15.3.

Now assume that the Federal Reserve increases the growth rate of the money supply such that the economy begins to experience an inflation rate of $\left[\frac{\Delta p_t}{p_t}\right]_0$. Because the actual inflation rate is now positive, employers and employees adjust their inflationary expectations upward from 0. Employees recognize that their money wages must rise to maintain their real wages. This recognition does not happen instantaneously. In the very short run, the economy can be expected to move along a curve like S_1, a short-run Phillips curve. But in the long run, employees will adjust their expected inflation rate to the new actual inflation rate, $\left[\frac{\Delta w_t}{w_t}\right]_0 = \left[\frac{\Delta p_t}{p_t}\right]_0$. The economy must eventually end up at point B in Figure 15.3. In the long run, the Phillips curve must be vertical. There is no long-run relationship between the rate of change in money wages and the rate of unemployment.

Just how employees determine the expected inflation rate, how long they take to adjust their expectations, and the role played by "sticky" money wages and prices are all points of controversy among economists. In terms of Figure 15.3, the path from A to B and the length of time it takes to travel this path are in dispute. Something like the dotted path shown in Figure 15.2 has been suggested by many economists. The first researchers to estimate Phillips curves quickly recognized that there were such "loops" around the estimated functions. Although this evidence was puzzling, economists did not initially associate these loops with any issues that threatened the stability of the estimated relationship. Thus, there were both empirical and theoretical storm clouds threatening on the horizon from the very beginning.

Testing the Natural-Rate Hypothesis

How can the natural-rate hypothesis be tested empirically? The approach most often used by econometricians is to rewrite Equation 15.4 as follows:

$$\frac{\Delta w_t}{w_t} = f(u_t) + \alpha \left[\frac{\Delta p_t}{p_t}\right]^* \tag{15.5}$$

The validity of the natural-rate hypothesis can be inferred from the size of α. If α is equal to 1, the natural-rate hypothesis is confirmed. The long-run Phillips curve is vertical. If, on the other hand, α is less than 1, the natural-rate hypothesis is not confirmed. The long-run Phillips curve has a negative slope.

The econometrician's task is to estimate α. But Equation 15.5 poses a problem. Some mechanism for generating expected inflation must be assumed to estimate Equation 15.5. This means that any test of the natural-rate hypothesis is a test of *both* the natural-rate hypothesis and the expectations-generating mechanism. The most common approach to defining the mechanism is to assume some adaptive solution. Expected inflation is determined through some lagged weighting of past inflation rates.

$$\left[\frac{\Delta p_t}{p_t}\right]^* = \sum_{i=1}^{n} v_i \frac{\Delta p_{t-1}}{p_{t-1}}, \quad \text{where } v_i \neq 0 \tag{15.6}$$

Tests of the natural-rate hypothesis are quite sensitive to the assumed adaptive mechanism. The adaptive expectations mechanism, discussed in Lesson 10, represents the weights as a declining geometric function over time. Many other weightings are possible, and economists have experimented with differ-

Figure 15.3
Short-Run and Long-Run Phillips Curves

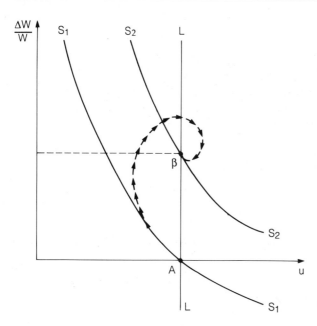

ent lag mechanisms. For example, R. J. Gordon tried three different mechanisms in his 1970 paper. His discussion of the different mechanisms indicates the kinds of issues economists were dealing with as they struggled with testing the natural-rate hypothesis in 1970.[6]

The lack of sample surveys or other consistent sets of evidence about the price level the average worker has expected at various dates presents an extremely difficult problem. Only indirect evidence is available. In my research, as in all previous research on price expectations, changes in the expected price level are assumed to be a function of past price changes. Three different methods of estimating the weights on price changes in various past periods were employed. First, weights are assumed to decline geometrically, with highest weights on the most recent period and regularly descending weights on successive periods in the past. This technique requires numerous tests of the wage equation, each for a different assumed weight for price change in the most recent period. Second, a relatively unrestricted and flexible weighting scheme is estimated by the computer as part of the process of estimating the wage equation. Third, since the level of the interest rate on bonds responds to changes in price expectations, the weights on past prices are estimated in an equation explaining the level of the interest rate on bonds as a function of past price changes.

Surprisingly, very similar results are obtained by the second and third methods. The wage equation in this paper uses the third method, with weights obtained from an interest rate equation described in Appendix B. In this equation about 70 percent of the weight in the formation of price expectations depends on price changes in the most recent year, and about 30 percent on price changes from one to three years ago. In the second method somewhat more weight is given to the most recent year.

Gordon did not find evidence to support the natural-rate hypothesis in 1970. In subsequent work, however, he was unable to statistically reject the null hypothesis that $\alpha = 1$. His 1970 analysis was interesting in that he found a shorter lag structure for price expectations than did most other researchers.

The fact that most researchers found expected inflation to be heavily dependent on actual inflation rates prevailing two to three years previous to the current year was intellectually troubling to many economists. Did it really make sense to argue that employers and employees look that far back in forming their current expectations? Or was this lag structure simply the lag structure that made the natural-rate hypothesis "work"?

Yet, as the evidence accumulated over the years, as the studies were reworked to reflect new data and more sophisticated econometric techniques, the weight of the evidence came to support a long-run vertical Phillips curve in the judgment of most economists. The Phillips curve is still a standard topic in most principles texts. But it is now discussed as being a long-run vertical relationship.

What if you want to know more about the natural-rate hypothesis, especially about more recent examinations of the hypothesis? A good source of this kind of information is the *Journal of Economic Literature*. If you have never used the *Journal of Economic Literature*, read Lesson Note 15.1.

Lesson Note 15.1

Using the *Journal of Economic Literature*

The *Journal of Economic Literature* is published four times a year by the American Economic Association. The *Journal* is written by professional economists for professional economists. The *Journal* contains an annotated listing of new books, reviews of selected new books, a listing of current articles, abstracts of selected articles, and review articles of economic issues and controversies. The *Journal* thus helps economists keep abreast of what is happening in their discipline. Of course, there are always lags in publishing, and the most recent work in economics takes awhile to appear in the *Journal*.

The book reviews are written by economists who specialize in the area. Thus, a review not only details what the book is about but also frequently gives the reviewer's evaluation of the arguments and analysis. The article titles are organized under journal names and a numerical classification system; the classification system is shown below. The editors of the *Journal* select some articles to be abstracted. The authors of these articles then write a brief description of their articles. Finally, every issue includes two or three articles devoted to a research issue or economic controversy. These articles are written by scholars who are actively involved in the issues being reviewed, and these articles are frequently valued as much for the authors' evaluations as for the extensive literature review.

On-line computer access to the *Journal of Economic Literature* is provided by the DIALOG Information Retrieval Service. Most universities subscribe to DIALOG; the service provided is invaluable to anyone interested in researching economic questions. An article in the December 1985 issue of the *Journal* by D. Ekwurzel and B. Saffran discusses the availability of on-line information retrieval for economists.[7]

Classification System for Articles and Abstracts

000 General Economics; Theory; History; Systems
    010   General Economics
        011   General economics
    020   General Economic Theory
        021   General equilibrium theory
        022   Microeconomic theory
        023   Macroeconomic theory
        024   Welfare theory
        025   Social choice
        026   Economics of Uncertainty and Information
    030   History of Economic Thought; Methodology
        031   History of economic thought
        036   Economic methodology
    040   Economic History
        041   Economic history: general
        042   North American (excluding Mexico) economic history
        043   Ancient and medieval economic history until 1453
        044   European economic history
        045   Asian economic history
        046   African economic history
        047   Latin American and Caribbean economic history
        048   Oceania economic history
    050   Economic Systems
        051   Capitalist economic systems
        052   Socialist and Communist economic systems
        053   Comparative economic systems

100   Economic Growth; Development; Planning; Fluctuations
    110   Economic Growth; Development; and Planning Theory and Policy
        111   Economic growth theory and models
        112   Economic development models and theories
        113   Economic planning theory and policy
        114   Economics of war, defense, and disarmament (including product and factor market topics)
    120   Economic Development Studies
        121   Economic studies of less industrialized countries
        122   Economic studies of more industrialized countries
        123   Comparative economic studies involving both industrialized and less industrialized countries; international statistical comparisons
    130   Economic Fluctuations; Forecasting; Stabilization; and Inflation
        131   Economic fluctuations
        132   Economic forecasting and econometric models
        133   General outlook and stabilization theories and policies
        134   Inflation and deflation

200 Quantitative Economic Methods and Data
    210   Econometric, Statistical, and Mathematical Methods and Models
        211   Econometric and statistical methods and models
        212   Construction, analysis, and use of econometric models
        213   Mathematical methods and models
        214   Computer programs

    220   Economic and Social Statistical Data and Analysis
        221   National income accounting
        222   Input-output
        223   Financial accounts
        224   National wealth and balance sheets
        225   Social indicators and social accounts

226 Productivity and growth: Theory and data
227 Prices
228 Regional statistics
229 Micro-data

300 Domestic Monetary and Fiscal Theory and Institutions
    310 Domestic Monetary and Financial Theory and Institutions
        311 Domestic monetary and financial theory and policy
        312 Commercial banking
        313 Financial markets
        314 Financial intermediaries
        315 Credit to business, consumer, etc. (including mortgages)
    320 Fiscal Theory and Policy; Public Finance
        321 Fiscal theory and policy
        322 National government expenditures and budgeting
        323 National taxation and subsidies
        324 State and local government finance
        325 Intergovernmental financial relationships

400 International Economics
    410 International Trade Theory
        411 International trade theory
    420 Trade Relations; Commercial Policy; International Economic Integration
        421 Trade relations
        422 Commercial policy
        423 Economic integration
    430 Balance of Payments; International Finance
        431 Balance of payments; mechanisms of adjustment; exchange rates
        432 International monetary arrangements
    440 International Investment and Foreign Aid
        441 International investment and capital markets
        442 International business
        443 International aid

500 Administration; Business Finance; Marketing; Accounting
    510 Administration
        511 Organization and decision theory
        512 Managerial economics
        513 Business and public administration
        514 Goals and objectives of firms
    520 Business Finance and Investment
        521 Business finance
        522 Business investment
    530 Marketing
        531 Marketing and advertising
    540 Accounting
        541 Accounting

600 Industrial Organization; Technological Change; Industry Studies
    610 Industrial Organization and Public Policy
        611 Industrial organization and market structure
        612 Public policy toward monopoly and competition
        613 Public utilities and government regulation of other industries in the private sector
        614 Public enterprises
        615 Economics of transportation
    620 Economics of Technological Change
        621 Technological change; innovation; research and development
    630 Industry Studies
        631 Industry studies: manufacturing
        632 Industry studies: extractive industries
        633 Industry studies: distributive trades
        634 Industry studies: construction

635 Industry studies: services and related industries
640 Economic Capacity
    641 Economic capacity

700   Agriculture; Natural Resources
710 Agriculture
    711 Agricultural supply and demand analysis
    712 Agricultural situation and outlook
    713 Agricultural policy, domestic and international
    714 Agricultural finance
    715 Agricultural marketing and agribusiness
    716 Farm management; allocative efficiency
    717 Land reform and land use
    718 Rural economics
720 Natural Resources
    721 Natural resources
    722 Conservation and pollution
    723 Energy
730 Economic Geography
    731 Economic geography

800   Manpower; Labor; Population
810 Manpower Training and Allocation; Labor Force and Supply
    811 Manpower training and development
    812 Occupation
    813 Labor force
820 Labor Markets; Public Policy
    821 Theory of labor markets and leisure
    822 Public policy; role of government
    823 Labor mobility; national and international migration
    824 Labor market studies, wages, employment
    825 Labor productivity
    826 Labor markets; demographic characteristics
830 Trade Unions; Collective Bargaining; Labor–Management Relations
    831 Trade unions
    832 Collective bargaining
    833 Labor–management relations
840 Demographic Economics
    841 Demographic economics
850 Human Capital
    851 Human capital

900   Welfare Programs; Consumer Economics; Urban and Regional Economics
910 Welfare, Health, and Education
    911 General welfare programs
    912 Economics of education
    913 Economics of health
    914 Economics of poverty
    915 Social security (public superannuation and survivors benefits)
    916 Economics of crime
    917 Economics of discrimination
920 Consumer Economics
    921 Consumer economics; levels and standards of living
930 Urban Economics
    931 Urban economics and public policy
    932 Housing economics (includes nonurban housing)
    933 Urban transportation economics
940 Regional Economics
    941 Regional economics

EXERCISE 15.2

Using the classification system in the *Journal of Economic Literature* is sometimes like a detective game. Using the topics shown in Lesson Note 15.1, indicate the topics where you would begin your search for information on the natural-rate hypothesis.

_____

_____

_____

A review article on the natural-rate issues discussed in this lesson was published in the June 1978 issue of the *Journal*. The article, by A. M. Santomero and J. J. Seater, is titled "The Inflation–Unemployment Trade-Off: A Critique of the Literature."[8] I have tried to draft this lesson to help you read this article, should you wish to know more about the Phillips curve story.

The Rational Expectations Challenge

Think for a moment about the implications of an expectations mechanism like that shown in Equation 15.6. If the economy experiences rising inflation over several quarters, an individual's expected inflation rate will be consistently too low. If the economy experiences falling inflation for several quarters, an individual's expected inflation rate will be consistently too high. Is it reasonable to assume that individuals will continue to use an adaptive mechanism like that described by Equation 15.6? A group of economists known as rational expectationists argue that the answer is "No."

These economists contend that a rational individual must hold expectations that are unbiased estimates of the actual economic variables, which are assumed to be generated by a stochastic process. If an individual's expectations consistently differ from the mean of the true process, the individual is simply irrational. A rational individual will adjust his or her expectations. Thus, the error in an individual's expectations must be random, with a mean of 0.

Estimating rational expectations models requires advanced econometric techniques. Expected values for future endogenous variables are used as explanatory variables. Further, rational expectations thinking requires that the expected values for future endogenous variables must be equal to the model's prediction of these values. This requirement imposes restrictions on parameters that are typically quite complex, requiring nonlinear, full-information, maximum likelihood estimators, not the subject of a beginning econometric class.

The major difficulty with assessing rational expectations arguments is that economists subscribing to this view go on to assume a great deal more. Specifically, they assume that markets return to equilibrium in the short run. Many feel that this market-clearing assumption is the major controversial element in rational expectations thinking, not the assumption of rational expectations per se. Historically, inflation does not consistently rise or fall quarter after quarter. Thus, individuals confront a learning process with a highly uncertain outcome and costly information. Is an adaptive mechanism like Equation

15.6 irrational for these individuals? The answer to this question is not clear. Equation 15.6 also assumes that the weights are constant. The rational expectationists are certainly correct when they suggest that this is an erroneous assumption. But how much damage does this do to models that assume weights are constant? Here again, the answer is not clear.

Answers to these questions will emerge over the coming years, as economists continue to test their theories against empirical data. Students opening a macroeconomic principles book ten years from now will very likely read about the Phillips curve. But they will also very likely read a different story than you do today.

Data Bank

World Bank and United Nations Data

CNAME	Alphabetic Name of Country (Text File)
WBC	World Bank Country Classification

    1. Low-Income Country (data cases 1–24)
    2. Middle-Income Country (data cases 25–72)
    3. Industrialized Country (data cases 73–90)
    4. Capital Surplus Oil Exporter (data cases 91–94)
    5. Centrally Planned Economies (data cases 95–106)

GNP60	Gross National Product per Capita in 1960 in 1980 U.S. Dollars
GNP80	Gross National Product per Capita in 1980 in 1980 U.S. Dollars
CPOP	Population (1984 estimate, in thousands)
RPOP	Annual Rate of Population Increase
DPOP	Population Density (population per square kilometer of surface area in 1983)
INFANT	Infant Mortality (deaths per 1000)
EXMEN	Expectation of Life at Birth: Men (years)
EXWOM	Expectation of Life at Birth: Women (years)
GFCF	Gross Fixed Capital Formation (percent of GDP)
PFCE	Private Final Consumption Expenditures (percent of GDP)
GFC	Government Final Consumption (percent of GDP)
AGR	Agricultural Output (percent of GDP)
GROWTH	Average Annual Growth Rate of GDP
GROPC	Average Annual Growth Rate of GDP per capita
LIT	Illiteracy Rate of Population Fifteen Years of Age or Older (all data from UNESCO)

NOTES: 1. Missing values are indicated by zero (0).

    2. Gross national product (GNP) measures a country's production of final product, without reference to where its citizens live. Gross domestic product (GDP) measures the amount of final product produced within a country's borders, without reference to who owns productive assets.

Meats Data

B1	Population: Number of People Eating from Civilian Food Supplies in the U.S., in Millions (1950–1984)
B2	Beef Production, Millions of Pounds (1950–1983)
B3	Beef Consumption, Millions of Pounds (1950–1983)
B4	Beef Consumption per Capita, in Pounds (1950–1983)
B5	Veal Production, Millions of Pounds (1950–1983)
B6	Veal Consumption, Millions of Pounds (1950–1983)
B7	Veal Consumption per Capita, in Pounds (1950–1983)
B8	Lamb Production, Millions of Pounds (1950–1983)
B9	Lamb Consumption, Millions of Pounds (1950–1983)
B10	Lamb Consumption per Capita, in Pounds (1950–1983)
B11	Pork Production, Millions of Pounds, Excluding Lard (1950–1983)
B12	Pork Consumption, Millions of Pounds , Excluding Lard (1950–1983)
B13	Pork Consumption per Capita, in Pounds, Excluding Lard (1950–1983)
B14	Chicken (Ready-to-Cook) Production, in Millions of Pounds (1950–1983)
B15	Chicken (Ready-to-Cook) Consumption, in Millions of Pounds (1950–1983)
B16	Chicken (Ready-to-Cook) Consumption per Capita, in Pounds (1950–1983)
B17	Fish (Fresh and Frozen) Production, in Millions of Pounds (1950–1983)
B18	Fish (Fresh and Frozen) Consumption, in Millions of Pounds (1950–1983)
B19	Fish (Fresh and Frozen) Consumption per Capita, in Pounds (1950–1983)
P1	Retail Price of Beef, per Pound, in Dollars
P2	Retail Price of Veal, per Pound, in Dollars
P3	Retail Price of Lamb, per Pound, in Dollars
P4	Retail Price of Pork, per Pound, in Dollars
P5	Retail Price of Chicken, per Pound, in Dollars
P6	Retail Price of Fish, per Pound, in Dollars
H1	Production of All Hogs and Pigs, in Thousands (1950–1983)
H2	Hogs and Pigs Kept for Breeding, in Thousands (1963–1983)
H3	Per Head Value of Hogs on Farm, as of Jan. 1, in Dollars (1950–1983)
H4	Hog–Corn Price Ratio, U.S.
H5	Hog–Corn Price Ratio, N.C.U.S.
H6	Price of Corn per Bushel, U.S., in Dollars
H7	Price of Corn per Bushel, N.C.U.S., in Dollars

NOTES:

1. All data are from Department of Agriculture Sources.

2. Price indices for deflating nominal values are found in the quarterly time-series section of the Data Bank.

Annual Time-Series Data

NOTE: Should you wish to use any of the quarterly data in the quarterly data section as yearly data, use the conversion procedure indicated by your econometric software. Instructions for this conversion are found under the heading "Converting Time Series" in your software instructions.

The following data, indicated by Cs, are taken from Allan H. Young and John C. Musgrave, "Estimation of Capital Stock in the United States," in Dan Usher, ed. *The Measurement of Capital, Studies in Income and Wealth*, vol. 45, Chicago: National Bureau of Economic Research, 1980. Data are recorded in five-year increments from 1925–1975.

C1	Constant Dollar Gross Stocks of Reproducible Tangible Capital in the Business Sector, in Billions of 1972 Dollars
C2	Constant Dollar Net Stocks of Reproducible Tangible Capital in the Business Sector, in Billions of 1972 Dollars
C3	Constant Dollar Gross Stocks of Reproducible Tangible Capital in the Government Sector, in Billions of 1972 Dollars
C4	Constant Dollar Net Stocks of Reproducible Tangible Capital in the Government Sector, in Billions of 1972 Dollars
C5	Constant Dollar Gross Stocks of Reproducible Tangible Capital in the Household Sector, in Billions of 1972 Dollars
C6	Constant Dollar Net Stocks of Reproducible Tangible Capital in the Household Sector, in Billions of 1972 Dollars

The following data, indicated by Ds, are taken from Robert Eisner, *How Real Is the Federal Deficit?* New York: The Free Press, 1986. All data are recorded for 1955–1984.

D1	Official Budget Surplus or Deficit (–)
D2	Official Budget Surplus or Deficit (–), Adjusted for Price Effects
D3	Official Budget Surplus or Deficit (–), Adjusted for Interest Effects
D4	Official Budget Surplus or Deficit (–), Adjusted for Price and Interest Effects
D5	High-Employment Official Surplus or Deficit (–)
D6	High-Employment Official Surplus or Deficit (–), Adjusted for Price Effects
D7	High-Employment Official Surplus or Deficit (–), Adjusted for Interest-Rate Effects
D8	High-Employment Official Surplus or Deficit (–), Adjusted for Price and Interest Effects
OKUN1	Potential GNP, Calculated by Survey of Current Business and DRI, Inc., in 1972 Dollars (1955–1984)
OKUN 2	GNP, in 1972 Dollars (1955–1984)
OKUN 3	Potential GNP, Calculated by Congressional Budget Office, in 1982 Dollars (1956–1986)
OKUN 4	GNP, in 1982 Dollars (1956–1986)
OKUN 5	Inflation Rate in Terms of Consumer Price Index (1955–1986)
OKUN 6	Civilian Unemployment Rate
OKUN 7	Civilian Labor Force Population
OKUN 8	Productivity
OKUN 9	Average Number of Hours Worked per Worker

Quarterly Time-Series Data

All the following quarterly data are in billions of dollars unless otherwise noted.

QTIME   Time Series Counter (1947.1–1987.4)

Q1   National Income, in 1982 Dollars (1947.1–1987.4)

Q2   Total Personal Income, in 1982 Dollars (1947.1–1987.4)

Q3   Disposable Personal Income, in 1982 Dollars (1947.1–1987.4)

Q4   Personal Consumption Expenditures, in 1982 Dollars (1947.1–1987.4)

Q5   Personal Consumption Expenditures for Durable Goods, in 1982 Dollars (1947.1–1987.4)

Q6   Personal Consumption Expenditures for Nondurable Goods, in 1982 Dollars (1947.1–1987.4)

Q7   Personal Consumption Expenditures for Services, in 1982 Dollars (1947.1–1987.4)

Q8   National Bureau of Economic Research Recession Periods, Indicated as 1; Nonrecession Periods Indicated as 0 (1947.1–1987.4)

Q9   Gross Private Domestic Investment, in 1982 Dollars (1946.1–1987.4)

Q10   Nonresidential Fixed Investment (structures plus producers' durable equipment), in 1982 Dollars (1946.1–1987.4)

Q11   Residential Fixed Investment, in 1982 Dollars (1946.1–1987.4)

Q12   Changes in Business Inventories, in 1982 Dollars (1946.1–1987.4)

Q13   Exports of Goods and Services, in 1982 Dollars (1946.1–1987.4)

Q14   Imports of Goods and Services, in 1982 Dollars (1946.1–1987.4)

Q15   Federal Government Purchases of Goods and Services, in 1982 Dollars (1946.1–1987.4)

Q16   State and Local Purchases of Goods and Services, in 1982 Dollars (1946.1–1987.4)

Q17   Gross National Product, in 1982 Dollars (1946.1–1987.4)

Q18   Domestic Auto Output, in 1982 Dollars (1947.1–1987.4)

Q19   Final Sales of New Autos to Consumers, in 1982 Dollars (1947.1–1987.4)

Q20   Final Sales of New Autos to Producers, in 1982 Dollars (1947.1–1987.4)

Q21   Sales of Imported New Autos, in 1982 Dollars (1947.1–1987.4)

Q22   Consumers Net Purchases of Used Autos, in 1982 Dollars (1947.1–1987.4)

Q23   Sales of New Trucks to Consumers, in 1982 Dollars (1947.1–1987.4)

Q24   GNP Produced in the Farm Sector, in 1982 Dollars (1947.1–1987.4)

Q25   GNP Produced in the Nonfarm Business Sector, in 1982 Dollars (1947.1–1987.4)

Q26   Corporate Profits with Inventory Valuation and Capital Consumption Adjustments, in 1982 Dollars (1946.1–1987.4)

Q27   Corporate Profits Tax Liability, in 1982 Dollars (1946.1–1987.4)

Q28   Wages and Salaries, in 1982 Dollars (1946.1–1987.4)

Q29   Personal Consumption Expenditures for Food, in 1982 Dollars (1946.1–1987.4)

Q30   Personal Consumption Expenditures for Clothing and Shoes, in 1982 Dollars (1946.1–1987.4)

Q31   Personal Consumption Expenditures for Gasoline and Oil, in 1982 Dollars (1959.1–1987.4)

Q32   Personal Income Taxes, in 1982 Dollars (1946.1–1987.4)

Q33   Contributions for Social Insurance, in 1982 Dollars (1946.1–1987.4)

Q34   Purchases of National Defense Goods, in 1982 Dollars (1946.1–1987.4)

Q35	Grants–in–Aid to State and Local Governments, in 1982 Dollars (1946.1–1987.4)
Q36	Transfer Payments to Persons, in 1982 Dollars (1946.2–1987.4)
Q37	Compensation of Military Employees, in 1982 Dollars (1972.1–1987.4)
Q38	Exports of Goods and Services, in 1982 Dollars (1947.1–1987.4)
Q39	Exports of Durable and Nondurable Goods, in 1982 Dollars (1947.1–1987.4)
Q40	Imports of Goods and Services, in 1982 Dollars (1947.1–1987.4)
Q41	Imports of Durable and Nondurable Goods, in 1982 Dollars (1947.1–1987.4)
Q42	Gross Saving, in 1982 Dollars (1946.1–1987.4)
Q43	Personal Saving, in 1982 Dollars (1946.1–1987.4)
Q44	Implicit Price Deflator for GNP, 1982 = 100 (1947.1–1987.4)
Q45	Implicit Price Deflator for Consumption Expenditures, 1982 = 100 (1947.1–1987.4)
Q46	Implicit Price Deflator for New Autos, 1982 = 100 (1947.1–1987.4)
Q47	Implicit Price Deflator for Food, 1982 = 100 (1947.1–1987.4)
Q48	Implicit Price Deflator for Gasoline and Oil, 1982 = 100 (1947.1–1987.4)
Q49	Consumer Price Index, 1967 = 100, Not Seasonally Adjusted (1948.1–1987.4)
Q50	Average Workweek of Production Workers in Manufacturing (1945.1–1987.4)
Q51	Average Weekly Overtime of Production Workers in Manufacturing (1948.1–1987.4)
Q52	Civilian Labor Force Participation Rate of Males 20 Years of Age and Older (1948.1–1987.4)
Q53	Civilian Labor Force Participation Rate of Females 20 Years of Age and Older (1948.1–1987.4)
Q54	Number of Persons Unemployed, from Labor Force Survey, in Thousands (1948.1–1987.4)
Q55	Unemployment Rate (1948.1–1987.4)
Q56	Average Duration of Unemployment, in Weeks (1948.1–1987.4)
Q57	Average Weekly Insured Unemployment Rate for State Programs (1949.1–1987.4)
Q58	Index of Help-Wanted Advertising in Newspapers, 1982 = 100 (1945.1–1987.4)
Q59	Number of New Business Incorporations (1947.1–1987.4)
Q60	Index of Unit Labor Cost in the Private Business Sector, 1982 = 100 (1947.1–1987.4)
Q61	Money Supply M1, in 1982 Dollars, Deflated by Consumer Price Index (1947.1–1987.4)
Q62	Money Supply M2, in 1982 Dollars, Deflated by Consumer Price Index (1947.1–1987.4)
Q63	Net Changes in Business Loans, in 1982 Dollars (1945.1–1987.4)
Q64	Net Change in Consumer Installment Credit, in 1982 Dollars (1945.1–1987.4)
Q65	Member Bank Borrowing from the FED, in Millions of 1982 Dollars (1947.1–1987.4)
Q66	Federal Fund Rate (1954.4–1987.4)
QTBILL	Discount Rate on New Issues of Ninety-One-Day Treasury Bills (1945.1–1987.4)
Q67	Yield on New Issues of High-Grade Corporate Bonds (1946.1–1987.4)
Q68	Yield on Long-Term Treasury Bonds (1945.1–1987.4)
Q69	Bank Rate on Short-Term Business Loans (1945.1–1987.4)
Q70	Average Prime Rate Charged by Banks (1945.1–1987.4)
Q71	Output per Hour in the Nonfarm Business Sector (1947.1–1987.4)
Q72	Index of Industrial Production for Durable Manufacturing, 1977 = 100 (1948.1–1987.4)
Q73	Capacity Utilization Rate in Manufacturing (1948.1–1987.4)
Q74	Michigan Survey of Consumer Sentiment, Not Seasonally Adjusted, 1966 = 100 (1953.1–1978.1)

Q75	Michigan Survey of Consumer Sentiment, Not Seasonally Adjusted, 1966 = 100 (1978.1–1987.4)
Q76	Ratio of Consumer Installment Debt to Personal Income
Q77	Index of Current Dollar, Average Hourly Earnings of All Employees in the Nonfarm Business Sector, 1977 = 100
Q78	Index of Real Dollar, Average Hourly Earnings of All Employees in the Nonfarm Business Sector, 1977 = 100
Q79	Civilian Noninstitutional Population, 16 Years and Over, Not Seasonally Adjusted, Thousands of Persons (1948.1–1987.4)

For Those Who Like Living Dangerously

SSPOT	Index of Sunspot Activity (1945–1987)
BBALL	Baseball Index: 1 Indicates Years That the National League Won the World Series, and 0 Indicates Years That the American League Won (1945–1987)

Seasonally Unadjusted Data

USALES	Monthly Department Store Sales (1970.01–1984.12)
UNEMP	Monthly Unemployment Rate (1970.01–1984.12)
MTIME	Monthly Time Index

JAN   JULY
FEB   AUG
MARCH   SEPT   } Dummy Variables for Months
APRIL   OCT
MAY   NOV
JUNE   DEC

States Data

STATEN	Alphabetic Name of State, by Observation (Text File)
EXES*	Expenditures on Elementary and Secondary Schools, in Millions of Dollars
NTE	Number of Elementary and Secondary Teachers, in Thousands
NPTE	Number of Public Elementary and Secondary Teachers, in Thousands
ADA	Average Expenditures per Pupil in Average Daily Attendance
EXED	State Government Outlays on Education, in Millions
EXCAP	State Government Capital Outlays, in Millions
EXPW	State Government Expenditures on Public Welfare, in Millions
DEBT	State Government Debt Outstanding, in Millions
POP*	Resident Population, in Thousands
POPU	Resident Population Living in Urban Areas, in Thousands
POPY	Resident Population Between Five and Seventeen Years of Age
POPW	White Resident Population, in Thousands
PY*	Personal Income, in Billions of Dollars
ASALT	Average Salary of Public Elementary and Secondary Teachers, in Dollars

ASAL	Average Annual Pay, in Dollars (for workers covered by state unemployment insurance laws and for federal civilian workers covered by unemployment compensation for federal employees—approximately 89 percent of the total civilian labor force)
UNITS	Number of Local Government Units
FAID	Total Federal Aid to State and Local Governments, in Millions of Dollars
SREV	State Government General Revenue Raised from Taxes, in Millions of Dollars
SCHA	State Government Revenue from Current Charges, in Millions of Dollars
SFED	State Government Revenue from Federal Government, in Millions of Dollars
EMP	Total Employment, in Thousands
UEMP	Total Unemployment, in Thousands
PMALE	Participation Rate of Males in the Labor Force
PFEM	Participation Rate of Females in the Labor Force
CCPI	Consumer Price Index for the Largest City in the State
ENER	Energy Consumption, in Trillions of BTU
AREA	Total Area, in Square Miles
NFOR	National Forest Land Within Boundaries, in Thousands of Acres
LOT	Revenue from Lottery, in Millions of Dollars
ENROL	Elementary and School Enrollment, in Thousands
PERHS	Percent of Population Completing at least Four Years of High School
PERC	Percent of Population Completing at least Four Years of College
POLICE	State and Local Police Protection Payroll, in Thousands of Dollars
ABOR	Abortions, Rate per 1000 Women Between Fifteen and Forty-four Years of Age
ARTS	State Legislative Appropriations for State Arts Agencies
MIG	Net Total Migration, in Thousands
BIRT	Total Births, in Thousands
DEA	Total Deaths, in Thousands
VCRIME	Violent Crime, Offenses Known to Police per 100,000 Population
PCRIME	Property Crimes, Offenses Known to Police per 100,000 Population
REPS	Number of Representatives in Congress
VOTE1	Percent of Votes Cast for Leading Party for U.S. House of Representatives
VOTE2	If Leading Party is Democratic, Coded 1 If Leading Party is Republican, Coded 0

NOTES:

1. All data are from the 1986 *Statistical Abstract for the United States*.

2. Data flagged with an asterisk (*) are recorded for all the years since 1975 as separate variables. They are indicated by a year designation. For example, POP80 is the total resident population for 1980.

Notes

Lesson 1

1. P. Temin, *Did Monetary Forces Cause the Great Depression?* (New York: Norton, 1976), 7–8.

2. R. J. LaLonde, "Evaluating the Econometric Evaluations of Training Programs with Experimental Data," *American Economic Review* 76 (Sept. 1986): 604–620.

3. Some assumption must be made about the *distributional form* of the random error term in order to construct confidence intervals and test hypotheses about parameters. It is convenient from the perspective of statistical theory to assume that the random error term is normally distributed. When the normality assumption is added to the list of assumptions, the classical linear regression model becomes the classical normal linear regression model.

4. Advanced econometric texts discuss the Gauss–Markov theorem. The proof proceeds by positing an alternative linear unbiased estimator and showing that the weights that minimize its variance are indeed the ordinary least-squares weights. In other words, the minimum-variance linear unbiased estimators of the regression slope and intercept must be the ordinary least-squares estimators.

Lesson 2

1. A **simple probability experiment** is a process that generates a single outcome, usually referred to as a **simple event**. The experiment must be repeatable, with the probability of each simple event remaining the same for each repetition. The set of all possible simple events associated with the experiment is called the **sample space**. For example, tossing a six-sided die is a simple probability experiment. The sample space consists of the simple events 1, 2, 3, 4, 5, and 6. The probability of observing one of the simple events remains the same as the die is repeatedly tossed. The probability of all simple events is assumed to be the same. A **random variable** is a numerically valued function defined over the sample space. When a random variable takes on discrete values, as it must for the die experiment, it is referred to as a **discrete random variable**. Possible random variables associated with tossing the die are:

>   Let Y be the number observed on the face of the die.

>   Let X be 2 if the die shows an even number and 5 if the die shows an odd number.

>   Let Z be 1 if the die shows 1, 2, 3, or 4 and 2 if the die shows 5 or 6.

The probability distributions for the random variables can be described as follows:

Y	$p(Y)$	X	$p(X)$	Z	$p(Z)$
1	1/6	2	3/6	1	4/6
2	1/6	5	3/6	2	2/6
3	1/6				
4	1/6				
5	1/6				
6	1/6				

2. This lesson deals only with discrete random variables. The mean and variance for a continuous random variable X are defined as follows: $\mu_x = \int Xf(X)dX$, and $\sigma^2 = \int (X - \mu_x)^2 f(X)dX$, where $f(X)$ is the probability density function for the continuous random variable.

Lesson 3

1. J. M. Keynes, *The General Theory of Employment, Interest, and Money* (New York: Harcourt, Brace, 1936), 90, 95–97.

2. S. Kuznets, *Uses of National Income in Peace and War* (New York: National Bureau of Economic Research, 1942), 30; R. W. Goldsmith, *A Study of Savings in the United States* 1 (Princeton, N.J.: Princeton University Press for NBER, 1955), 22.

3. J. S. Duesenberry, *Income, Savings, and the Theory of Consumer Behavior* (Cambridge, Mass.: Harvard University Press, 1949).

Lesson 5

1. A. M. Okun, "Potential GNP: Its Measurement and Significance," American Statistical Association, *1962 Proceedings of the Business and Economics Statistical Section* (Washington, D.C.: ASA), 98–104.

2. For Okun's own view of how the four variables changed, see A. M. Okun, "Upward Mobility in a High-Pressure Economy," *Brookings Papers on Economic Activity* 1973: 1 (Washington, D.C.: The Brookings Institution, 1973): 207–52.

3. G. H. Moore, "Inflation and Statistics," in *Essays in Contemporary Problems 1980* (Washington, D.C.: American Enterprise Institute for Public Policy Research, 1980); W. H. Wallace and W. E. Cullison, *Measuring Price Changes: A Study of the Price Indexes*, 4th ed. (Federal Reserve Bank of Richmond, 1981).

Lesson 6

1. Z. Griliches, "Hybrid Corn and the Economics of Innovation," *Science* 132 (29 July 1960): 275–280.

2. W. F. Shughart, II, and R. Tollison, "Corporate Chartering: An Exploration in the Economics of Legal Change," *Economic Inquiry* 23 (Oct. 1985): 585–599.

Lesson 7

1. The CES production function is defined as

$$Q = A[\delta K^{-\rho} + (1 - \delta)L^{-\rho}]^{-1/\rho},$$

where K and L are the factors of production capital and labor, and A, δ, and ρ are parameters. The paramters are assumed to obey the following restrictions: $A > 0; 0 < \delta < 1;$ and $-1 < \rho = 0$.

2. E. E. Leamer, *Specification Search* (New York: Wiley, 1978), 5–9.

3. Leamer, *Specification Search*, 4.

Lesson 8

1. Murray, Alan. "Seasonal Variations Seen Causing Big Savings in Economic Statistics," *The Wall Street Journal*, 13 March 1984: 33.

Lesson 10

1. D. E. W. Laidler, *The Demand for Money: Theories, Evidence, and Problems* 3d ed. (New York: Harper & Row, 1985), 81–86.

2. E. Ames, and S. Reiter, "Distributions of Correlation Coefficients in Economic Time Series," *Journal of the American Statistical Association* 56 (Sept. 1961): 637–656.

3. Your text may or may not include a section on time-series analysis. If you want to see several examples of time-series models, including models with different error processes, see Part 3 of Robert S. Pindyck, and Daniel L. Rubinfield, *Econometric Models and Economic Forecasts*, 2d ed. (New York: McGraw-Hill, 1981).

4. D. Cochrane, and G. H. Orcutt, "Applications of Least Squares Regressions to Relationships Containing Autocorrelated Error Terms," *Journal of the American Statistical Association* 44 (1949): 32–61.

5. G. Hildreth, and J. Y. Lu, "Demand Relations with Autocorrelated Disturbances," *Michigan State University Agricultural Experiment Station, Technical Bulletin* 276 (Nov. 1960).

Lesson 11

1. L. M. Koyck, *Distributed Lags and Investment Analysis* (Amsterdam: North-Holland, 1954).

2. We have not yet discussed consistency as a desirable estimator property. The topic of consistency is taken up in Lesson 14. Suffice it to say here that inconsistent estimators are not desirable.

3. O. Eckstein, *Core Inflation* (Englewood Cliffs, N.J.: Prentice-Hall, 1981), 72–76.

Lesson 12

1. T. M. Brown, "Habit Persistence and Lags in Consumer Behavior," *Econometrics* 20 (July 1952): 355–371.

2. M. Friedman, *A Theory of the Consumption Function* (Princeton, N.J.: Princeton University Press for the NBER, 1957). The formulation of the life-cycle theory of the consumption function is found in A. Ando, and F. Modigliani, "The 'Life Cycle' Hypothesis for Saving: Aggregate Implications and Tests," *American Economic Review* 56 (March 1963): 55–84.

Lesson 14

1. The ordinary least-squares line does not pass directly through p_1 and p_3. Samples of data represent vertical slices through the parallelogram. This causes the regression line to flatten slightly.

2. This discussion follows the presentation in J. Johnston, *Econometric Methods* 3d ed. (New York: McGraw-Hill, 1972). For a discussion of some definitional ambiguities associated with the large sample properties of estimators, see G. S. Maddala, *Econometrics* (New York: McGraw-Hill, 1977), 148–151.

Lesson 15

1. A. Kaplan, *The Conduct of Inquiry* (San Francisco, Calif.: Chandler, 1964), 3–11.

2. A. W. Phillips, "The Relationship Between Unemployment and the Rate of Change of Money Wage Rates in the United Kingdom, 1861–1957," *Economica* 25 (Nov. 1958): 283–299.

3. Phillips, "The Relationship Between Unemployment and the Rate of Change of Money Rates in the United Kingdom, 1861–1957."

4. R. M. Solow, "Down the Phillips Curve with Gun and Camera," in D. A. Belsley et al. (eds.), *Inflation, Trade, and Taxes* (Columbus: Ohio State University Press, 1976), 4–5.

5. M. Friedman, "The Role of Monetary Policy," *American Economic Review* 58 (March 1968): 1–17; E. Phelps, *Inflation Policy and Unemployment Theory* (New York: Norton, 1973).

6. R. J. Gordon, "The Recent Acceleration of Inflation and Its Lesson for the Future," *Bookings Papers on Economic Activity* 1970:1 (Washington, D.C.: The Brookings Institution, 1970), 16.

7. D. Ekwurzel, and B. Saffran, "Online Information Retrieval for Economists—The Economic Literature Index," *Journal of Economic Literature* 23 (Dec. 1985): 1728–1763.

8. A. M. Santomero, and J. J. Seater, "The Inflation–Unemployment Tradeoff: A Critique of the Literature," *Journal of Economic Literature* 16 (June 1978): 499–544.